Sociological Research Methods in Context

FIONA DEVINE and SUE HEATH

MACMILLAN

First published 1999 by
MACMILLAN PRESS LTD
Houndmills, Basingstoke, Hampshire RG21 6XS
and London
Companies and representatives
throughout the world

ISBN 0–333–66631–3 hardcover
ISBN 0–333–66632–1 paperback

A catalogue record for this book is available from the British Library.

This book is printed on paper suitable for recycling and
made from fully managed and sustained forest sources.

10 9   8   7   6   5   4   3   2   1
08 07 06 05 04 03 02 01 00 99

Editing and origination by
Aardvark Editorial, Mendham, Suffolk

Printed and bound in Great Britain
by Creative Print & Design (Wales) Ebbw Vale

To our past and present students
at the Universities of
Liverpool, Manchester and Southampton

Contents

List of Tables

List of Figures

Acknowledgements

As is inevitable in the production of a book of this nature, there are many people we would like to thank. First, we are hugely indebted to the researchers upon whose work we have drawn: Maírtín Mac an Ghaill; Janet Finch and Jennifer Mason; Annie Phizacklea and Carol Wolkowitz; Peter Saunders; Kaye Wellings, Julia Field, Jane Wadsworth, Anne Johnson and Sally Bradshaw; Dick Hobbs; Nicky Gregson and Michelle Lowe; and Sasha Roseneil (listed in the order in which their work is discussed within the book). We would particularly like to thank them for their generosity in allowing us to undertake such a detailed critique of their work. It is rarely a comfortable experience to have one's work subjected to such close critical gaze, and we are extremely grateful to them for the gracious nature of their individual responses to this project. In all cases we received insightful comments and additional material which have enhanced our understanding and evaluation of their work. Nonetheless, the views that are advanced in this book remain very much our own.

We would both like to express our sincere thanks to Peter Halfpenny for reading through the entire manuscript and subsequently providing us (as ever) with very useful commentary and advice. We are similarly grateful to Macmillan's anonymous reviewer. Sue Heath would like to thank Carol Vincent for her useful comments on Chapter 2, and her former SY1440 students at Manchester University (1994–97), who were the guinea pigs for some of the material covered here. In particular, she would like to thank Steve New for invaluable and always enjoyable discussions concerning many of the issues raised in the book. Fiona Devine would like to thank Dave Marsh for inviting her to write a chapter on methodological issues in *Theory and Methods in Political Science*, which subsequently led to the initial approach from Macmillan to write a methods text, and for his subsequent support for the underlying ideas behind the book; and Graham Crow for his willingness to read the final version of Chapter 1 at short notice. Kathryn

Isaacs deserves a special mention for her help in editing the draft manuscript, as does Catherine Gray for her editorial support.

We would also both like to thank colleagues in our respective departments for their interest in this project, with particular thanks to Liz Kenyon for patiently tolerating Sue's divided commitments during the last stages of writing. A big thank you, too, to our families, and to our friends – both old and new. And finally, a moment of sheer self-indulgence: a huge thank you to each other. This has been a fully collaborative venture – and great fun!

FIONA DEVINE
University of Manchester

SUE HEATH
University of Southampton

The authors and publisher wish to thank the following for permission to use copyright material:

Routledge: J. Finch and J. Mason, *Negotiating Family Responsibilities* (1993); N. Gregson and M. Lowe, *Servicing the Middle Classes* (1994) and P. Saunders, *A Nation of Home Owners* (1990).
Penguin: K. Wellings *et al.*, *Sexual Behaviour in Britain* (1994).
Open University Press: M. Mac an Ghaill, *The Making of Men* (1994) and S. Roseneil, *Disarming Patriarchy* (1995).
Sage: A. Phizacklea and C. Wolkowitz, *Homeworking Women* (1995).
Oxford University Press: D. Hobbs, *Doing the Business* (1988).

Every effort has been made to trace all the copyright holders but if any have been inadvertently overlooked the publishers will be pleased to make the necessary arrangements at the first opportunity.

Chapter 1

Introduction

The purpose of this book is to discuss issues of method within the context of current empirical research. It focuses on how the choice and use of particular methods and techniques shape the substantive findings of such research. This is achieved by way of a critical evaluation of eight pieces of recent research in core areas of the discipline of sociology: education, family, employment, housing, health, crime, class and political activism. All published in the last decade, the studies capture some of the most important economic, social and political changes in Britain in the last 50 years or more. They typify the long tradition of empirical research in British sociology on which the high reputation of the discipline is based. The book is especially concerned with the real life problems of doing social research, including the compromises which sometimes occur, the constraints which are not easily surmounted as well as the initial hunches which are undermined, and the surprises which emerge out of the process of research. Practical issues, therefore, loom large in the discussion of the key texts, but that is not to say that the focus is prosaic or mundane. Rather, a consideration of real life research inevitably raises wider issues to do with the ethics of conducting research, as well as political issues which underpin the choice of method and how research actually gets done.

Practical, ethical, political and epistemological issues were similarly the central concern of Colin Bell and Howard Newby's groundbreaking book, *Doing Sociological Research*, which was first published in 1977. They broke away from the tradition of prescriptive methods books which told students how research should be undertaken in an abstract, albeit straightforward, way. Their text was descriptive in focusing on how research has been done in real life by way of seven personal accounts of doing sociological research. The contributors offered autobiographical accounts which reflected on the initial motives for their research, how it was conducted, its consequences and the subsequent use of the substantive findings. They emphasised that research is rarely straightforward, that it is often beset by false starts, initiated with badly thought-out ideas, sometimes compromised by the personal difficulties of working with others, constrained by time and money, and so on. Bell and Newby's approach to these themes generated a much more reflexive consideration of issues of method, and their influence today is most obvious in other autobiographical collections on the research process (see, for example, Bell and Roberts 1984; Hobbs and May 1993; Roberts 1981; Stanley 1990).

Arguably, the influence of Bell and Newby's book is wider still in the plethora of methods books which is increasingly student friendly. Accessibility has been achieved by discussing the plurality of methods available to researchers, including both quantitative and qualitative research methods and techniques (Bryman 1988; Brannen 1992; Mason 1996; Silverman 1997). It has also been achieved by drawing more on real life research as a way of presenting issues of method (Gilbert 1993; Hammersley 1992; O'Connell Davidson and Layder 1994). Far more attention, therefore, has been devoted to understanding, interpreting and explaining the process of doing social research than was the case in the past. There has been a tendency, however, to draw on short abstracts from empirical research with the result that the practical, ethical and political issues of doing research have not always been discussed fully. Students, for example, have been unable to see how the choice of methods – the means by which the research actually gets done – shapes the substantive findings which emerge. More important, there has been a tendency to draw on classic, yet outdated, examples of empirical research, such as Paul Willis' *Learning to Labour* which was first published over twenty years ago (Willis 1977). Of course, drawing on such studies has many virtues. The unintended consequence, however, is that more recent empirical research has been ignored. That is to say, the kinds of social issues and substantive topics which are most likely to generate interest and enthusiasm among current generations of students tend not to be drawn upon for a discussion of research methods.

Against such a background, this book is written for students by focusing on some of the most recent empirical research. In doing so, it addresses issues which are relevant to all our daily lives and are also, therefore, engaging. We hope that the grounded discussion of the topics under investigation encourages students to address issues of method as well. Each of the chapters asks probing questions about how the research was done, whether the choice of methods was appropriate, what setbacks were experienced and how they were overcome and, finally, whether the substantive results were valid and reliable. In doing so explicitly, we hope to encourage students to put aside their initials fears about asking such questions of published research and thus assist them in acquiring the skills and confidence to critically evaluate empirical research for themselves. From this vantage point, students should then be in a stronger position to engage in empirical research of their own, with a realistic awareness that the research process is usually far from straightforward. The challenge is to confront the mundane *messiness* of empirical research by addressing the practical, ethical and epistemological issues which present themselves during the research process. Of course, it is always much easier to cast a critical eye over someone else's research. The empirical studies in this book have been subject to unusually close scrutiny, about which their authors have been most gracious. We might add that, influenced partly by the legacy of Bell and Newby (1977), the authors upon whose work we focus have made our project easier by being more open about their research than previous generations of sociologists perhaps tended to be. We are firmly of the belief, however, that evaluating the empirical work of others is an important first step before embarking on research of one's own. It is for this reason that it is so crucial that issues of method are discussed in the context of recent empirical research.

The choice of studies

Our choice of studies was governed by several criteria. First, we sought to include first-class research which, at the time of writing, had been published in book form in the last ten years. Consequently, all of the work considered has appeared since 1988, and the books should be readily available on library bookshelves. Second, we wanted to embrace research which covered the main sub-disciplines of sociology and addressed important parts of people's daily lives. While we did not specifically choose studies on gender or race, these issues – along with class divisions – were often integral to our chapters and reflect the importance of social stratification in British sociology. Third, it was important to discuss a variety of different research methods and techniques. Interestingly, all of the studies in this book employed a variety of methods, with many drawing on a mix of quantitative and qualitative techniques (see Figure 1.1). The studies, therefore, highlight the virtues of methodological eclecticism – a theme which is considered further in Chapter 10. They also show that the debate about the virtues of quantitative versus qualitative data can become rather sterile (Bryman 1988; Brannen 1992) and that the more immediate practical challenge is to bring together the results of different methods and techniques. Fourth, and finally, we concentrated on books where there was an explicit discussion of how the research was done, what the pitfalls had been and how they were circumvented. Indeed, many of the authors of the studies under investigation have reflected on their research methods in separate publications and we also drew on this material where appropriate. The authors of the studies, in other words, have been themselves reflexive about how they did their research. In sum, we would venture to suggest that the studies evaluated in this book are examples of *good practice* in social research.

Author	Title of study	Methods
Maírtín Mac an Ghaill	*The Making of Men*	Observation, interviewing, case studies, diaries, surveys
Janet Finch and Jennifer Mason	*Negotiating Family Responsibilities*	Local survey, in-depth interviews
Annie Phizacklea and Carol Wolkowicz	*Homeworking Women*	National survey, in-depth interviews, case studies
Peter Saunders	*A Nation of Home Owners*	Local surveys including open-ended questions
Kaye Wellings *et al.*	*Sexual Behaviour in Britain*	National survey
Dick Hobbs	*Doing the Business*	Observation, in-depth interviews
Nicky Gregson and Michelle Lowe	*Servicing the Middle Classes*	Content analysis, local surveys, in-depth interviews
Sasha Roseneil	*Disarming Patriarchy*	Observation, interviews, documentary analysis

Figure 1.1   Methods used in the eight case studies

The structure of each chapter is the same. After a short introduction to the study under the spotlight, the research is located in the context of recent debates in its particular sub-discipline. This review of the literature shows how the research was shaped by previous work, how it might offer a new contribution to the topic in question and how the aims and objectives of the research were developed. In some cases, it will be seen that methods employed by other researchers influenced how the research in question was undertaken. The main substantive findings of the research are then summarised so that they are known to the reader before the critical evaluation of the study begins. This not only serves to illustrate the link between the conduct of a study and the type of results subsequently presented, but also firmly locates the issues of method raised by each study in the context of their empirical grounding. The most important component of each chapter, however, is the critical evaluation of how the research was undertaken. This task is achieved through an exploration of two or three issues of method in each chapter, although reference is also made to methodological issues raised in other chapters. It should be said that all of the authors commented on our assessment of their work. They sometimes disputed aspects of our evaluation and if, in our view, a convincing case was made then we amended the chapters accordingly. More often than not, however, the authors provided additional comments on the points we made and acknowledged the issues raised. A final overview of the methods and findings of the research is provided in each chapter's conclusion. Finally, additional readings are provided at the end to facilitate further exploration of both the substantive topics and issues of method discussed.

Inevitably, our choice of books influenced the range and nature of issues of method we address in this book. In highlighting the messiness of much sociological research – of how research rarely proceeds through its various stages without some setbacks, constraints, complications, detours and so forth – three issues emerged on numerous occasions across the chapters. First, despite the increasingly reflexive nature of much sociological practice, the vexed problems of politics and bias surfaced especially in Maírtín Mac an Ghaill's ethnographic study of masculinities in a state comprehensive school, Dick Hobbs' participant observation of petty criminals and local CID detectives in the East End of London and Sasha Roseneil's case study of the experiences of women at the Greenham Common peace camp of the 1980s. Second, methods of sampling (especially minority populations for whom there are no sampling frames) and their implications for the generalisability of findings emerged most notably in Annie Phizacklea and Carol Wolkowitz's national survey of homeworking women (1995), Peter Saunders' three towns survey of home ownership (1990) and Kaye Wellings and her colleagues' national survey of sexual attitudes and lifestyles (1994). Third, while the virtues of mixing methods have long been emphasised, the challenge of making sense of different findings arose in Janet Finch and Jennifer Mason's study of family obligations (based on a random sample and in-depth interviews) (1993) and Nicky Gregson and Michelle Lowe's research on the use of waged domestic labour in dual career families (derived from an analysis of advertisements in *The Lady*, case studies in the North East and South East of Britain and in-depth interviews) (1994). Furthermore, the emphasis on the untidiness of much sociological research raises another issue to do with the scientific claims of sociology. That is to say, if sociological research rarely proceeds in an uncomplicated fashion, can it be regarded as a scientific practice? Is sociology a rigorous social science? How might it be rigorous? These issues are now considered more fully with reference to the case studies discussed in detail in each chapter.

Politics, bias and field relations

The case studies in this book illustrate that the problem of bias can take numerous forms, in that both funders' and researchers' views can influence the conduct of research – and even whether it proceeds at all. Wellings and her colleagues (1994) encountered such difficulties. In the context of a moral panic about AIDS, their survey of sexual attitudes and lifestyles was halted at a late stage by government intervention at the highest level and only rescued by the intervention of the Wellcome Trust. In his study of home ownership in Britain, Saunders' (1990) prior commitment to the benefits of home ownership, individualism and private property (as his attitudes have shifted to the right of the party political spectrum) was an important influence on his decision to place less emphasis than other sociologists in the field on class differences in the accumulation of wealth in the housing market. These examples of bias, of course, raise the issue of the politics of research and how sociological research is influenced by the political context in which it is undertaken (Bell and Newby

1977; Bell and Roberts 1984). However, there are less obvious ways in which bias and politics can influence the process and output of research. A researcher's personal biography, their prior commitment to particular beliefs and values and the nature of field relations – whether they are close or distant to the people involved (Pearson 1993) – can influence the choice of research topic, the means of information gathering and the presentation of substantive findings. It is now widely agreed that such 'effects' are integral to social science research and they cannot be eliminated in the search for an objective social science. That said, there is a growing commitment to reflexivity whereby researchers are aware of, reflect on and are explicit about the ways in which different forms of bias affect their research (see, for example, Hobbs and May 1993). Of course, reflexivity does not mean that the issue of bias and the politics of research are no longer problematic. It does make it easier, however, to consider the implications of these issues on how the research was conducted and the substantive findings that emerged.

Issues of bias and the politics of research are most apparent in the work of Mac an Ghaill, Hobbs and Roseneil. Mac an Ghaill's book, *The Making of Men: Masculinities, Sexualities and Schooling* (1994) is based on an ethnography of life at 'Parnell School'. As a sociologist of education, Mac an Ghaill's work is at the cutting edge of current debates concerning the construction of masculinities in the context of schooling. Specifically, his research raises questions about 'taking sides' and the legitimacy of 'standpoint' epistemologies, including whether involvement in research can be seen as a form of empowerment. Mac an Ghaill's loyalties and political allegiances are self-evident in his book and there is no mistaking his political commitment to excluded and marginalised young adults. Such an explicit political commitment is not without its problems, however, and can lead to some selectivity in the use of data, a problem which is evident to some degree in Mac an Ghaill's work. There are also difficulties associated with according greater validity to the accounts of oppressed individuals over others, an issue which Mac an Ghaill has acknowledged in more recent reflections on his research (Haywood and Mac an Ghaill 1998). Moreover, 'empowerment' (however defined) and 'giving a voice' are not necessarily synonymous. Identifying with a powerless group can lead to a simplistic polarisation between 'goodies' and 'baddies', when in reality all groups may deserve some sympathy, albeit for different reasons.

Questions of bias and politics in relation to personal biographies and field relations loom large in the discussion of Hobbs' *Doing the Business* (1988), an ethnographic study of petty criminals and local CID detectives in the East End of London. Hobbs' central argument is that a unique working-class culture – which celebrates entrepreneurship – shapes the activities of both the policed and the police in the locality. These issues are contextualised within a social history of the development of the British police and an economic history of the East End from which the culture of the locality emerged. The ethnographic research consisted of both overt and covert participant observation of the policed (criminals) and the police (non-uniformed CID) in a variety of different settings, including local pubs and clubs. Hobbs grew up in the East End and he is certainly honest about his partial insider status. That is not to say, however, that his position was unproblematic. It is arguable that Hobbs proffers a less critical account of malpractice within the Metropolitan CID than might have been the case if a non-local had researched the same topic, while his reliance on informal access to the CID, together with the nature of his relations with a small number of detectives, may well have provided him with only a partial picture of police malpractice. Hobbs' corroboration of material derived from his various drinking sessions with material from other sources could, for example, have been discussed explicitly. Further, his personal closeness to a group of local criminals leads him to paint a relatively benign view of their activities, while he also makes light of the ethics of his own involvement in criminal behaviour and of the likely consequences if he had been caught by the police. Yet it is hard not to conclude that only a cockney-turned-academic could have written such an interesting account of the East End: that Hobbs was part of the world he studied undoubtedly contributed to the richness of his ethnography.

Issues of biography, prior commitments, and loyalties to research participants appear, albeit in a different fashion, in Roseneil's *Disarming Patriarchy* (1995). Her book is a fascinating chronicle of the experiences of women involved in the Greenham Common peace camp during the 1980s, and it describes an important moment in the history of the women's movement in Britain. It is as much based on Roseneil's own memories as it is on those of the 35 women she interviewed in depth as part of her study, as she herself joined the camp as an 18 year old, having abandoned her 'A' level studies in order to do so. Roseneil's research is based on what she calls 'retrospective auto-ethnography', an approach whereby she subjected her own personal experiences, alongside those of other Greenham women, to the rigours of a variety of qualitative methods of data collection and analysis. A term like 'dislocated ethnography' might be more accurate, better capturing the varying degrees of overlap, both in time and space, between Roseneil's experiences and those of the women involved in her research. Her commitment to feminist methodology also raises questions of prior loyalty and self-censorship within the research process. Roseneil's feminism leads to an incontrovertible alignment with Greenham women, but it also means, somewhat disappointingly, that she is rather obscure about some aspects of intra-camp rivalries. Finally, although she claims to 'tell it like it is', Roseneil is rather more open about tensions and conflicts between the majority of Greenham women who shared a broadly pro-feminist position than she is about conflicts between such women and the small minority of women who, despite being active participants in the peace camp, were nonetheless hostile to the feminist politics of Greenham.

Overall, these three studies illustrate the inherently political nature of sociological research: it invariably serves certain interests over others. In this respect, then, all research has a political dimension. The work of Mac an Ghaill, Hobbs and Roseneil also raises questions of value freedom in sociology. Can sociological research be value free? Is it important, or necessary, for researchers to declare their own values or standpoint? Should researchers prioritise some people's accounts over others? Does giving a voice to people involved in research empower them? If so, in what sense is this so? It is now more commonplace for researchers to consider the impact of political and other potential sources of bias on the conduct of their research, as well as to weave these issues into research reports. Without doubt, this is a favourable development in sociology. It reminds us, for example, of the dilemmas surrounding the ongoing maintenance of good relations with contacts in order to facilitate the collection of further information from them. It is apparent, however, that reflexivity does not *solve* the issue of bias in sociological research, although it does have two major advantages. First, it enhances the researcher's awareness of the likely impact of politics and issues of bias on their research. Second, it forces all of us – both as researchers and as consumers of research – to think about the implications of such bias for the substantive findings and the conclusions which can be drawn from them. We would venture to suggest that greater attention could still be paid to the second advantage, if the knock-on effects of such issues are to be fully acknowledged. The sociological enterprise would be all the more robust for this move.

Sampling techniques and generalisability

A broad range of sampling techniques are employed in the studies discussed in this book. Sampling refers to 'the selection of people, places or activities suitable for study' (Lee 1993: 60). Various sampling techniques are used in both quantitative and qualitative research. An important distinction exists between *probability* sampling and *non-probability* sampling. In the case of the former, the chances of inclusion in a sample are either equal or, if not equal, calculable; in the case of the latter, it is impossible to estimate the probability of inclusion. Within the quantitative research tradition, methods of sampling and the effective use of different sampling frames – pre-existing lists from which one can select a sample, such as membership lists or registers of various kinds – crucially affects two key issues. These are the *representativeness* of the sample (the degree to which the sample accurately reflects the characteristics of the broader population, whether that population consists of all British citizens, all ferret owners, or all flower pot factories) and the *generalisability* of the research findings (the degree to which one can say with confidence that the findings from one setting are likely to apply to similar settings). The use of an inadequate sampling frame could place a question mark over both the representativeness and generalisability of research findings if the membership of the population it lists is not exhaustive. An obvious example is related to the much discussed inadequacies of the electoral register as an effective sampling frame; not all household members are registered to vote, with a particular tendency for younger and more geographically mobile individuals to be omitted.

In comparison, qualitative research does not seek to be either representative or generalisable in quite the same manner as quantitative research, or at all. However, this is not to suggest that the choice of sampling methods or the use of sampling frames are any less important than in quantitative research. Finch and Mason's research on family support and help (which is discussed more fully in the next section) offers an excellent discussion of the theoretical sampling strategy (sometimes referred to as purposive sampling) which they employed within the qualitative part of their research. They did not automatically draw a sub-sample of respondents from their main sample. Rather, they drew on just some of their respondents and their kin in order to focus quite selectively on the social groups most likely to have been involved in the (re)negotiation of family relationships and responsibilities (namely, young people in the 18–24-year-old age group and people who had been divorced and/or remarried). Finch and Mason's work illustrates that methods of sampling should be as systematic and rigorous as strategies associated with quantitative sampling techniques. A failure to justify one's sampling strategies in any research, therefore, only undermines the strength of the claims that can be made about the data.

Issues of sampling and generalisability also arise in Saunders' book, *A Nation of Home Owners* (1990). Saunders considers the phenomenal growth of home ownership in Britain this century and its consequences for people's daily lives – be they home owners or council tenants – and its wider impact on the character of British society. A wide array of secondary sources, including government statistics and other academic and non-academic surveys, are used by Saunders. His principal method of enquiry, however, involved local surveys of 450 households in three working-class towns: Burnley, Derby and Slough. Saunders' decision to undertake a set of three surveys rather than a nationally representative survey is worthy of note, not least because he does not fully explore the local dimension of his surveys except in relation to capital gains. He effectively uses them as if they constituted a nationally representative survey and he often generalises from his empirical findings in three towns to British society as a whole. However, his sample size is relatively small: arguably *too* small – particularly for drawing out differences between groups or categories of respondents – to make generalisations. Moreover, his response rate, especially on the council estates in Slough, was disappointing. Consequently, it may be that Saunders generated a sample of respondents who were very positive about their experiences of home ownership by virtue of the fact that those with less positive views declined to be interviewed. The low response rate, therefore, raises some doubts about the representativeness and generalisability of his findings. It should of course be stressed that this problem is not peculiar to Saunders' research, in that all random sample surveys which achieve less than 100 percent response rate are likely to be problematic in this respect.

Sampling issues, especially the difficulties of sampling minority populations, also arise in Phizacklea and Wolkowitz's *Homeworking Women* which was published in 1995. Homeworking – paid work at home – is one way in which women combine employment with child-care and domestic commitments and is especially prevalent among ethnic minority women. That said, Phizacklea and Wolkowitz wanted to look at all types of homework undertaken by different groups of women. In order to capture this diversity, they employed a variety of research methods including a postal question- naire included in the women's magazine *Prima*, in-depth interviews with white and Asian women homeworkers in Coventry, and a series of case studies of organisations which had developed teleworking schemes. Their use of a readership of a women's magazine for a postal questionnaire elicited a limited response from a highly select group of women derived from an already skewed group of readers, while they also encountered considerable difficulties in generating a sample of homeworkers for their in-depth study. An initial attempt to contact homeworkers via adverts in the local press met with limited success, especially with regard to Asian women homeworkers. A second strategy of contacting them through community workers proved somewhat more successful in generating a sample of white women in a range of non-manual and manual occupations and a smaller number of Asian women homeworkers, all in manual occupations. It was nonetheless disappointing that they achieved only a small sample of Asian women homeworkers based only in manual occupations. Their research therefore highlights the consid- erable difficulties of generating a sample from a relatively small and hidden workforce. That said, their intensive case study research powerfully captures the diverse experiences of working-class Asian women homeworkers performing low-skilled tasks for which they were paid very little, as against the experiences of white middle-class women teleworkers undertaking high-skilled work for which they were well remunerated.

Finally, the difficulties of gaining access to a hidden population which arise in a large, national sample survey can be seen in the discussion of Wellings *et al.*'s study, *Sexual Behaviour in Britain: The National Survey of Sexual Attitudes and Lifestyles* (1994). Against the background of the emergence of the human immune deficiency virus (HIV) epidemic, the rationale for the study was the need to gather information that might help to assess and prevent its future spread.

Wellings' research team noted that previous studies had focused on high-risk groups and had been based on clinic and volunteer samples, resulting in a lack of knowledge concerning the sexual attitudes and behaviours of the broader population. It was crucial, therefore, to find out whether or not people from high-risk groups differed significantly from the wider population. A lot of attention was given to the development of sensitive questions within the survey, with broad acknowledgement of the likely difficulties arising from differently understood definitions of commonly used phrases and terminology. As others have noted, however, respondents were given positive encouragement to 'admit' to heterosexual behaviour, yet were given slightly less positive encouragement to speak of homosexual practices. More importantly, disputes about the findings concerning the incidence of homosexual practice in Britain raised issues relating to the survey's representativeness. Arguably, difficulties in locating the 'hidden population' of actively gay men and lesbians led to an underestimation of the incidence of homosexual behaviour. Again, therefore, the reliability of some of the key findings has been called into question by some critics.

As the studies in this book demonstrate, gaining access to a group of people – especially a hidden population – is no simple matter. The choice of sampling procedures and sampling frames, therefore, has major consequences for the status of one's research findings. It should also be noted that issues of sampling are not simply confined to the early stages of a piece of research and easily forgotten once completed. On the contrary, sampling issues are integral to the entire research process, especially for projects using the mixed method approach, which will inevitably require different sampling methods and frames for different components of the research at various times over the duration of the project. Indeed, issues of sampling within qualitative research are often ongoing, particularly if strategies such as snowballing are used (a strategy whereby successfully located respondents are asked if they know of other similarly placed individuals who might be interested in being involved in the research). Most importantly, the studies in this book demonstrate that choices about sampling techniques and sampling frames require careful deliberation. The decision-making process has to be systematic and rigorous and not arbitrary and idiosyncratic. We would argue that this simple point applies with equal force to quantitative and qualitative research and that these issues should be discussed explicitly in all research reports. To date, however, quantitative researchers have tended to be much better than qualitative researchers at discussing sampling issues. We hope this situation will be rectified in the future since a full justification of sampling strategies can only enhance the strength of the claims that can be made about the material collected. In turn, the reliability of the research findings – whether similar results would be produced if the research was replicated by other researchers – would also be improved.

The challenges of mixing methods

While a mixed approach was not one of the original criteria on which the studies discussed in this book were chosen, all of the researchers employed a variety of methods, often drawing on a mix of both quantitative and qualitative research techniques. Contrary to Bell and Roberts' earlier conclusion (Bell and Roberts 1984: 5), both sociology as a discipline and individual sociologists as practitioners have now become increasingly pluralistic. It has become commonplace to reject the old debate about the relative advantages and disadvantages of quantitative and qualitative research, and instead the virtues of combining methods are widely applauded (Bryman 1988; Brannen 1992). We would not dissent from this consensus although we are also of the opinion that some of the difficulties of employing a range of methods are often neglected. Epistemological issues still loom large – as will be discussed in Chapter 10 – and practical problems persist. It cannot be assumed, for example, that an expert in the field of survey research is also equally proficient in ethnography, and vice versa. Moreover, proper attention has yet to be devoted to making sense of some of the contradictory findings that frequently emerge from different methods and techniques. It is easy enough to select snippets from qualitative interviews to 'flesh out' the data from quantitative research. A more important issue arises, however, when qualitative material does *not* confirm or even *challenges* quantitative findings (and vice versa). Should one or other data source be conveniently discarded? How does a researcher try to reconcile contradictory findings? What criteria should be applied? Some of these issues are yet to be fully addressed in the welcome although not totally unproblematic shift towards methodological eclecticism.

The studies by Phizacklea and Wolkowitz, Finch and Mason and Gregson and Lowe stand out as research which combines methods taken from both the quantitative and qualitative traditions. As we have already seen, Phizacklea and Wolkowitz used a national survey, in-depth interviewing and case studies to capture the heterogeneity of homeworking in Britain. Finch and Mason's *Negotiating Family Responsibilities* (1993), briefly discussed in the previous section, is worth considering more fully here. Their work is an exploration of the extent to which the provision of family support and help is governed by normative rules and assumptions about appropriate behaviour and obligation. It involved a face-to-face survey of 978 randomly sampled adults followed by semi-structured interviews with 88 people. Thirty-one of them had been respondents to the survey and eleven members of this sub-group gave their consent for other members of their family to be interviewed. Their work provides the opportunity to focus on the validity of triangulation as a method in the social sciences alongside their use of the vignette technique and its advantages and disadvantages. Finch and Mason distance themselves from a narrow interpretation of triangulation which sees it merely as a way of using one part of the research to check the validity of the other. Rather than assume that different methods will produce substantially the same results, they acknowledge that inconsistent results can – and often do – emerge, and their work provides a number of worked examples of how they made analytical sense of these tensions.

The difficulties of mixing methods can also be seen in Gregson and Lowe's *Servicing the Middle Classes,* which appeared in 1994. They examine the 'crisis in social reproduction' in work-rich dual career households in which both women and men work in demanding professional and managerial careers, and how they increasingly draw upon waged domestic labour to cope with the demands of work and family. They focus specifically on the resurgence of the demand for and supply of nannies and cleaners, and did so by employing three distinct methods of research. First, they analysed advertisements drawn from the national magazine, *The Lady,* and from local newspapers in their case study areas of Newcastle and Reading. Second, they conducted a survey of middle-class households in the two localities in which both partners worked full time. Third, they conducted in-depth interviews with a small number of nannies and cleaners and their employers in the two locales. The adverts in the national magazine and the local newspapers showed an upward trend in the demand for waged domestic labour – especially for nannies – although the reliability of these data as a basis for estimating the national demand for domestic labour is open to some doubt. Interestingly, their workplace surveys in Newcastle and Reading showed that the use of waged domestic labour in middle-class households is not very extensive and it is the cleaner rather than the nanny who is the more frequently used form of waged domestic labour. In other words, the findings diverged in terms of the *extent* of the demand for waged domestic labour and the *nature* of the labour that was in demand. This discrepancy raises doubts about whether the crisis in social reproduction of domestic labour in middle-class households is as great as they claim. That said, their research raises important issues about the relationship between class and gender and is one of the more novel pieces of work to explore these issues in recent years.

It is readily apparent, therefore, that it is not unusual for sociologists to use a combination of methods rather than just one method in isolation. The work of Phizacklea and Wolkowitz, Finch and Mason and Gregson and Lowe, in particular, is distinctive in the way in which they combine methods drawn from two very distinct traditions: namely, data gathered via a quantitative survey, and more qualitative methods such as in-depth interviews, case studies and documentary analysis. We are of the view that these studies are good examples of how different methods and techniques can be used to produce a full and rich picture of the topic under investigation. Nevertheless, we are aware of the difficulties of methodological eclecticism especially in relation to the integration of different types of data. A mixed method approach requires researchers to make decisions over how to deal with inconsistencies between sources of data and to consider whether or not one data source should take priority over another, and the authors of the studies considered in this book are not unaware of these issues. Both Finch and Mason and Gregson and Lowe consider the issues explicitly in their monographs and how they square different substantive findings is plain to see. Social researchers are increasingly familiar with the challenges and difficulties posed by methodological pluralism. We would argue that this development is most welcome, and that a recognition of the issues at stake will only enhance the strengths of sociology in the future.

Messiness, sociology and science

The emphasis of this book is that sociological research rarely proceeds in a neat and tidy fashion, and it is often beset with difficulties – some of which can be anticipated while others cannot. Practical, ethical and political issues frequently confront the survey researcher or ethnographer at different stages of the research process. If we acknowledge the messiness of sociological research, what are the implications for the scientific claims of sociology? Is sociology a rigorous social science? The long-standing debate about whether sociology is a science invariably leads to a comparison between the social sciences and the natural sciences. The first point to make, then, is that research in the physical sciences does not proceed in an uncomplicated fashion either. As sociologists of science have long argued, practical, ethical and political problems present themselves to the physicist as much as they do the sociologist (Barnes *et al.* 1996; Fuller 1997). Bias, for example, can influence the definition of a scientific problem, the subsequent conduct of research and the interpretation of empirical findings in the natural sciences in comparable ways to the social sciences. At the same time, however, the social and natural sciences do not confront the same dilemmas because they focus on different worlds. The study of people is different to research in the physical world because people are conscious human beings who attach meaning to where they are and what they do. The sociologist has to understand these meanings (although not be bound by them) if he or she is to make sense of the subject or topic under investigation. The advantage is that most social researchers can observe, talk to and participate in their respondents' activities. The difficulty with such relations, however, is that informants may alter their behaviour, often to please the researcher. There are therefore some practical, ethical and political problems which are distinct to the *social* sciences.

So, is sociology a science? We answer in the affirmative – a definite yes – since sociology is based on theoretical thinking, systematic methods of empirical investigation and data analysis, and the logical assessment of arguments to develop a body of knowledge concerning aspects of the social world. Sociology is scientific, therefore, in being a disciplined search for knowledge on a particular subject matter based on the collection of evidence to support its claims. That sociological research does not proceed in a neat and tidy fashion does not necessarily undermine its claims to be a science. It is possible, as the authors of the studies in the book show, to confront the constraints of research head on, acknowledge the compromises that have been made, discard the initial hunches which proved to be wrong and deal with contradictions and inconsistencies in a logical and systematic fashion. Practical, ethical and political issues, therefore, need to be tackled directly rather than pushed aside if the claim to scientific status is to be upheld. These issues cannot be ignored since the social world is, after all, a messy and complicated place. Acknowledging this fact makes the practice of sociological research a demanding and challenging one. Embedded in this discussion is a definition of what good sociological research looks like. Good sociological research requires integrity on the part of the researcher, a willingness to face difficult questions, an openness to new and different ideas, an acceptance that some strategies of research can go wrong, an ability to adapt to different ways of doing things and so on. The way in which practical, ethical and political issues arise in all research demands pragmatism, but a pragmatism which is systematic and rigorous. In this respect the studies chosen for this book are examples of good practice.

Some caveats

Inevitably, a book of this kind is not as comprehensive as a prescriptive methods text. The advantage of the standard approach to issues of method is that it provides a useful vehicle for a systematic appraisal of the advantages and disadvantages of many research methods. It is less easy for a book such as ours to be as exhaustive, and there are three omissions of which we are keenly aware. First, it would have been useful to draw on research on a social issue which had used documentary sources of information, especially of a historical nature. This would have provided the opportunity to discuss the use of documentary sources in empirical research. While there are many studies which draw on such evidence, however, there is rarely an explicit discussion within such studies of the uses and limitations of particular documents. Scott's (1990) introductory text on documentary sources provides a useful discussion of the ways in which such evidence can be evaluated. However, it proved difficult to find a piece of recent research, which explicitly discussed the use of documents, on which to apply his criteria of appraisal. Second, it would have been interesting to draw on some innovative research in the burgeoning area of culture. There is a mass of general texts on the subject and an increasing number of research monographs on a range of cultural practices from the phenomena of raves to the advent of cybercafés. To date, however, there are no studies published in book form – at least none of which we are aware – which deal *explicitly* with issues of method as part of their general presentation of research findings. This situation will undoubtedly change in the future, and in this respect we welcome the recent publication of two methods textbooks aimed specifically at students of cultural studies (McGuigan 1998; Seale 1998). Finally, although we have included various pieces of survey research, we do not examine a study based on the secondary analysis of a survey data set. Again, it was difficult to find a monograph based exclusively on this method which *also* included an explicit discussion of issues of method. We suspect that research of this kind is more widely published as academic articles in journals rather than in books although, once again, this situation may change. Nevertheless, despite these three omissions, we believe we have considered eight recent empirical studies which cover a wide range of research methods and techniques and which students will find interesting and enjoyable to read. It is our intention that the discussion of the topics under investigation will stimulate students to think more explicitly about issues of method, critically to evaluate how social research is done and to reflect upon the implications of the research methods used for the substantive findings which emerge. In doing so, we hope that they will acquire some basic research skills which will prepare them to conduct research of their own. By avoiding an abstract and dry discussion, we have sought to tackle issues of method in a fresh and invigorating way. The welcome consequence of such an endeavour has been to draw on published work which is testimony to the continued strength of the empirical research tradition within British sociology.

Chapter 2

Education: Mac An Ghaill's *The Making of Men*

Introduction

Maírtín Mac an Ghaill's *The Making of Men: Masculinities, Sexualities and Schooling* was published in 1994 at a time when reporting of the so called 'crisis of masculinity' was beginning to reach fever pitch within the British media. The publication that summer of GCSE results which proclaimed an ongoing reversal in the relative academic fortunes of boys and girls was seen by many commentators to give added legitimacy to this perceived crisis. Moreover, not only were girls purportedly outstripping boys in the academic rat race, but they were deemed guilty of outstripping their male peers in the race to find work in the diminishing youth labour market. A BBC Panorama documentary screened in autumn 1995, for example, was unequivocal in its suggestion that young men were now 'losing out' to young women, who were 'fighting back' against young men in the employment sphere (Panorama 1995). It was claimed that young men in their final years of schooling were demoralised as never before, lacked a sense of purpose in life, and were the new victims of an education system which had succumbed to the 'political correctness' of feminist teachers and educators (Heath 1999). Six months later, the Chief Inspector of Schools was arguing that 'the failure of boys, and in particular white working-class boys, is one of the most disturbing problems we face within the whole education system' (Woodhead 1996). Mary Kenny, writing in *The Daily Express*, was more brutal in her assessment of the changing times: 'What we want for our sons is not "equal" women, but good wives; we don't want them to be intimidated by tough, competitive women who humiliate men and do them down' (Kenny 1996).

It is within this broader context of arguments concerning the relationship between gender, education and employment that the importance of Mac an Ghaill's work becomes apparent. *The Making of Men*, an ethnographic study of the role of schooling in creating and reinforcing various student and teacher 'masculinities', undoubtedly highlights the lack of direction which many young men experience as they move through their final years of compulsory schooling into a radically restructured labour market (Haywood and Mac an Ghaill 1996). However, it similarly highlights the complex nature of this process, and in particular it puts a question mark over the popular notion that young women are universally and unproblematically reaping the benefits of recent social shifts. As Linda, a young woman attending 'Parnell School', Mac an Ghaill's case study site, noted perceptively:

> Nearly everyone we know around here has been unemployed sometime... It's just terrible, if that's all you've got to look forward to. You can see it with a lot of the boys round here. They've just got no future and it's not their fault. But the teachers are wrong, *it's not the girls' fault either.* (Mac an Ghaill 1994: 141 – emphasis added)

This chapter begins with a consideration of the significance of Mac an Ghaill's work for the sociology of education, the sub-discipline within which his work is situated. His work contains many important insights into the complex role of modern schooling in reproducing existing inequalities within society, and highlights the strategies of resistance and accommodation adopted by different pupil subgroups. The main part of the chapter will highlight Mac an Ghaill's overt political commitment to working towards an 'emancipatory curriculum' and his desire that, as part of that vision, research should be a source of empowerment for those involved. This commitment raises broader methodological questions about the place of the researcher's own values and agenda within the research process. Fortunately, these are issues about which Mac an Ghaill himself has written widely, providing valuable insights into his practice as a politically motivated researcher beyond those contained in the text of *The Making of Men*.

Researching schooling and masculinities

Since the mid-1960s and the pioneering work of the 'Manchester School' (Hargreaves 1967; Lacey 1970; Lambert 1976), the sociology of education has benefited from a rich tradition of detailed ethnographic studies of life in school. Indeed, the ubiquity of the educational sociologist reporting on the realities of life in the classroom was neatly captured by the title of a study conducted in the early 1980s, *The Man in the Wendy House* (King 1984): clearly, no classroom was safe from the roving ethnographer! These early studies, based on observation, in-depth interviews with pupils, teachers and parents, and analysis of school archives, were produced largely as a reaction to the more quantitative tradition which had dominated educational sociology in the immediate post-war period. This earlier style of work, often referred to as 'political arithmetic', was concerned with assessing the role of schooling as an engine of social class mobility, and fed into Labour Party debates on the merits of comprehensive reform of the education system. However, while political arithmetic importantly revealed a great deal about inequitable educational outcomes, it could offer little by way of an explanation of the processes within schools which led to such outcomes. In contrast, ethnographic methods provided an ideal tool for exploring the day-to-day operation of school life. Not only did they place an emphasis on studying teachers and pupils in their 'natural settings', but allowed researchers to develop understandings of the *symbolic* meaning of classroom behaviour and interaction.

Early school ethnographies remained focused on issues of class inequality and social mobility, albeit within a framework which questioned the assumed meritocratic basis of schooling. For example, studies such as *Hightown Grammar* (Lacey 1970) revealed some of the processes by which working-class pupils who had succeeded in entering grammar school were nonetheless consistently disadvantaged in their schooling. Later ethnographic studies, most notably *Learning to Labour* (Willis 1977) and *Beachside Comprehensive* (Ball 1981) similarly placed great emphasis on the role of schooling in reproducing class-based inequalities within society. With the rise of feminist and anti-racist influences from the mid-1970s onwards, these earlier studies attracted criticism for their tacit assumption that all pupils shared the same experiences as the white working-class boys they investigated. In response, later ethnographies focused rather more systematically on other dimensions of pupil experience. *Typical Girls?* (Griffin 1986) is often cited as the classic feminist riposte to *Learning to Labour,* while other studies highlighted the intersection of gender and race in producing differentiated experiences of, and responses to, schooling (Fuller 1980; Mac an Ghaill 1988; Mirza 1992; Troyna and Hatcher 1992). Others focused explicitly on the differential experiences of pupils from affluent backgrounds, including those educated outside the state education system (Aggleton 1987; Roker 1993; Walford 1986).

Despite these developments, school-based ethnographies which have focused largely on the experiences of boys have tended to celebrate the more macho elements of their sub-cultures in a rather uncritical fashion. This is certainly true of Willis' treatment of his 'lads' in *Learning to Labour,* and Walker's treatment of 'the footballers' and 'the Greeks' in the Australian ethnography *Louts and Legends* (Walker 1988). In both studies, the sexist, racist and homophobic behaviour of these groups is interpreted as a form of working-class resistance to the authority of the school, rather than 'a legitimation and articulation of power and domination' over other pupils (Skeggs 1993). Accordingly, a central theme in the work of many feminist sociologists of education has been the day-to-day exercise of male power and privilege within schools. Some of this work, however, has been weakened by a tendency to present a rather undifferentiated view of the behaviour of boys and men in schools (for example, Jones and Mahoney 1989; Mahoney 1985). The implication of much of this work has been that all males within a school are, for example, potential harassers of women, or that all males are motivated by misogyny in their behaviour towards women. Such a stance overlooks the possibility that certain groups of young men are *also* marginalised by the power relations of the school. In this respect, Connell (1987 and 1995) has argued that the 'gender regimes' of schools (in common with other social institutions) are characterised by the simultaneous existence of 'hegemonic' and 'subordinated' masculinities. So, while certain forms of masculinity are given tacit approval and hold sway within an institutional setting, other forms are seen as inferior and consequently marginalised and often ridiculed. Moreover, Connell argues that hegemonic masculinities do not exist within a vacuum, but are constructed in relation to both subordinated masculinities *and* femininities. Neither do they remain static, but are subject to historical change and redefinition. It is within the context of this particular theoretical debate that Mac an Ghaill places his own work, arguing that schools should be viewed as highly gendered and sexualised arenas. As he puts it:

> This social scaffolding of modern state secondary schooling is informed by differentiated masculinities and femininities and the power relations that are contained within them. (Mac an Ghaill 1994: 4)

The Making of Men

The Making of Men is based on an ethnographic study of 'Parnell School', an 11–18 co-educational comprehensive in an industrialised inner-city area of the Midlands, an area of high unemployment and widespread poverty. Mac an Ghaill tells us that the school's student intake is predominantly working class, and reflects the ethnic diversity of the local population. At the time of the study, in the early 1990s, the school was heavily involved in the restructuring of the curriculum as a consequence of the ongoing influence of 'new vocationalism'. This sought to align schooling more closely with the needs of the labour market, and Mac an Ghaill argues that this shift was responsible for the emergence of new forms of work-identified masculinity among both pupils and teachers. This was also a period during which increased emphasis was being placed on parental choice and the operation of a 'market' in education. Mac an Ghaill points out that the need to market the school was also having an impact on the way in which the school dealt with certain forms of (predominantly male) pupil (mis)behaviour.

The bulk of the research reported in *The Making of Men* took place between 1990 and 1992, although Mac an Ghaill had already been conducting related research in Parnell School for the previous two years. Moreover, throughout this period he was himself employed as a teacher within the school, a point which is relevant to later discussions within this chapter. For a three-year period, Mac an Ghaill collected a vast amount of data via a range of methods associated with ethnographic research: most importantly, through observation of school life (which he wrote up on a daily basis), as well as through diaries and questionnaires (the latter often created by the students themselves, highlighting issues about which they wanted to write), and through formal and informal group and individual interviews with both pupils and teachers. The bulk of the data relates to a cohort of male and female students who were in their last year of compulsory schooling during the 1990–91 academic year, although he also draws on material from an earlier study of the schooling experiences of gay students, some but not all of whom had attended Parnell School. By combining these varied approaches, Mac an Ghaill was able to build up a series of in-depth case histories on which to base his analysis.

The resulting book is divided into five empirically based sections:

- dominant teacher masculinities at Parnell School
- dominant pupil masculinities
- the construction and reinforcement of dominant sexualities
- the responses of young women to the exercise of hegemonic masculinities by both male pupils and teachers
- the experiences of gay pupils within an arena characterised by 'compulsory heterosexuality'. (Rich 1980)

It is, of course, impossible to do justice to these themes in one short chapter. However, Mac an Ghaill opens the book with a striking account which sets the tone of the ethnographic analysis which follows. He recalls an occasion from earlier in his teaching career when a male student had presented him with a bouquet of flowers in the playground as a gesture of thanks, having just passed an exam. As a consequence, the student had got caught up in a fight while fending off homophobic abuse from his peers, and shortly afterwards Mac an Ghaill found himself being summoned to the headteacher's office. On arrival, he was informed that he had 'gone too far this time', to which Mac an Ghaill responded that he could not be held responsible for a fight between pupils. However, the headteacher had actually heard nothing about the fight:

> Suddenly, I realised the symbolic significance of our playground perfor-mance: the exchange of flowers between two males was institutionally more threatening than the physical violence of the male fight. (Mac an Ghaill 1994: 1)

This is an extraordinarily revealing incident, yet Mac an Ghaill argues that it is not at all extraordinary in the context of the everyday running of the modern state secondary school. The significance of the lack of fuss over the fight, he contends, is that such behaviour is consistent with a hegemonic masculinity in which emphasis is placed on authority, heterosexuality, aggression and power. The act of exchanging flowers between men transgressed all of these characteristics, indeed undermined them, and the resulting physical aggression was thereby rendered *comprehensible*. In contrast, the actions of Mac an Ghaill and the male pupil were *incomprehensible* to those who witnessed them.

This complicity between certain teachers and pupils in reinforcing a particular form of dominant masculinity within the school is a strong theme running throughout *The Making of Men*. Mac an Ghaill identifies a range of differentiated masculinities among the young men involved in his research – the Macho Lads, the Academic Achievers, the New Enterprisers and the Real Englishmen (although he stresses that these were not 'fixed' categories, none remaining static during the entire period of research). He argues that the first of these groups, the Macho Lads, had for some time represented the hegemonic version of masculinity within Parnell School (although curriculum changes meant that their ascendancy was being eroded by the New Enterprisers). Theirs was an unashamedly anti-school sub-culture, based around active resistance to the authority of the school and the teachers who represented that authority. However, Mac an Ghaill argues that many male teachers in the school were far more comfortable with the Macho Lads' version of masculinity than that of the other groupings of boys within the school, and also felt better able to cope with the anti-school behaviour of the Macho Lads than with that of certain groups of female pupils. This arose partly because these teachers sympathised with the Macho Lads given the socio-economic climate in which they would leave school. However, Mac an Ghaill also argues that many teachers themselves identified with and positively valued the 'macho' values which the Macho Lads represented, but which as 'responsible adults' they were themselves unable to express.

Many other points could be drawn out from Mac an Ghaill's work in order to highlight its importance to the rapidly growing literature on the way in which certain forms of masculinity are reinforced in day-to-day school life. Having very briefly considered some of its central arguments, the rest of the chapter will consider two key methodological issues which are raised by *The Making of Men*, both of which are related to the politics of conducting sociological research. These are the question of 'taking sides' in research, and whether or not the research process can be viewed as a source of empowerment for those involved. That we are able to discuss these points with the benefit of various published insights from Mac an Ghaill himself is a further strength of his work, which has always been very methodologically self-conscious (see for example Haywood and Mac an Ghaill 1998; Mac an Ghaill 1991 and 1993).

Taking sides

The question of whether or not sociologists should allow their own values and beliefs to affect their research cuts to the heart of a long-standing and complex epistemological debate within the social sciences. As we shall see, views on the appropriate relationship between the conduct of research and a researcher's own values are extremely polarised. The classical positivist position has traditionally placed great emphasis on the desirability of achieving 'value freedom' within the research process, as part of the claim of social science to be a 'true science' on a par with the physical sciences (a position which of course assumes that the latter are value free, an assumption which was questioned in Chapter 1). Regardless of the desirability of maintaining a clear distinction between facts and values, critics of this position have questioned whether this is actually *possible* to achieve, given that sociological research is overwhelmingly concerned with gaining an understanding of the operation of value systems within society. Moreover, sociological researchers cannot be divorced from their autobiographies, and will inevitably (whether consciously or otherwise) bring their own values to bear on the types of research they choose to pursue, the ways in which they pursue that research and the ways in which they interpret and analyse their data. From this perspective, it is often argued that the best way forward is not to pretend to be value neutral, but to be honest about one's own perspectives on any given research topic and to then seek to represent the data in as objective a way as possible: 'In this way, value freedom involves not taking sides with those whom we investigate, despite the existence of our own value positions' (Williams and May 1996: 116). This is a stance often associated with a Weberian approach to sociological research. However, this particular debate, over the relative merits of a value-free versus necessarily value-influenced stance within the research process, has not only remained largely unresolved in recent years, but has been superceded by a much more radical debate concerning the inherently political nature of social research and the importance of a researcher's standpoint within the research process.

Indeed, some writers have argued that sociologists have a *duty* to adopt a much more overtly politicised approach to their research. Such a stance is not synonymous with a total rejection of objectivity, but is based on the view that the notion of value freedom is in itself value laden, and tends covertly to serve certain interests above others. In the early 1970s, for example, conflict methodologists in the United States argued that the reluctance of sociologists to 'take sides' in their research had, by default, resulted in a collusion between power elites and the sociological community. They argued that sociologists had a public responsibility to use their research skills for politically motivated ends: 'This responsibility is borne insofar that special skills and available time affords the sociologist a better position in which to investigate matters in the public interest' (Christie 1976: 518). A similar view was proposed by critical theorists influenced by the Frankfurt School, who argued that social theorising should be used as a tool for the emancipation of society. As such, critical theorists still identify with and work towards the political ends of a range of oppositional social movements. As Poster has argued, 'Critical theory springs from an assumption that we live amid a world of pain, that much can be done to alleviate that pain, and that theory has a crucial role to play in that process' (Poster 1989: 3).

In the introduction to *The Making of Men*, Mac an Ghaill acknowledges his own debt to feminist critical theory, highlighting in particular the work of Patti Lather, who has written widely in the field of education (see, for example, Lather 1986, 1991). Mac an Ghaill describes feminism as a 'standpoint' epistemology, a position which takes on board the idea that:

> Human activity not only structures but sets limits on understanding. If social activity is structured in fundamentally opposing ways for different groups, one can expect that the vision of each will represent an inversion of the other, and in systems of domination the vision available to the rulers will be partial and perverse (Skeggs 1992: 1, quoted in Mac an Ghaill 1994: 175).

Feminist standpoint epistemology, therefore, gives priority to the voices of the less powerful and the marginalised. While that certainly means giving a voice to women (although with an increasing recognition of the diversity of women's experiences), it may also mean giving a voice to other groups who find themselves located on the margins of patriarchal society – such as the voices of marginalised masculinities identified by Mac an Ghaill. Standpoint methodologists, then, are not only open about their particular values and beliefs, but are also transparent concerning their prioritising of certain accounts over others, whether in the sense of claiming that those accounts are somehow closer to the truth or simply by giving voice to previously silenced groups. (Chapter 9 includes a further discussion of this theme in the context of Sasha Roseneil's research on the Greenham Common peace camp.)

Having very briefly sketched out the terrain on which the question of partisan research is situated, we now turn specifically to the response of Mac an Ghaill to this issue. On even a cursory reading of his work, Mac an Ghaill's loyalties and political allegiances are self-evident. In *The Making of Men*, as in his earlier work *Young, Gifted and Black* (1988), there is no mistaking where his sympathies lie in relation to the topics he is researching. Mac an Ghaill is politically committed to the excluded, to those whose experiences tend to be marginalised within the context of the school. Throughout *The Making of Men* his commitment to gay students and to those marginalised by a refusal to engage in behaviours associated with hegemonic masculinities is clear. Indeed, a reviewer of the book in the *Times Educational Supplement* described Mac an Ghaill as 'an eloquent, principled and caring contestant on the side of the oppressed'. Nowhere is this more clearly signalled than in the book's front page dedication: 'In support of gay and lesbian students'. He also notes that 'in lessons and in informal situations I presented a pro-gay perspective' (Mac an Ghaill 1994: 154), while one of the aims of the book is 'to present a critique of the Neo-Conservative New Moralism and its accompanying media campaign of demonisation of feminists and the gay and lesbian movement' (ibid: 14). No mincing of words, then!

It is important to note at this point that educational sociology has had a long-standing association with political engagement of this kind. Given that education is intrinsically linked to social mobility and issues of social justice, many contemporary educational sociologists view their research as necessarily having a strong political dimension, whether with a small or a large 'p'. We have already noted for example the links which existed in the immediate post-war years between the tradition of political arithmetic and Labour Party campaigns for comprehensive schooling. In the last twenty years, feminist and anti-racist researchers have similarly worked closely with teachers and policy makers to promote greater equality within the education system (Heath 1997, Weiner 1994). In researching the education system, therefore, it would nowadays seem to be very difficult, if not impossible, to leave one's own values and beliefs out of the picture.

However, not all researchers have been completely at their ease over such developments. For example, Peter Foster, Roger Gomm and Martyn Hammersley, writing in various combinations, have singled out sociologists of education, above all other groups of researchers, as being particularly culpable of using research for 'inappropriate' political ends (a viewpoint endorsed by Tooley and Darby's (1998) much publicised and highly controversial OFSTED-commissioned review of educational research). In an echo of the Weberian stance outlined earlier, Hammersley and Gomm (1996) acknowledge that sociologists will inevitably hold particular political values, and then state that 'while there is nothing wrong even with having strong views and commitments about the phenomena being studied, research must not become a vehicle for these' (Hammersley and Gomm 1996: 20). They continue by arguing that a concern among sociologists of education to promote equality of opportunity particularly with respect to race and gender has led to a distortion of the process of enquiry. Indeed, they go so far as to suggest that this development 'represents an abandonment of research in favour of the production of propaganda' (Foster *et al.* 1996: 178). They conclude that increasing pressure for research to 'serve political ends' has not only resulted in partisanship being prioritised over methodological rigour, but has also led to a consequent weakening of the sub-discipline's influence in the political sphere.

In addition to these general concerns, Foster and Hammersley (1996) raise two further points which are of particular relevance to an assessment of Mac an Ghaill's methodology in *The Making of Men*. First, they are critical of what they regard to be the selective use of data by standpoint researchers. Second, they criticise such researchers for necessarily prioritising pupils' comments and experiences over those of teachers. These two aspects of their argument are highlighted here not just because they seem apposite to *The Making of Men* and to the broader discussion on 'taking sides', but also because Foster and Hammersley cite Mac an Ghaill's earlier work, *Young, Gifted and Black*, as a specific example of the style of politically motivated research of which they are so critical. It is not unlikely, therefore, that they would extend their criticisms to his more recent work.

First, then, Foster and Hammersley (1996) argue that all too often researchers committed to a standpoint epistemology assume that their audiences share their value judgements, and consequently do not provide comprehensive evidence for their arguments. Rather, they are selective with their data, particularly (but not exclusively) within the qualitative research tradition, 'where individual instances of unequal treatment are recounted, like atrocity stories, and treated as evidence of systematic and widespread discrimination' (Foster and Hammersley 1996: 19). Can Mac an Ghaill be accused of such selectivity in *The Making of Men*? On a detailed reading, what is striking about the book is the relative *absence* of atrocity tales, something which makes the book stand out within an ethnographic tradition not usually shy about including as much blood and gore as possible! So, for a study which regarded participant observation as being 'the core methodology of the book' (Haywood and Mac an Ghaill 1998: 125), there are actually remarkably few directly observed events included and commented on within the narrative. Rather, the book heavily relies on material taken from interviews with teachers and pupils.

However, one of the most powerful first-hand incidents to which Mac an Ghaill refers – the account of the exchange of flowers with which he opens the book – happened not in Parnell School but in a school where he had previously taught. The incident is an excellent example of the general point which Mac an Ghaill advances within *The Making of Men* concerning the reinforcement of certain dominant forms of masculinity within state secondary schools, but it is perhaps rather disingenuous of him to use such a powerful example without including similar accounts directly relating to Parnell School. Mac an Ghaill describes the flower incident as a 'key moment' – that is, a moment 'in which you begin to reconceptualize "what's going on" in the research arena' (Mac an Ghaill 1994: 2). By definition, then, key moments are unlikely to happen every day. However, the fact that he does not include any similar 'key moments' from his five years of observations at Parnell School has the unfortunate effect of weakening his argument in as much as we are left wondering whether this event was a 'one off' or, rather, typical of secondary schools in general. If this is a form of selectivity, then Mac an Ghaill is guilty as charged.

Foster and Hammersley's second point is that researchers concerned with educational inequality (a concept which, they argue, is invariably defined on the researcher's own terms) are often guilty of subjecting certain accounts to closer scrutiny than others. *Young, Gifted and Black* is picked out for special attention in this respect, and they point to what they regard as Mac an Ghaill's tendency to accept the accounts of pupils at face value, in contrast to the 'sustained ideology critique' to which teachers' accounts are subjected. Readers must judge for themselves whether this is a fair criticism of Mac an Ghaill's earlier work. However, in deciding whether he is similarly guilty with respect to *The Making of Men*, let us consider the following example, taken from a discussion of male teachers' and female pupils' views of the role of the school in 'producing' appropriate pupil femininities. Both the teacher and the pupils are referring to the new 'care work' courses which had been introduced under the auspices of the new vocationalist agenda:

> Mr Middleton: These girls lack confidence... They will tell you that the care courses we have devised for them give them back that confidence... The new vocational courses have given them new skills and most importantly confidence in themselves that comes from acquiring those skills.

> Kelly: The teachers told us to write down what we had learned from the caring course. I told him nothing. And then he said what about all the stuff you learned about child care. What a stupid man. I couldn't even begin to tell him, that's not learning. I do all that at home...

> Kerry: When he asked me what I had learned, I told him 'I've learned that you are trying to make us housewives'. He went mad, saying that we were learning lots of new skills. That's rubbish, it's just common sense; to us anyway.

In his subsequent analysis of these and similar statements made by both teachers and pupils, Mac an Ghaill clearly places greater weight on the pupils' accounts, even labelling the teachers' comments as 'patronising'. Does Mac an Ghaill, therefore, prioritise the pupils' accounts over those of the teachers? The answer, we think, is a clear and unequivocal 'yes', but this is not an act to which Mac an Ghaill is ashamed to admit: 'As feminist research has shown, teacher discourses and male academic representations of working-class young women have served to marginalise their experiences and make invisible their responses to schooling' (Mac an Ghaill 1994: 119). So, Mac an Ghaill's claim in the book's introduction that he is committed to giving 'high status to research participants knowledges, understandings and feelings' (ibid: 14) needs to be qualified slightly. He is undoubtedly faithful in reporting a variety of angles on the issues being discussed throughout the book but, as a political act, is not hesitant in prioritising some participants' voices over others, namely the voices of those whom he argues have previously been marginalised and spoken for.

In more recent methodological writing, however, Mac an Ghaill has problematised his former stance:

> One of the key areas of debate in critical social and cultural research is that concerning the explanatory status of experience... In fieldwork situations there is the possibility of members of a subordinated group... sensitising the researcher to alternative perceptions of *what is going on.* However, it does not necessarily follow that there is a need to argue that as a result of their subordinated position, groups speak a truth. (Haywood and Mac an Ghaill 1998: 128 – emphasis in original)

Thus, Mac an Ghaill appears to have moved away from his earlier allegiance to a form of standpoint epistemology which *necessarily* accorded greater validity to the accounts of oppressed individuals. Instead, he presents a case for acknowledging the 'high epistemological status' of marginalised groups relative to more powerful groups, 'without ascribing a simple truth to them' (ibid: 130). While this may be his position now, it is not at all clear that his thinking had moved on this far within *The Making of Men,* which clearly prioritises certain accounts over others, regardless of where the truth may lie.

In giving greater status to certain accounts in this way, however, Mac an Ghaill is nonetheless able to capitalise on the creative tension which arises *between* the very often, if not invariably, conflicting accounts of teachers and pupils. From the earlier example, we can see how, by placing these different perspectives alongside each other, an invaluable insight is gained into the 'gendered cultural gap' between the male teacher and his female students, regardless of whose account (if anybody's) is 'right'. Seeing through the eyes of the people being studied is, of course, a keynote of qualitative research, yet Bryman (1988) notes that many studies are flawed by a failure to acknowledge the existence of competing viewpoints. Mac an Ghaill, however, not only manages to present a variety of perspectives, but develops important insights from the tensions that are thus generated.

Research as empowerment: empowerment for whom?

In providing a convincingly authentic account of the experiences of marginalised groups of young men, Mac an Ghaill reveals another closely related aspect of his agenda as a researcher: a commitment to 'giving a voice' to those otherwise lacking a platform for their views and experiences. In *Young, Gifted and Black*, Mac an Ghaill gave a voice to the Asian Warriors, the Rasta Heads and the Black Sisters. Likewise, in *The Making of Men* he gives a clear voice to a number of marginalised groups – in particular, to female students and to gay students. Mac an Ghaill also notes in a number of places that he viewed the research as a collaborative exercise, marked by reciprocity and mutual respect. This is perhaps most obvious in his discussion of gay students' experiences of the education system. The topics which formed the subject matter of this aspect of the research were chosen by the students themselves, and Mac an Ghaill's close affinity with the group is self-evident. There is a stark contrast to be drawn here between Mac an Ghaill's rich portrayal of the experiences of both gay and straight young men who feel marginalised because of their refusal to adopt the values of hegemonic masculinity, and Jim Walker's attempts to do justice to the experiences of the similarly marginalised 'three friends' in the aforementioned *Louts and Legends* (Walker 1988). Whereas Mac an Ghaill's work problematises hegemonic rather than subordinated masculinities, Walker treads warily around what he regards as the ambiguous sexualities and masculinities of the three friends, labelling their responses to the aggression of the Footballers and the Greeks as 'banding together in adversity', rather than representing a valid sub-cultural form of its own.

It is also refreshing to hear the voices of the 'Academic Achievers' – a group of diligent working-class male pupils – represented within a sympathetic context. School ethnographers have often denigrated the commitment to hard work and conformity of 'non-deviant' pupils, in contrast to a noisy celebration of 'resistant' anti-school sub-cultures.

Indeed, by now we know a fair amount about male anti-school sub-cultures from the work of ethnographers such as Hargreaves, Lacey, Willis and Walker. The similarities both over time and across different cultures between the anti-school groups identified by these writers are striking: the importance of racism, sexism, homophobia and violence to their daily lives have been hammered home repeatedly, often with a less than critical gaze. In contrast, one of the strengths of *The Making of Men* is the way in which it taps into the experiences of young people who are situated on the margins of what is deemed acceptable 'masculine' behaviour. (This is also a refreshing aspect of another relatively recent ethnography, *Divide and School* (Abraham 1995), where we are introduced to the 'Gothic Punks', a group of boys who were viewed with suspicion by both teachers and pupils alike for being interested in 'arty' subjects and for treating female pupils as peers.)

In *The Making of Men* Mac an Ghaill flags up his desire 'to operationalise an emancipatory research method... with its emphasis on collaboration, reciprocity and reflexivity' (Mac an Ghaill 1994: 5), and the process of giving a voice to powerless groups is, he argues, an essential part of the empowerment process. Mac an Ghaill was, however, criticised by the late Barry Troyna on this point (Troyna 1994). Troyna's argument – with reference to *Young, Gifted and Black* – was that Mac an Ghaill was guilty of conflating the process of *giving a voice to* marginalised groups (an achievement which Troyna did not dispute) with the process of *empowering* those groups, whether as individuals or collectively. Responding to a similar, earlier criticism by Troyna, Mac an Ghaill had disagreed with Troyna's assessment, arguing that 'my study operated within an anti-racist and anti-sexist framework and did empower the students who were involved in it' (Mac an Ghaill 1993: 162). The main drift of Troyna's argument, however, was that while the young people involved in Mac an Ghaill's research on racism in schools had undoubtedly gained a platform for their views, it was not entirely accurate to claim that this process had empowered them, as their situation within the school and within broader society had not tangibly improved as a result of their involvement, even if they now had a much greater understanding of their oppression. Similarly, it is hard to see how the gay students and the other marginalised groups represented in *The Making of Men* were empowered by their involvement: they still remained at the bottom of the pecking order in the school, they were still very much the outsiders in an environment where aggression and 'macho' authority were the dominant masculine values.

Mac an Ghaill has always been adamant that involvement in research tends to produce an enhanced sense of self-awareness and therefore of confidence, and that these are important forms of empowerment, even if material conditions remain largely unchanged. One respondent notes for example that his involvement in the research had represented a milestone in his life:

> I've talked to you in a way that I've never talked to anyone and still don't, can't. At home we never talk like that about how we feel or even show how we care about each other... It's really a shame because it really helps you sort your head out and all the rest of it. (Mac an Ghaill 1994: 174)

We could no doubt argue long and hard over whether Mac an Ghaill's research did or did not empower his respondents in any tangible sense. The important point to note, however, and one which Mac an Ghaill himself readily concedes, is that 'empowerment' (however defined) and 'giving a voice' are not necessarily synonymous. Indeed, Troyna and Carrington (1989) point to examples of research on black communities where 'giving a voice' has actually served to reinforce stereotypical images of black people as victims or problems, while Finch (1984) has also written of her fears that her research which gave voice to working-class organisers of pre-school playgroups could have been used to bolster stereotypes of working-class women as inadequate mothers.

The discussion so far assumes that it is self-evident who the powerless groups are within *The Making of Men*. It has been assumed that Mac an Ghaill was primarily concerned with empowering both gay and marginalised male students, and female students, rather than other groups within Parnell School, yet there are grounds for arguing that it is actually not at all clear cut who the powerless groups are within the study. Mac an Ghaill expresses greatest empathy with the students who are on the margins on account of their rejection of hegemonic masculinity, and he eloquently demonstrates how such young men, by failing to meet up to the requirements and expectations of hegemonic masculinity as constructed within Parnell School, are consistently marginalised in the life of the school. They are bullied by classmates, teased by teachers, and generally consigned to the sidelines. In contrast, the Macho Lads and their various hangers on are very much at the top of the school's masculinity pecking order, even gaining tacit support from certain male teachers. As one female teacher, speaking of certain of her male colleagues, tells Mac an Ghaill:

> Oh, they'll be tough with the yobs but at the same time you can see them passing on the masculine codes that boys will be boys. All the usual male bonding that cuts across age and status differences. (Mac an Ghaill 1994: 49)

Nonetheless, on leaving school it is precisely these young men, rather than the other groups with whom Mac an Ghaill sympathises, who will in all probability be more prone to unemployment and social exclusion, and on this basis it would be conceivable to create a case for siding with *this* group rather than other groups. As another (male) teacher argued:

> I'm not trying to condone the irresponsibility of the working-class lads. They're tough and at times quite a handful but at least they're more straightforward than those half hippie middle-class kids... You can be sure that none of them with all their connections will end up on a training scheme or on the dole. (ibid: 48)

Thus their hard macho response to their schooling could be interpreted as an understandable reaction, or a form of resistance, to their perceived lessened chances of post-school success: hence the indulgent attitude of some of the teachers. In this sense, it could be argued that it is the Macho Lads who are truly on the margins, the longer term losers, the unwitting victims of current social and economic change (Haywood and Mac an Ghaill 1996). As such, do not the Macho Lads deserve our greater sympathy?

By what criteria, then, does Mac an Ghaill choose to identify with one group of pupils rather than another? In *Young, Gifted and Black*, he justifies his commitment to black and Asian pupils on the basis of Becker's classic argument that sociologists not only *should* not, but *cannot*, sit on the fence in the conduct of their research (Becker 1967). Rather, they are compelled to side with either the 'underdogs' or the 'overdogs'. On reading his earlier work, one is easily convinced that the underdogs are the groups of pupils affected by racism, whereas the overdogs are those who benefit from the school's endemic racism. In the context of *The Making of Men*, however, Becker's view is less helpful, even though in the context of school life the students who fail to meet up to the requirements of hegemonic masculinity are undoubtedly the underdogs in relation to the Macho Lads. The problem is that more generally such a simplistic polarisation between 'goodies' and 'baddies' seems inappropriate, as there are sound reasons for arguing that both groups of pupils deserve a show of solidarity, albeit for very different reasons. The following comments perhaps help us to understand Mac an Ghaill's position:

> If (partisan) sociologists are to act in the role of arbiter between interest groups... there must be some appeal to a body of ethical principles if justice is to be realised. Ultimately... 'it is to values, not to factions that sociologists must give their most basic commitment'. (Troyna and Carrington 1989: 207, quoting Gouldner 1975)

Thus Mac an Ghaill's identification of groups other than the Macho Lads as the underdogs within his study, presumably arises from his previously stated ethical commitment to the values of feminism and gay liberation. This causes him to oppose any behaviour which is oppressive in nature, even though the perpetrators might *themselves* experience oppression, albeit of a different kind. Nonetheless, he is careful to avoid representing the Macho Lads as 'one-dimensional oppressors', and writes of them with some sympathy, acknowledging the increasingly restrictive labour market conditions which they will soon have to face. Ultimately, however, Mac an Ghaill's chief sympathies lie with the young men who share in a subordinated form of masculinity within Parnell School, particularly those whose sexuality represents an overt challenge to hegemonic masculinities. Such critical distance is in keeping with his stated aim 'to deconstruct earlier male academic representations of the schooling of young males' (Mac an Ghaill 1994: 14). Interestingly, he notes that this stance tended to surprise male teachers, who often assumed that, 'as a male researcher I would collude in the reproduction of the invidious "normality" that serves to mystify the mechanisms through which male heterosexual privilege and domination operate' (Mac an Ghaill 1994: 155).

Conclusion

The Making of Men is an important book for anyone interested in the role of schooling in constructing and reinforcing dominant

forms of masculinity, and in marginalising subordinate masculinities and sexual identities. It is also an important book for methodological reasons, and within this chapter we have highlighted just
two of the issues of method that the book is likely to raise among its
readership: the appropriateness of taking sides in the research
process, and the extent to which the research process can be a source
of empowerment for those involved. By so doing, we have argued
that value-free research is an impossibility, and that any research
inevitably will be affected by the values of the researcher – regardless
of whether their value position is made explicit. Moreover, a
researcher's own values and biases may lead them to prioritise
certain accounts over others – even if unwittingly. Throughout the
book Mac an Ghaill makes no secret of his political stance and this
has a major impact on the style both of the conduct of his research
and of the writing up of his findings. This is by no means a
criticism, but is rather an inevitability in research of this kind,
written from the perspective of critical theory. The alternative is for
the researcher to adopt a rather bland persona, to become all things
to all people (Measor 1985), but by so doing leaving people second
guessing about one's own stance. *The Making of Men* would have
been a very different book if Mac an Ghaill had taken that route.
Instead, the sections of the book which are concerned with subordinated masculinities, particularly the experiences of gay students, are
extremely revealing and detailed, precisely because of his readiness
to identify with those subordinated masculinities.

Regardless of the strongly argued merits and demerits of this
approach, Mac an Ghaill's work therefore stands within an
established tradition of political activism among educational sociologists. Michael Apple, the noted American educational sociologist,
recently argued in an introduction to a book on this topic (Gitlin
1994) that:

> Too often the idea that educational research must be politically engaged
> is reduced to a slogan. It is a purely rhetorical point in which researchers
> assert their organic connections with various oppressed groups but then
> go about their business in ordinary ways. (Apple 1994: ix)

On the evidence of this book, these are accusations that Mac an
Ghaill can shrug off with some confidence.

Additional reading

For more on the theoretical ideas underpinning Mac an Ghaill's work, see Bob Connell's *Masculinities* (1995), while Debbie Epstein and Richard Johnson's *Schooling Sexualities* (1997) provides an interesting discussion of some of the more substantive issues raised by *The Making of Men*. Andrew Gitlin's edited collection *Power and Method: Political Activism and Educational Research* (1994) provides further examples of research informed by a very explicit political agenda, while Mary Maynard and June Purvis' *Researching Womens Lives from a Feminist Perspective* provides additional insights into feminist standpoint epistemology (1994).

Chapter 3

The Family: Finch and Mason's *Negotiating Family Responsibilities*

Introduction

Consider the following questions: do you expect anyone to help you pay off your overdraft when you graduate? Do you hope that someone will provide you with emergency accommodation if you ever find yourself unable to afford a place of your own? What if you ever fall seriously ill: is there anyone you can rely on to look after you? Implicit in each of these questions is the assumption that we rather hope that we will have someone to fall back on in a time of need. For many people that someone will be a partner or a close friend, but it is also very likely that relatives such as parents, older siblings, grandparents even, will also come to mind as potential sources of help. But will they help you? And if they do, will accepting their help make you feel obligated to them? Will anything be expected of you in return? What if you cannot reciprocate? Or maybe you expect your relatives to help because you have supported them in some way in the past?

Such dilemmas and calculations lie at the heart of Janet Finch and Jennifer Mason's *Negotiating Family Responsibilities*, a broad-ranging multi-method study of contemporary family relationships, especially their significance as sources of practical and financial help. Are there rules concerning the giving and receiving of help within families? If so, how do they operate? As Finch and Mason's work demonstrates, these are important questions to be asked in contemporary Britain, not least because many social welfare policies are based on the assumption that the family will act as the primary provider of certain types of care and support. The removal in 1988 of 16- and 17-year-olds' benefit rights, for example, was based in part on the premise of family support, while care in the community policies likewise assume the existence of relatives who are ready and willing to provide help. Similarly, there are many assumptions concerning family support built into the system of student loans and fees for higher education. But are these assumptions accurate? Often they are not; we all know of penniless students whose parents are unable or unwilling to provide financial assistance to them, or of media horror stories of elderly relatives being abandoned on the steps of hospitals and nursing homes by their families. As Finch and Mason argue:

> At a time when public statements about the decline in family life are commonplace, we are trying to find out whether these relationships within kin groups do have any real meaning. We were especially interested in whether concepts of family responsibility, or duty or obligation make any sense to people living in contemporary Britain. (Finch and Mason 1993: 1)

Researching the family

In his book *Family Connections*, David Morgan (1996) provides a useful overview of the development of the sociology of the family. He tells the tale of a marginalised sub-discipline, despite the centrality of 'the family' in some shape or form to most people's lives. However, he also notes that research on the family has nonetheless flourished within certain sociological traditions, even if not specifically referred to as 'the sociology of the family'. Community studies of the 1950s and 60s, for example, focused on the overlap between kinship networks and close community ties. Young and Willmott's study of Bethnal Green, *Family and Kinship in East London* (1957), is perhaps one of the best known examples of this genre. Drawing heavily on the theoretical frameworks and methodology of social anthropology, it produced what many critics regarded as a mythical and overly-romanticised representation of working-class family life (Crow and Allan 1994). (Quite what these researchers would have made of

Walford, of *Eastenders* fame, is hard to imagine!) These early community studies were largely based on participant observation, often augmented by other methods, such as in-depth interviewing and diary keeping. Moreover, they tended to be based on one very specific locale, raising questions of how generalisable the findings of any given study could ever be – even over time within the *same* location, as demonstrated by the inconsistent findings of area restudies.

By the late 1960s and early 1970s the study of the family had become integral to the development of certain strands of feminist sociology, particularly (but by no means exclusively) within the Marxist feminist tradition. These studies were based very much around theoretical and empirical explorations of inequalities within family life as part of a much broader analysis of gender relations within modern society (Gittens 1993). Key themes included the relationship between the family and the state, issues concerning sexual violence within the home, and the relationship between sexual divisions of labour within the domestic sphere and within the public sphere. While earlier studies focused very much on the institution of marriage, and parenthood within marriage, later studies attempted to unpack the very concept of 'family', in order to challenge the stereo-typical notion of the nuclear family composed of mum, dad and 2.2 children and to consider alternative ways of 'doing family'. More recent research has, for example, focused on the 'families of choice' of gay and lesbian individuals, and on the extended kinship networks brought about by complex stepfamily relationships.

These early feminist studies of the family were characterised by a strong reliance on qualitative research methodology, particularly in-depth qualitative interviewing. This preference arose out of broader debates concerning feminist epistemology and whether or not one could talk of a distinct feminist research methodology and of associated feminist methods (Maynard and Purvis 1994; Stanley and Wise 1992). Qualitative methods were seen as being particularly appropriate to the study of women's experiences of the family, allowing women to speak out for themselves within a sphere where men all too often had spoken on their behalf. As a legacy of both the community studies approach and the influence of feminism, qualitative methods have remained the predominant approach within sociological research on the family. There is nonetheless a strong strand of more quantitative research on the family, based largely on the secondary analysis of large data sets such as the General

Household Survey, census data in various forms and, more recently, the British Household Panel Survey.

Conceptually speaking, much recent family-related research has attempted to steer a middle course between the polarised representation of the family as *either* a uniformly oppressive structure *or* a constant source of unfailing love, support and harmony. As Morgan argues, focusing on one aspect at the expense of the other ignores the complexities of family life:

> Family relationships are also about unities and patterns of cooperation. To recognise this is not to return to some reified notion of marriage or family as undifferentiated wholes. However, it is also the case that family members do have some sense of solidarity and unity, for whatever reasons, and these identities do have wider consequences'. (Morgan 1996: 9)

Morgan argues that much of this focus on family cooperation and solidarity has arisen from a growing interest in the concept of the life course, with sociologists developing a strong interest in intergenerational support and care across its various phases. This has brought together sociologists who do not necessarily view themselves as family sociologists *per se*. For instance, sociologists of youth are increasingly focusing on young people's family relationships, due to increased levels of dependency upon parents and changing patterns of household formation (Allatt and Yeandle 1992; Irwin 1995; Jones 1995), while sociologists of ageing are also looking at the exchange of support across generations (Pilcher 1995). All of this proves Morgan's point that there is a great deal of interest in the family, albeit not always expressed under the label 'sociology of the family'.

Negotiating Family Responsibilities

Negotiating Family Responsibilities is a study which reflects this middle way. It is based on the findings of the Family Obligations Project, an initiative funded by the Economic and Social Research Council, and carried out in the Greater Manchester area between 1985 and 1989. The study involved a two-stage research strategy: a face-to-face survey of 978 randomly sampled adults, and semi-structured interviews with 88 people, 31 of whom had responded to the survey. Some people were interviewed more than once, yielding 120 interviews in total. The survey was designed to explore the normative values people hold with respect to family responsibilities: what do the public think *ought* to be done by family members under particular sets of circumstances? In contrast, the interviews were designed to explore the significance of normative views *in practice*, and were based around discussion of specific examples of negotiations over family responsibilities. Of the original 31 interviewees, 11 gave their consent for relatives to be contacted, and in these cases between three and eight family members were also interviewed, bringing the total number of interviewees to 88. Together, these two approaches formed a complementary whole, focusing on both public and private meanings of 'family', and allowing Finch and Mason to compare expressed beliefs with the realities of family relationships. In other words, the chosen method-ology allowed the researchers to explore both the normative and the negotiated aspects of family responsibilities.

The key method used within the survey was the vignette technique. Vignettes present third-party, hypothetical situations in which people may find themselves, and respondents are then asked how they think the situation should be resolved. (Figure 3.1 reproduces one of the vignettes used in the survey.) Vignettes are used with increasing frequency in survey research, and are seen as particu-larly useful for tapping into information on 'attitudes to, or courses of action in, complex social situations' (Courtenay 1986: 5). Once the analysis of the survey data had begun, however, it emerged that there was no general consensus on 'the right thing to do', and that there were remarkably few circumstances in which people agreed that the responsibility to help clearly lay with relatives. Rather, in general, the survey respondents were strongly divided in their views on appropriate levels of help from family members as opposed to other potential sources of help.

Suppose that a couple with a young child have returned from working abroad and can't afford to buy or rent anywhere to live until one of them gets a job. Should any of their relatives offer to have the family in their own home for the next few months?

Figure 3.1   Example of a short vignette (Finch and Mason 1993: 198)

Nonetheless, there were three common features of the circumstances where people *did* think the family should be the first port of call. First, family help tended to be endorsed where a need was seen as entirely legitimate and where the person requiring help was regarded as being faultless: in other words, they were *deserving* of help. Second, people felt that offers of help were more likely to be forthcoming when fairly limited assistance was required, whether in terms of time, skill, effort or material aid. Third, the parent–child relationship was accorded a special status, and came closest to being viewed as having associated fixed responsibilities, although support flowing from this relationship was not regarded as automatic or unlimited. Thus, although people believed that help was more likely to be given in certain situations than in others, whether or not that help would be provided, and the specific form of that help, was subject to negotiation on the merits of the case.

The second stage of the research, based around qualitative interviews, revealed that most people could indeed report many examples of either giving or receiving help from their kin, yet there were still no obvious 'rules' determining whether or not help should be provided. The interviews did, however, reveal some of the processes by which help is given and received, including the centrality of reciprocity, legitimate excuse making, and moral reputation. Reciprocity was a very important theme and, although the receiving of a gift clearly created the expectation that a counter-gift would be proffered at an appropriate time, it was still seen to be very important to get the balance right and not feel oneself beholden to kin. It was also clear, however, that some people were nonetheless able to legitimately avoid commitment to other family members, and being unable, rather than unwilling, to provide support proved to be the key to this process of legitimate excuse making. For example, the father of one interviewee had needed full-time care following hospitalisation. As none of the siblings was able to move into the family home to nurse him, they insisted that their father's estranged wife move back in, her objections being viewed as evidence of an unreasonable unwillingness to help, rather than an inability.

Finally, respondents were very conscious of their own moral reputation, and it was clearly important for many family members that their action (or lack of action) be seen in a good light. Whether to ask for help or wait until help was freely offered was a case in point, and seemed to depend on what was being asked for and how one asked. Thus, requests for gifts were out, but requests for loans were acceptable. Similarly, appearing to *expect* help was a definite no-no, even where help had previously been given by the person now in need. Even the act of 'being generous' became a complex moral minefield, with the potential for causing resentment on the part of the recipient because of an inferred obligation.

Such are the main substantive findings of Finch and Mason's study. Above and beyond the considerable interest which the study has generated among family sociologists, however, it also raises many interesting issues of method. In common with the other studies discussed in this book, the authors are themselves aware of these issues and have written specifically about various aspects of their research methodology (Finch 1987; Finch and Mason 1990a; Mason 1994, 1996). This chapter is concerned with three particular issues. First, we will focus on the challenge of combining data derived from different research methods. We will then consider the limits of the vignette technique; and third, we will explore the use of theoretical sampling, the strategy used within the interview phase of the research. These are issues which are partly rooted in debates concerning the different epistemological assumptions underpinning quantitative and qualitative research, a theme returned to in greater depth in Chapter 10; the discussion in the current chapter relates more to the *practical* difficulties which arise when trying to combine approaches drawn from different research traditions.

Combining methods

It is quite common for researchers to rely on a variety of methods within the one study, although more often than not they tend to combine either different qualitative methods or different quantitative methods, depending upon their methodological leanings or the research question in hand. Nonetheless, it is not uncommon for researchers to combine methods from *both* approaches, and in his important text, *Quantity and Quality in Social Research*, Bryman (1988) provides numerous examples of studies which have done just that. He argues, however, that priority often tends to be given to one or other method: in other words, qualitative research may be used as a preparatory stage to an essentially quantitative study, or vice versa. In such cases, the different methods are not accorded equal status; rather, one approach is used to facilitate the other, by identifying salient points which will form the basis of a more detailed exploration. In contrast, Finch and Mason argue that equal status was given to *both* aspects of their two-stage research design, albeit for different reasons:

> Not only were we employing different methods to generate different types of data, but we anticipated that these would tell us about different aspects of family obligations. We were explicitly *not* following the more conventional model of using a survey to provide a broad picture of a phenomenon, and a qualitative study to cover a more limited area of the same ground, but in more depth. (Mason 1994: 90 – emphasis in original)

We would argue that such an approach represents a form of 'methodological triangulation'. This term is used to describe techniques which attempt to obtain a rounded picture of a particular phenomenon by studying it from multiple viewpoints, of necessity drawing on different data sources, and invariably involving the use of a variety of different research methods. While on occasions these different methods are drawn solely from *either* the quantitative *or* the qualitative tradition, methodological triangulation often involves the use of methods drawn from *both* traditions. Crucially, each of the methods used is given equal weighting, rather than one being subordinated to another. As we have seen, this was the intention behind the two-stage research strategy of the Family Obligations Project. Each stage was important in its own right, shedding light on a different aspect of family relationships – including both the public face and the private face of kinship responsibility.

However, Mason is cautious about using the term 'triangulation' to describe her work with Finch: 'We were not using our two-stage research design as a method of "triangulation", at least not in the sense of using one part of the study to check the validity of the other part' (Mason 1994: 104). Elsewhere, she argues even more strongly that:

> At its worst, the logic of triangulation says that you can use different methods, or data sources, to investigate the same phenomenon, and that in the process you can judge the efficacy or validity of the different methods and sources by comparing the products... This is problematic because... different methods and data sources are likely to throw light onto different social or ontological phenomena or research questions. Furthermore, it implies a view of the social world which says that there is

one, objective, and knowable social reality, and all that social researchers have to do is to work out which are the most appropriate triangulation points to measure it by. (Mason 1996: 148–9)

The perspective which Mason rejects has indeed tended to base triangulation's main strength on the vulnerability of the single method approach within the social sciences. Cohen and Manion (1985) argue, for example, that researchers who rely exclusively on one particular method are potentially open to the accusation of bias in the picture they develop from their research. By contrast, they suggest that a multi-method approach allows the researcher to say with greater confidence that their 'results' are not simply an artefact of a particular research method. This argument tends to assume, however, that different methods will produce broadly comparable data, and that they thus allow the researcher to get nearer to some notion of 'objective truth' than would data generated by reliance on a single method alone. As Mason rightly points out, this argument is perilously close to concluding that there is only one 'correct version of social reality', which can only be discovered through producing essentially similar findings from different data sources and methods focusing on the same phenomenon. Thus, rather than arguing that the strength of triangulation lies in its capacity to reveal different, but equally valid, facets of a social phenomenon, writers such as Cohen and Manion argue instead that the strength of the approach lies in its ability to build up overlapping layers of truth, each layer essentially confirming all other layers.

This is a position which Finch and Mason are right to reject, linked as it is to a spurious claim to the achievement of enhanced validity through the use of multiple methods. However, not all social researchers view triangulation in this narrow sense. Indeed, Bryman argues to the contrary that, 'it is in the spirit of the idea of triangulation that inconsistent results may emerge', but importantly 'it is not in the spirit that one should simply opt for one set of findings rather than another' (Bryman 1988: 134). This points to the way in which triangulation can be used effectively to explore the dynamics of complex social phenomena, highlighting the multi-layered and often contradictory nature of social life. Indeed, it is within these contradictions that one can begin to gain a richer understanding of human behaviour, which is precisely what Finch and Mason argue they set out to do through their multi-method approach: 'Our view was that an understanding of kin obligatedness *in practice* would require an analysis of the relationship between the two data sets and the social processes they expressed' (Mason 1994: 91 – emphasis in original).

A particularly good example of how Finch and Mason sought to analyse this relationship can be found in their creative use of the apparent tensions between the two data sets in relation to the impact of divorce and remarriage on the negotiation of family obligations. One might reasonably suppose that many ex-spouses would cease to feel any sense of obligation to their in-laws following marital breakdown, and vice versa, with potentially far-reaching consequences for the provision of support such as child care and elder care. Finch and Mason (1990b) sought to interrogate this assumption, first by exploring normative beliefs concerning the 'right thing to do' in the event of divorce within a kinship group, and then by examining particular instances of family breakdown cited by respondents from within the qualitative data set.

1. Jane is a young woman with children aged 3 and 5. She was recently divorced. She wants to go back to work and she needs the money. But if she has a job she must find someone to mind the children after school. Her own family live far away but her former mother-in-law Ann Hill is at home all day and lives nearby. Jane has always got on well with her former mother-in-law.
Should Ann offer to look after Jane's children?

2. Ann *does* offer to help and Jane goes back to work. Some years later Ann has a stroke and needs regular care and help in the home.
Should Jane offer to give up her job and look after her former mother-in-law?

3. Jane *does* give up her job. A year later Jane remarries.
Now that Jane has remarried, should she go on helping her former mother-in-law?
Why do you think she should go on helping/should stop helping?

Figure 3.2   'Jane and Ann Hill' vignette (Finch and Mason 1993: 34–5)

A number of the survey vignettes alluded to the renegotiation of relationships post-divorce, and Finch and Mason were surprised to discover that the 'clean break' solution was by no means the universally favoured option. In particular, they point to the responses to a vignette based around 'Jane and Ann Hill' (Figure 3.2). The responses revealed overwhelming support for continuing contact between the former daughter-in-law (Jane) and the former mother-in-law (Ann) for the purposes of childcare, a mixed response to the idea that Jane should give up her job to care for Ann (although 43 per cent were nonetheless in favour), and overwhelming support for continued assistance to Ann following Jane's remarriage. The responses to parts one and three, then, seem to point to a widespread view that under certain circumstances divorce and subsequent remarriage are irrelevant to the continuation of relationships between former in-laws.

In this light, and following comparison with other similar vignettes, Finch and Mason concluded that the lower level of consensus over whether or not Jane should give up her job to care for Ann can be interpreted as an ambivalence over the wisdom of a younger person sacrificing their paid employment to care for *anyone*, rather than a judgement on kin relationships following divorce *per se*. In contrast, only a minority of the survey respondents felt that divorce should alter the relationship between Jane and Ann, causing the authors to conclude that:

> In terms of publicly expressed beliefs about the morality of family obligations, divorce and remarriage are treated as morally neutral events. This may seem surprising, especially at a common sense level, where these events are infused with blame, guilt and recriminations. But our evidence suggests that people regard continuing relationships with former in-laws at the very least as permissible, and that they positively should continue if a mutually supportive and good relationship has been built up. (Finch and Mason 1990b: 227)

From the responses to this vignette, one might suppose that the qualitative interviews would have revealed a whole series of examples of strong post-divorce relationships between former in-laws. However, in practice there were very few examples of ongoing support of this nature. It should be noted, of course, that the interview sample was not intended to be statistically representative; nonetheless, one might have expected rather more cases of this kind to have emerged from a group of 88 individuals. Initially, one might be tempted to view these differences between the data sources as *discrepancies*. To do so, however, highlights a fundamental error which can easily be made within research, of attempting to read off actions from beliefs. There is rarely a straightforward, one-to-one correspondence between these two facets of social life, and the challenge which Finch and Mason explicitly set themselves was to try to understand the nature of the relationship between them. So, rather than concluding that one or other source was 'wrong', the apparent incongruity between them formed the basis for a creative analysis of the features which were shared in common by both the vignette responses and instances within the interview data of similarly supportive relationships.

So how was this achieved? The method of analysis adopted by Finch and Mason is a form of analytic induction, described by Glaser and Strauss as a method which is:

> Concerned with generating and proving an integrated, limited, precise, universally applicable theory of causes accounting for a specific behaviour... It tests a limited number of hypotheses with *all* available data, consisting of numbers of clearly defined and carefully selected cases of the phenomena... theory is generated by the reformulation of hypotheses and redefinition of the phenomena forced by constantly confronting the theory with negative cases, cases which do not confirm the current formulation. (Glaser and Strauss 1967: 104)

First, then, a case was sought from the interview data which corresponded most closely to the situation of the Hills. This was by no means straightforward, partly as a consequence of the specificity of the vignette, but also because among the eighteen divorced people in the qualitative sample there were very few examples of friendly *and* – crucially – practically supportive relationships continuing after the breakdown of a marriage. The case that came closest to the Hill vignette was that of Mary Mycock (a pseudonym), who although now remarried had maintained a close and supportive relationship with both her ex-husband's mother and his siblings, and – rather more unusually – had also developed a friendship with her current husband's former father-in-law (see Finch and Mason 1990b for a detailed account of her circumstances). By means of a close analysis of Mary Mycock's situation, five features were identified which were also broadly implicit within the Hill vignette. These were: a history of reciprocal support between former in-laws, the quality of relationships while the marriage lasted, a desire to maintain relationships between grandparents and grandchildren, the process of divorce consolidating the relationship rather than undermining it, and the discovery of an acceptable basis for post-divorce relationships. Comparisons were then made right across the data set, looking in particular at cases either where similar circumstances had led to different outcomes or, conversely, where different circumstances had led to similar outcomes.

By this process of comparing both similar and dissimilar cases, it was possible to explore the relative importance of these five features to an understanding of whether or not post-divorce relationships with in-laws were likely to survive in other situations. Finch and Mason concluded that the key to good post-divorce relationships between in-laws was a history of good relationships before the divorce. At first glance this might seem to be a rather obvious point, but it is a point which needs to be qualified, as even good pre-divorce relationships were not always sufficient for their later maintenance. There were, for instance, a number of cases where this factor had been present yet, due to a strong sense of divided loyalties (particularly on the part of parents-in-law), relationships had eventually lapsed. More generally, Finch and Mason concluded that people do not *expect* to maintain post-divorce relationships with in-laws, yet are happy when they are able to do so: 'This echoes evidence about how people treat in-law relationships in general, regarding themselves as rather "lucky" if they work out well' (Finch and Mason 1990b: 243). Further, these conclusions make sense of, and complement, the findings of the survey data, which had revealed that the majority of people felt that a strong post-divorce relationship was feasible and desirable in the case of Jane and Ann Hill, even though the interview data revealed that in practice such relationships were unusual.

The strength of this analysis is, of course, highly contingent on the robustness of the vignette technique as a method for collecting normative data, and Finch (1987) has provided a strong defence of the technique and its usefulness within the Family Obligations Project. Nonetheless, the next section will briefly consider two potential difficulties associated with the vignette technique, both of which are relevant to the previous discussion of the relationship between the two data sets.

The limits of the vignette technique

In contrast to the abstract, non-contextualised attitude statements which are more commonly used within surveys to understand normative beliefs, vignettes are highly contextualised. Indeed, this is one of their major strengths, with respondents not asked to make general statements, but to think about appropriate forms of action in very specific circumstances. Thus, 'it is a method which acknowledges that meanings are social and that morality may well be situationally specific' (Finch 1987: 106). The specificity of the vignette situation, Finch argues further, is of benefit to researchers, as they do not need to make any prior assumptions about whether a normative response is transferable to a different situation. However, these strengths can also be viewed as a source of weakness. First, if the situation to which people respond is so very specific, then surely it is almost impossible to generalise beyond the vignette or to make judgements on the transferability of responses to different, possibly even very similar, situations. While an undoubted weakness of attitude statements is that they are too general, a weakness of vignettes is that they may be *too specific*. Could we argue from the Jane and Ann Hill vignette, for example, that similar responses would be generated if the children were older – 10 and 13, for example, rather than 3 and 5 – or if Ann herself had a job? The simple answer is 'no': the only way we could test this would be to use vignettes which included these variations, possibly through using different versions of the vignette with sub-sections of the main sample. Relatedly, how important to the assessment of a vignette are respondents own assumptions concerning factors such as the race, gender, class background and age of people within the vignette? Again, only by deliberately varying these characteristics could we comment with any confidence on the significance of these details, yet by varying the vignette for different groups, comparability across the whole data set would be lost. Moreover, using multiple variations is rarely likely to be feasible in practical terms.

Second, the specificity of a vignette is bound to make respondents think about similar situations from their own lives. Indeed, Finch has argued that respondents tend to 'enter very much into the spirit of this soap opera style of questioning, identifying with the characters as people who faced real dilemmas' (Finch 1987: 109). However, the danger of close identification is that respondents do not make normative statements about what *should* be done in the outlined circumstances, but rather judge the situation in terms of their *own* likely response. In such cases, they may well disregard the specific characteristics of the person at the centre of the vignette and instead judge the vignette in their own terms: what they would like to think they would do, perhaps, or what they have indeed already done in a similar situation. This suggests that it is impossible to know on what basis a view of appropriate behaviour is being advanced. Mason agrees that this is an area of uncertainty, yet argues that for the purposes of the Family Obligations Project *it did not really matter.*

> In the survey, we were less interested in the reasoning process, than in whether people were giving replies which could be taken to represent their sense of *appropriate* answers (however they reached that conclusion). We concluded that it was reasonable to interpret our data as – at the very least – reflecting what people saw as appropriate in this way. (Mason 1994: 100 – emphasis in the original)

Thus, to Finch and Mason, the possible conflation of both impersonal and personal interpretations of the vignettes was not viewed as a major problem, as both approaches produced responses based on a sense of 'the proper thing to do'. This implies that unlike much survey research, which seeks to minimise the extent to which respondents produce answers which they may consider to be acceptable in the interviewer's eyes, in Finch and Mason's exploration of normative behaviour 'acceptable answers' paradoxically became valid forms of data, hinting at a shared awareness of a public morality concerning kinship responsibilities. Where this argument would, however, break down is if respondents provided answers on the basis of what they would *realistically* do, or had even done in the past, as opposed to what they think they ought to do, or what they think 'people in general' ought to do. A realistic appraisal of one's own likely course of action would be much more constrained by (unspecified) material concerns, and consequently would not tap into normative views in quite the same way. Unfortunately, we cannot know how the vignettes were interpreted, and it is unlikely that the respondents themselves would even be able to unravel the objective and subjective elements that they took into account in arriving at their answers.

Undoubtedly, vignettes can be a very useful method, but they are also an essentially flawed method, with very real question marks hanging over the broader claims that can be made from them. Nonetheless, Mason argues that in an imperfect world they remain one of the best methods for getting at public normative views: they *do* succeed in getting interviewees involved in a third-party event, and in getting them to give consideration to relevant factors and circumstances. Nonetheless, the use of vignettes within qualitative settings may perhaps be more fruitful, with respondents being asked to 'think aloud' by explaining exactly *why* they arrived at a particular decision. Similarly, the wider contextual information which is often sought by respondents when vignettes are used in qualitative settings – respondents asking an interviewer whether the person at the centre of a vignette is employed, for example, or whether the person has children – is often very revealing of people's decision-making processes, as well as highlighting the specificity of different courses of action depending on the particular imputed characteristics of an individual.

Theoretical sampling

In this final section we turn to a consideration of the sampling strategy that underpinned the qualitative aspect of Finch and Masons work. In order to explore the factors which were important in determining ongoing support between in-laws in the example we considered earlier, it was not necessary for the cases selected from the interview material to be representative of the broader population. Rather, Finch and Mason deliberately sought out cases from the interview material which would help to either confirm or refute the theoretical ideas they were developing. Indeed, taking one step further back, the individuals they chose to interview in the first instance were not chosen on the grounds of their typicality but on the grounds of being more likely than others to have experienced the (re)negotiation of family responsibilities. Thus they were chosen to fulfil a particular purpose within the research and subsequent theoretical analysis.

We have already seen that the survey and interview phases of Finch and Mason's research each had a very different underpinning logic in terms of their purpose within the project. Reflecting their divergent research objectives, the two phases adopted sampling strategies which similarly had very different rationales, the one underpinned by the logic of representative sampling, the other by the logic of *theoretical sampling*. Theoretical sampling is closely associated with the 'grounded theory' approach of Glaser and Strauss (1967), whose influence on Finch and Mason was noted earlier in connection with their use of analytic induction as a method of data analysis. Indeed, theoretical sampling is central to this method of analysis, as it allows researchers to sample cases which will serve to either confirm or refute their developing theories, in the case of the latter causing the researcher to modify their theory to take into account the negative case. Random sampling and theoretical sampling do not, therefore, set out to do the same thing:

> Theoretical sampling is done in order to discover categories and their properties, and to suggest the interrelationships into a theory. Statistical sampling is done to obtain accurate evidence on distributions of people among categories to be used in descriptions or verifications. Thus, in each type of research the 'adequate sample' that we should look for... is very different. (Glaser and Strauss 1967: 62–3)

The starting point for Finch and Mason's own 'adequate sample' came from the respondents to the phase one survey, many of whom had indicated a willingness to be involved in further research. However, inclusion in the initial survey alone was not sufficient reason to be selected for interview, as Finch and Mason wanted to ensure that the individuals they eventually selected would be in a position to talk about their own experiences of kinship support. A random selection would not necessarily have produced a sample possessing the relevant range of experiences to enable Finch and Mason to develop their theoretical ideas. Thus, they were deliberately looking for individuals who fell into one of two possible categories: people who had been divorced and/or remarried, and people who were aged 18 to 24. The rationale for these categories was simple: both contained people who were more likely than most to have been involved in (re)negotiating family relationships and their contingent responsibilities. Thus, divorced and remarried people were likely to have been involved in delicate negotiations over relationships with steprelatives and ex-in-laws, while 18- to 24-year-olds were likely to have been involved in negotiations over their changing states of dependence on, or independence from, family members. Clearly, other individuals outside these two categories were also likely to be involved in negotiating a variety of family responsibilities, and as a contingency plan Finch and Mason were prepared to look at other sub-groups – such as women who were in the middle of a younger and older generation – if these categories had failed to produce sufficient relevant cases. Nonetheless, a *random* selection from survey respondents would probably have yielded fewer relevant cases.

Finch and Mason did not choose these groups in order to draw straightforward comparisons between them, or to try to differentiate between rules governing each different type of negotiation. To have done so would have been to assume that the negotiations involved were substantially different on the grounds of belonging to one or other group. This was not a logic which underpinned the initial sampling, however; rather, the two groups were chosen as slightly different examples of essentially the same general phenomenon. As such, Finch and Mason actually played down the specific differences, and were as keen – if not keener – to explore the points of *similarity* between the experiences of individuals in the two groups.

It is important to note that theoretical sampling of this kind is a rigorous and systematic strategy: respondents are not simply chosen at random or because they happen to be in the right place at the right time. They are selected because of their capacity to take forward the analysis in a specifically defined way, and to enable case-by-case comparisons to be made in the interrogation of emergent theoretical hunches. This is a point which is sometimes missed by researchers who are more accustomed to the statistical rigour of probability sampling techniques. Nonetheless, a failure to provide a solid and convincing justification for *any* sampling strategy – whether used within the qualitative or the quantitative tradition – can seriously weaken the strength of the claims which can be made from a data set. Finch and Mason's considered rationale should be contrasted, for example, with the following statement taken from a recent interview-based study of 'successful people':

> Finding respondents did not present a problem. It did cross my mind initially that in finding a sample of successful people I could simply write about those whom I knew at school and university who have gone on to greater things… It was a tempting thought and I am sure that for old times' sake they would have agreed to be interviewed. However, an ego-centred sample is just that, so I went for chums of chums or people I met at parties instead. Sociologists typically do not use the phrase 'chums of chums' but dress up their less than random procedures with pretentious talk of the network and snowball technique or similar… My chosen method was to adopt a form of *purposive sampling* which, for the benefit of future textbook writers, I would like to distinguish from arbitrary or capricious sampling. Unlike those ethnographers who spend much time with respondents who are unbelievably tedious and confusing, I tried to find productive and cost-effective respondents and, by and large, the purposive sampling method was very successful. (Pahl 1995: 197–8 emphasis in original)

If this is truly the chief criterion for inclusion in Pahl's interview sample, then we are not overly convinced by the rigour of his strategy: it does indeed sound like arbitrary or capricious sampling! It is certainly the case that on occasions researchers are guilty of dressing up the reality of what is in effect a somewhat pragmatic approach to sampling, so in this sense perhaps Pahl is merely being more honest than most. But it is somewhat disingenuous of him to make this observation and then to engage in a similar exercise himself. While the terms 'theoretical sampling' and 'purposive sampling' are sometimes used interchangeably, Pahl's use of the term bears little relation to the way in which theoretical sampling is put into practice within the grounded theory approach to qualitative research. Most researchers are not being at all pretentious in their use of technical terminology, but are rather attempting to provide serious justifications for difficult sampling decisions.

It is ironic that Pahl based his sampling strategy at least in part on a judgement about the likely cost effectiveness of potential respondents, as this was an issue which arose as a point of concern within the Family Obligations Project. An important aspect of the interview phase of the research was to interview key relatives of individual respondents in order to understand kinship negotiations from the perspectives of all those involved, rather than to rely on the account of one person in isolation. Accordingly, in addition to the 31 interviewees who had been involved in the initial survey, a further 57 relatives were selected for interview. In cases where kin were to be followed up, the original respondent would be interviewed at least one more time, and this was where the problem arose:

> The core of the problem... was that we were worried that we were being seduced into following up the kin groups of people whom we found interesting to interview and who made it easy for us to spot situations apparently concerning negotiations in their kin group. Some of our respondents made very 'good informants' in the sense that they talked about their families using concepts that were quite close to our own, whereas others presented material in a more bland way... Were we in danger of missing the full range of experiences open to us by tending to follow up the people who were – on our distinctive definitions – most articulate and interesting? (Finch and Mason 1990a: 40)

This statement, coupled with Pahl's, points to an important issue which is rarely discussed publicly by researchers. It is undoubtedly the case that certain interviewees *are* more interesting, more pleasant, more engaging than others, and, just as in our personal lives we would rather spend time with people whose company we enjoy, it is very tempting to apply these criteria to our research sampling strategies. If the logic of probability sampling is applied to selection, then researchers have no legitimate excuse for excluding someone from fieldwork on grounds other than their refusal to participate. However, within the framework of theoretical sampling, the potential for allowing sampling decisions to be influenced by factors other than previously identified selection criteria is high, and unlikely to be subject to such close external scrutiny as random sampling procedures. In this context, it is refreshing to see this temptation acknowledged in print by both Finch and Mason and Pahl, although Pahl's decision to go ahead and exclude certain people on grounds of their 'quality' as respondents – how 'tedious' or 'confusing' they were likely to be – would seem to be unfortunate.

Finch and Mason decided upon a rather different solution, one which also highlights the benefits of a team approach to research. Rather than leaving the decision of whether to follow up someone's kin to the original interviewer, decisions were reached jointly, but only after the second researcher had listened to the recording of the interview. Invariably in cases of supposedly 'bland' interviews, the researcher who had not been present found the exchange far more interesting than the researcher who *had* been present, and was often able to point out the potential benefits of following up that person's kin group. By these means, the process of selection became much more systematic and much less susceptible to subjective interpretations of research utility. It may well have been the case that certain interviews were harder work than others as a result of this strategy, but the inclusion of the occasional 'challenging' interview respondent was probably a small price to pay for maintaining a broad spread of experience across the sample. It also seems particularly dangerous to exclude certain interviewees on grounds of inarticulateness alone within a sampling strategy which does not otherwise place too great an emphasis on controlling for factors such as educational background and social class.

Conclusion

Finch and Mason's work is widely regarded as an important contribution to the sociology of the family. In particular, it has demonstrated conclusively that the extended family is still alive and well, and has a tangible reality in most people's lives. However, it has also led them to conclude that the giving and receiving of support are not so much *common* experiences as *unremarkable* experiences, and that family members are not necessarily the first port of call in times of crisis. Rather, for most of the time, people do not expect to draw on the support of their kin, spouses excepted. Indeed, Finch and Mason argue that much of their data suggest that most people will go to great lengths to *avoid* having to call on their kin too often!

A major strength of Finch and Mason's research lies with their choice of a multi-method approach. A survey alone would only have told half of the story, as would in-depth interviews alone. In order to understand the dynamic nature of the relationship between normative beliefs and actual practices, it was essential that both phases of the research be conducted, and then for the apparent tensions between the two data sets to be interrogated systematically. Analytic induction, with its roots in Glaser and Strauss's grounded theory approach to data analysis, provided a properly thorough and rigorous way of approaching this task.

Again influenced by grounded theory, the underpinning logic of Finch and Mason's second-phase selection strategy was that of theoretical sampling. This should not be confused with the adoption of an ad hoc – or even post-hoc – rationalisation for otherwise haphazard selection criteria, and those who portray it in such terms do not do the research community any favours. Theoretical sampling calls for the same level of rigour required of random sampling techniques, and the strength of claims arising from the findings of both quantitative *and* qualitative research equally stand or fall on the validity and water tightness of their respective sampling procedures.

To conclude, *Negotiating Family Responsibilities* is not only a sociologically interesting piece of research, but it is also a timely and policy-relevant study. Its conclusions reveal the serious limitations of social policies which operate around a central assumption that the family is the automatic backstop for support and help in times of need. Finch and Mason's work is, therefore, a good example of applied sociological research, with direct implications for the formulation of policy, as well as for sociological theorising more generally. In such a context, methodological rigour is an absolute necessity, and Finch and Mason's work is more than adequate to the task.

Additional reading

David Morgan's *Family Connections* (1996) provides a very readable introduction to current research and theorising within the sub-discipline of the sociology of the family, while Lynn Jamieson's *Intimacy: Personal Relationships in Modern Society* (1998) explores the theme of the changing nature of intimate relationships both within and outside of the traditional family setting. Alan Bryman's *Quantity and Quality in Social Research* (1988) remains the classic text on mixing methods in social research, while Julia Brannen's edited collection *Mixing Methods: Qualitative and Quantitative Research* (1992) includes a wide variety of perspectives on this theme.

Chapter 4

Work: Phizacklea and Wolkowitz's *Homeworking Women*

Introduction

The world of work and employment has undergone fundamental change in the last 50 years. Employment in Britain is no longer dominated by men working full time in manufacturing; instead we have seen the huge growth of women's employment, frequently part time, in the service sector (Bradley 1997; Brown 1997). Allegedly, women's employment is flexible for both employers who treat women as a contingent workforce and for women who combine the responsibilities of paid work and unpaid work in the home (see Pollert 1994 for the debate on flexibility). Homeworking – working at home – is another way in which women combine employment and childcare and is especially prevalent among ethnic minority women. There is a huge body of academic research (Allen and Wolkowitz 1987; Bisset and Huws 1985; Phizacklea 1990) that has shown that manufacturing homeworking is invariably low-skilled and poorly paid work. More recently, however, there has been a growing interest in highly skilled, better paid homeworking facilitated by the explosion of new technology (Gorz 1985; Hakim 1987a, b). The former image of homeworking is a relic of the pre-industrial past while the latter image of homeworking is a portent of the post-industrial future. These 'two very contrasting and extreme images of homeworking' are the subject of *Homeworking Women: Gender, Racism and Class at*

63

Work by Annie Phizacklea and Carol Wolkowitz (1995: 2). In their book, they aim to demonstrate that: 'Homework in Britain today reflects all types of work carried out by women in the external labour market as well as the different experiences and material circumstances of women in a racialized and class-divided society.'

Phizacklea and Wolkowitz are keen to capture the heterogeneity of homeworkers and the ways in which race, gender and class shape the workforce at home. In addition, they seek to challenge the notion that homeworking women are 'grateful slaves' who have chosen to work at home and happily do so (Hakim 1991). Rather, they emphasise the constraints on women's choices – not least in the material and cultural context of the home – although they acknowledge that choices and constraints vary according to ethnic and class background (Phizacklea and Wolkowitz 1995: 16–18). Against this background, they adopted a wide definition of homeworkers to include all those working in their homes who describe themselves as employees, self-employed, homeworkers or 'teleworkers' in manual and non-manual employment (Phizacklea and Wolkowitz 1995: 21). In the knowledge that different methodologies uncover different types of homeworkers, they also employed a variety of methods. First, in order to get a national picture of homeworking, they published a questionnaire in *Prima*, a popular women's magazine. Second, in conjunction with the homeworking officer in the Economic Development Unit of Coventry County Council, they conducted a small in-depth study of homeworking in that city to capture ethnic differences in homeworking. Third, they conducted case studies of six organisations in the private and public sectors which had devised information and communication technology (ICT) 'teleworking' initiatives, while the experience of 'teleworkers' themselves was gleaned from women who responded to a questionnaire in the newsletter of the Working Mothers' Association (WMA) as well as the respondents from the *Prima* survey (Phizacklea and Wolkowitz 1995: 39–44).

The difficulties of locating a seemingly hidden workforce and the problems of their own choice of methods is explicitly acknowledged by Phizacklea and Wolkowitz. They provide a full account of how their research was done in the hope that it 'will not only help others to look critically at methodological alternatives but also enhance the credibility of our research findings' (Phizacklea and Wolkowitz 1995: 44). Given the commitment to 'more open and frank accounts of how research is done', it is highly appropriate that their research is considered here. The remainder of this chapter is divided into three sections. First, Phizacklea and Wolkowitz's study is located in the context of debates on the extent and nature of homeworking in the 1980s and 90s. Second, the key substantive findings arising out of the research are summarised. Third, the study is evaluated by focusing on three related issues: locating Asian women homeworkers via in-depth research; women's magazines, postal questionnaires and responses rates; and the use of contacts and its impact on case study research. Phizacklea and Wolkowitz encountered considerable difficulties in finding Asian women homeworkers in Coventry willing to be interviewed and it was somewhat disappointing that they managed to locate so few of them. The women's magazine elicited a limited response from a highly selective group of women derived via an already skewed group of *Prima* readers. Finally, the reliance on one contact for the case studies of 'teleworkers' may well have limited the research geographically to the south east and neglected routine non-manual clerical homeworking (which may be neither poorly paid nor well paid). Nevertheless, Phizacklea and Wolkowitz manage to capture the heterogeneity of homeworking and, without doubt, the different experiences of white and ethnic minority women homeworkers is the most powerful feature of the book.

Researching the contingent workforce

There is a long tradition of research by campaigners – including homeworking officers and the Low Pay Unit – which has documented the poor terms and conditions of employment of homeworkers in manufacturing (Bisset and Huws 1995; Greater Manchester Low Pay Unit 1986, Mitter 1986). More recently, however, academic researchers have turned their attention to the extent and nature of homeworking in Britain. The first major study was undertaken by Sheila Allen and Carol Wolkowitz (1987), who carried out the West Yorkshire Homeworking Survey between 1979 and 1980 (although Wolkowitz was not involved in the research when the survey was completed). This project involved a doorstep survey of 4,000 households across four working-class neighbour-hoods which yielded 90 interviews with home-based workers. Included within this group were ten Asian women homeworkers. Allen and Wolkowitz (1987: 29) rejected the myth that homeworking is a marginal form of waged work but rather emphasised that it is an integral part of economic life in capitalist societies, and they sought to bring it more clearly into view. They also challenged assumptions about the circumstances in which women, especially ethnic minority women, become homeworkers. Homeworking, they argued, is a way in which women combine paid and unpaid work in a way that men do not have to do and it must, therefore, be understood as part of the sexual division of labour (Allen and Wolkowitz 1987: 86). Examining homeworking as a method of production, they found it to be highly advantageous to suppliers since the flexible use of labour and the reduction in the costs of production are the main source of their profits. They also found that homeworkers rarely enjoy autonomy since suppliers exercise various mechanisms of control in the hours, pace and quality of work undertaken by homeworkers (Allen and Wolkowitz 1987: 133). In all of these respects, therefore, Allen and Wolkowitz undermined the myths and highlighted the realities of homeworking in Britain.

The main findings of the Department of Employment's research programme on homeworking, which were published in the same year, painted an altogether more favourable picture (Hakim 1987a, b; see also Hakim 1980, 1984). The inclusion of a one-off question on homeworking in the 1981 Labour Force Survey generated a sample of 576 homeworkers who were subsequently interviewed in the autumn of 1981 by the Office of Populations, Censuses and Surveys. A wide definition of homeworking was employed to include 'people who work *at* home and people working *from* home as a base' (Hakim 1987a: 1 – emphasis in original). Hakim, like Allen and Wolkowitz, found that the majority of home-based workers (especially those working at home) were women although, contrary to Allen and Wolkowitz's findings, she argued that they enjoyed high levels of satisfaction with their work. Asked why they worked at or from home, the majority of the survey respondents emphasised autonomy and flexibility while caring for young children. In contrast, the disadvantages of homeworking were noted by only a small minority of the sample. Only 3 per cent, for example, highlighted the problems of health and safety in their work. Three-quarters of the respondents expressed satisfaction with their rates of pay while two-thirds of them felt they controlled the amount and pace of work they undertook (Hakim 1987b). Overall, therefore, Hakim emphasised the positive advantages of homeworking over other forms of employment for women with domestic and childcare responsibilities. In subsequent publications, Hakim (1991, 1992, 1995) has argued that women's low level of commitment to paid work and their primary concern with home and family accounts for high levels of satisfaction with low-skilled poorly paid work. Indeed, homeworking women are the example *par excellence* of what she terms 'grateful slaves'. The contrast with Allen and Wolkowitz's analysis of the gendered nature of homeworking could not be greater.

Hakim is a controversial figure in the study of women's employment in general. In this, she shares a similar status to Saunders with respect to housing and class, as discussed in Chapter 5. Her views have generated considerable controversy (Crompton and Harris 1998; Devine 1994; Ginn *et al.* 1996). Leaving this more general debate aside, Hakim's research on home-based employment has not been without criticism either. Phizacklea and Wolkowitz argue that problems of sampling and interpretation cast considerable doubt on some of her key findings: namely, her claim that manufacturing homeworking is becoming increasing rare and that ethnic minorities are underrepresented among the home-based workforce. The random sampling procedures on which the Department of Employment research was based could not capture the concentration of manufacturing home-based employment in London and other major cities or the residential concentration of ethnic minorities in Britain. It is these features of homeworking which more in-depth research – including Phizacklea's (1990) work on the fashion industry – have identified. That said, the most recent research from the Department for Education and Employment (DfEE) and the Department of Trade and Industry (DTI) by Felstead and his colleagues (1996) also notes the continued importance of manufacturing homeworking (homework being defined more narrowly in this research, however). Drawing on an analysis of 1991 Census data, a doorstep survey of home-based workers and in-depth interviews in four localities, Felstead *et al.* (1996: 91) found that sewing was the most prominent form of homeworking activity (54 per cent) while other activities such as packing (12 per cent), clerical-type work (11 per cent), routine assembly (4 per cent) and knitting (3 per cent) were far less prevalent. Moreover, the locality research generated a large sample of ethnic minority homeworkers (54 per cent) although, of course, the size of the ethnic minority workforce varied according to the areas studied. The study, therefore, captured the concentration of ethnic minority homeworkers – especially in the clothing industry – in particular areas in Britain.

It is in the context of these debates about homeworking (and women's employment) that Phizacklea and Wolkowitz's work needs to be located. The aim of their research was to look at all types of homework, from the purported glamour of teleworking to the sweated labour of manufacturing in the home. They sought to examine both the advantages and disadvantages of homeworking among women in different occupations, thereby highlighting also the similarities and differences in terms and conditions of employment. They also sought to show that, despite the heterogeneity of the home-based workforce, gender, class and race shape the labour force who work at home. With these aims in mind, we now turn to the key substantive findings of their research.

Homeworking Women

Phizacklea and Wolkowitz examined racialised divisions in homework by way of a case study of homeworkers – 30 white and 19 Asian women – in the West Midlands city of Coventry. The nine white-collar workers, who had relatively good terms and conditions of employment, were all white. The other white women (21) were spread across a range of manual occupations including packing, electrical assembly and knitting. The Asian women homeworkers in their sample were concentrated in manual work and all of them were engaged in clothing production – often for Asian employers – as sewing machinists and so forth (Phizacklea and Wolkowitz 1995: 52).

While the average hourly rate of white and Asian manual homeworkers was the same, the distribution of levels of earning by ethnic group was distinctive. Just under half (13) of the white women homeworkers were paid less than £1.49 an hour compared with over two-thirds (16) of the Asian women homeworkers (Phizacklea and Wolkowitz 1995: 55) (see Table 4.1). Phizacklea and Wolkowitz also found that Asian women worked far longer hours than their white counterparts with an average working week of 48 hours compared with 26 hours for white manual homeworkers and twelve hours for white-collar homeworkers. The Asian women also experienced pressure through periods of excessive rush to meet orders. This situation reflected economic need in that over half (12) of the Asian women – with more young children at home – were on income support. Not surprisingly, white women emphasised the advantages of flexibility of working at home while the Asian women stressed financial concerns (1995: 58). There were clear differences between the choices and experiences of the white and Asian women homeworkers. Phizacklea and Wolkowitz concluded:

> In our sample, the latter (Asian women) are much more likely to be dependent on benefit and/or trying to manage on a very low income, in consequence they are thrown into homework which is so badly paid that they need to work very long hours; the pressure of work (and the additional stress created by irregularity of work) typical of the clothing sector then compounds the problem. (1995: 60)

Table 4.1 Distribution of clerical and manual homeworkers' hourly earnings (Coventry sample)

Hourly rate (£)	White	Asian
<0.25	2	2
0.25–0.49	2	–
0.50–0.74	3	I
0.75–0.99	3	5
1.00–1.24	I	2
1.25–1.49	2	6
1.50–1.74	–	–
1.75–1.99	2	–
2.00–2.24	3	I
2.25–2.49	2	–
2.50–2.74	2	I
2.75–2.99	4	–
3.00–3.24	–	–
3.25–3.49	2	–
3.50–3.74	–	I
3.75–3.99	–	–
4.00–4.24	–	–
4.25–4.49	–	–
5.00+	I	–

Source: Phizacklea and Wolkowitz (1995: 55)

The *Prima* survey was used to establish the variety of homework, the terms and conditions of employment and the advantages and disadvantages of working at home. The overwhelming majority of the 403 respondents were young women with children of pre-school or primary school age. Clearly, homework is 'an attempt by women in their child rearing years to combine childcare and paid work in the home' (Phizacklea and Wolkowitz 1995: 74). Thus, their sample worked at different occupational levels in manufacturing and services.

While 24 per cent of the respondents were employed in professional and managerial occupations and 21 per cent were employed in clerical work, 41 per cent of women were engaged in manual occupations (Phizacklea and Wolkowitz 1995: 76) (see Table 4.2). While hours of work varied, the mean was between 20 and 36 hours per week. Earnings also varied, with a median between £50 and £59 per week. The women home-based workers, therefore, were often working long hours for low pay (Phizacklea and Wolkowitz 1995: 80).

Table 4.2   *Prima* homeworker occupations

Occupation	Percentage
Professional/managerial	
Manager/owner	7.7
Private teacher	3.0
Other professional	13.7
Total	24.4
Clerical	
Book-keeper	4.2
Clerk	3.2
Typist	7.0
Sales	2.1
Secretary	4.0
Total	20.5
Manual	
Dress and upholstery	11.5
Sewing	7.0
Knitters	4.5
Other crafts	3.7
Assembly	3.0
Child-minding	11.0
Total	40.7
Other	14.2
n=377	

Note: Percentages may not total 100.
Source: Phizacklea and Wolkowitz (1995: 76)

The majority of women (54 per cent) cited the ability to look after their children as the main advantage of working at home. The flexible nature of work came a distant second (18 per cent) and was enjoyed more by high-level non-manual workers than manual homeworkers. Phizacklea and Wolkowitz emphasise that home-based work is a way of helping women deal with their constrained options. There were disadvantages also in terms of low earnings, unpredictable work, long hours, isolation and mess in the home. While earnings varied by occupation, the majority of the sample (53 per cent) earned less than £3.00 an hour. One-third (31 per cent) found it difficult to get away from often stressful work. Phizacklea and Wolkowitz (1995: 98) concluded that 'the advantages cited for homework partly reflect differences in occupations, whereas perceptions of the disadvantages are more widely shared'.

Finally, Phizacklea and Wolkowitz (1995: 101) examine whether ICT provides 'a more relaxed, autonomous and better rewarded form of homeworking'. Their research uncovered 30 large private sector companies and ten large public sector organisations – all based in the south-east – who had adopted some form of ICT scheme. The private sector companies (for example, banks and legal practices) adopted homeworking practices as a way of retaining professional women whose high level of skill was in short supply, while the spread of low-skilled clerical homeworking in the public sector organisations (local and central government employers) was the result of increased demand for administrative workers (Phizacklea and Wolkowitz 1995: 104). Given this, it was not surprising to find that levels of supervision varied in that the professional ICT workers enjoyed greater autonomy than the low-skilled clerical workers. Drawing on interviews with a small number of women (nine) who belonged to the Working Mothers Association, they found that ICT homework is often used to avoid career breaks by a group of privileged women. In occupations such as systems analysis and accountancy, earnings were high with an average of £9.00 per hour (in 1990). Moreover, the women came from affluent households with average household income of £519 per week (Phizacklea and Wolkowitz 1995: 112–3). The interviewees emphasised their preference for looking after children themselves (rather than employing nannies and child-minders) and a desire to avoid travelling to and from work (often within London), while isolation and the difficulty of separating home and work were seen as the main disadvantages to homeworking. In sum, Phizacklea and Wolkowitz emphasise the diversity of experiences between high-skilled and low-skilled homeworkers. Technology, they conclude, does not 'guarantee a more agreeable, autonomous or better rewarded way of working at home unless the skills and experience that a particular worker combines with that technology are in short supply' (Phizacklea and Wolkowitz (1995: 122).

Overall, examining the wide range of homework undertaken by women allowed Phizacklea and Wolkowitz (1995: 124) to 'see how homework is cut across by the impact of gender, class and "race" and therefore eludes facile generalisation'. There are different groups of homeworkers – casualized employees, micro-entrepreneurs, self-employed professionals, very small businesses and technical and executive level employees – who enjoy different levels of pay, protection and autonomy. However, most of the jobs are undertaken by women who combine family and work with varying degrees of choice and constraint. It is in this respect that they share an interest in improved terms and conditions of employment, 'recognising that it is illegitimate to deny women these rights because they are unable to work according to patterns established by men as the norm' (Phizacklea and Wolkowitz 1995: 127). In conclusion, they examined a number of strategies which homeworkers' organisations might advance in the future – such as lobbying for a range of legislative measure and creating the conditions for self-organisation – to promote the interests of homeworking women. In a clear political stance, they conclude:

> The main point is that the framework for considering future developments needs to focus on the projects homeworkers themselves advance, as well as the policies which firms seek to implement, and to ensure that platforms exist on which homeworkers can make their views known. (1990: 132)

Against this background, issues of method and their implications for the substantive findings will now be discussed.

Sampling a hidden workforce

In order to explore ethnic variations in homeworking, Phizacklea and Wolkowitz decided to undertake a small in-depth study drawing on a non-random sample in their home town of Coventry. This was done in conjunction with Coventry City Council, which appointed a

Punjabi-speaking homeworking officer within their Economic Development Unit since the Phizacklea and Wolkowitz project in Coventry was only just getting off the ground. Phizacklea and Wolkowitz originally intended to devise a questionnaire which would be placed in a local newspaper to be returned by respondents in a pre-paid envelope. However, the homeworking officer was 'emphatic' that this method would not work with Asian women home-based workers and 'we had therefore to reassess the question of access at the local level' (Phizacklea and Wolkowitz 1995: 41). Instead, adverts were placed in the local press asking home-based workers to telephone the researchers and arrange an interview. English language advertisements were placed in the local daily newspaper and in a free weekly paper. The advertisement was also translated into the four main south Asian languages spoken in Coventry and placed in a multilingual free advertising newspaper. The response, however, was disappointing in that some women responded to the English language adverts but only two women replied to the Asian adverts. As a second strategy, Phizacklea and Wolkowitz decided to contact minority home-based workers through community workers who approached homeworkers known to them. This method of gaining access to Asian women homeworkers proved somewhat more successful. Overall, the different methods resulted in a sample of 30 white, English-speaking women homeworkers and 19 Asian home-based women workers. All of the informants were interviewed in their homes using a semi-structured interview schedule. The Asian women homeworkers were interviewed in their mother tongue if they so wished (Phizacklea and Wolkowitz 1995: 41–2).

It is extremely difficult to establish the extent and nature of homeworking, particularly among ethnic minorities. First, there is the problem of sampling minority populations and, moreover, populations for which there is no sampling frame. Ethnic minority homeworkers often live in inner-city areas where it is increasingly difficult to undertake research of any kind (see also Saunders' difficulties discussed in Chapter 5). In areas of deprivation where crime and violence may be prevalent, people are increasingly reluctant to open their doors to strangers. Of course, this applies to all potential respondents although the added fear of racial violence may mean that ethnic minorities are even more reluctant to participate in research. Hakim's survey research on homeworkers, for example, only achieved a response rate of 43 per cent in London which might explain, as Phizacklea and Wolkowitz (1995: 31) claim, why ethnic minorities were underrepresented in the Department of Employment's research. Second, it is more difficult to establish a relationship of trust with informants in this context. Again, achieving a rapport is important for all research (see also the discussion on Hobbs' work in Chapter 7). It is all the more difficult to achieve, however, with vulnerable groups of people such as Asian women homeworkers. As we have seen, they are a highly disadvantaged group of workers under pressure to work long hours for low pay and whose work is often not on the books. Not surprisingly, therefore, it is almost impossible to approach potential respondents cold. As Phizacklea and Wolkowitz (1995: 33–4) note, the most successful studies of ethnic minority homeworkers (Huws 1994) have relied on ethnic minority outreach workers and campaigning groups to generate adequate numbers. Another way of establishing cooperation and trust is to interview ethnic minority groups such as Asian women in their mother tongue rather than English if they prefer (Phizacklea and Wolkowitz 1995: 42). It is a way of allowing Asian women to feel comfortable in the company of an interviewer who can speak their mother tongue and this may facilitate a more frank discussion of the advantages and disadvantages of homeworking.

It was not altogether surprising that the attempt to contact Asian women homeworkers through the media was not a success. What was disappointing, however, was that their subsequent attempt at contact through the homeworking officer and the community workers met with limited success. They made contact with more white English-speaking homeworkers than Asian homeworkers, when they had hoped to focus on the latter rather than the former. It may be that the absence of a home-based workers' project in Coventry hampered their chances of success. That said, there is the problem that this method might generate a biased sample in which campaigning and more visible homeworkers are overrepresented. We do not know how far the homeworking officer and the community workers were known and trusted by homeworkers in different parts of the city. Their association with Coventry Council, for example, may have been a source of suspicion and fear. Thus, Phizacklea and Wolkowitz did almost everything within their powers to generate a reasonable number of Asian women homeworkers, yet they still encountered considerable difficulties in achieving an in-depth non-random sample of sufficient size. Their research highlights the very real difficulties of gaining access to and subsequently sampling from, a seemingly hidden workforce. Interestingly, the recent DfEE/DTI study (Felstead *et al.* 1996) encountered similar problems. Part of the research involved a doorstep survey and in-depth interviews in four localities with high ethnic minority populations. Over 15,000 doors were knocked and a member of over 7,000 households answered a short questionnaire. It revealed 246 households (3 per cent) in which at least one member of the household had done paid work at home in the last twelve months. Only 99 of these persons were willing to be interviewed (Felstead *et al.* 1996: 21). The doorstep survey, therefore, was not very successful in generating a sample of respondents and networks links and snowballing with ward residents was used to identify more homeworkers for in-depth interviews. Phizacklea and Wolkowitz are far from alone, therefore, in encountering difficulties in generating a sample from a comparatively small and hidden workforce.

What must also be noted in Phizacklea and Wolkowitz's favour is that they still had sufficient numbers of Asian women homeworkers to make a comparison with white, English-speaking homeworkers feasible. They found, as we saw, some important similarities and differences in the terms and conditions of employment between the two groups. Their findings on the severely disadvantaged position of ethnic minority women – excluded from non-manual homeworking and ghettoised in the declining clothing industry – are extremely powerful (Phizacklea and Wolkowitz 1995: 62). The variation in choices and constraints among women is stark. It could, of course, be argued that we do not know whether the findings on ethnic minority women homeworkers are generalisable. The more recent DfEE/DTI study, however, confirms their findings. Of their sample of 338 homeworkers, 91 per cent were women, over half of them (54 per cent), as was noted earlier, were of ethnic minority origin and 34 per cent were of Asian origin specifically (Felstead *et al.* 1996: 25). Over half (54 per cent) were engaged in sewing, where they worked long hours for low rates of pay. The main reasons for working at home for the ethnic minority women was money and the opportunity for childcare (Felstead *et al.* 1996: 51). There is a high degree of fit, therefore, between their two rather different pieces of research, which only enhances the robustness of each set of results. Despite the fact that they generated only a small sample of ethnic

minority women homeworkers for in-depth interview, Phizacklea
and Wolkowitz's research on racialised divisions in homework is
fully vindicated.

The national picture

In order to get a reasonable national picture of homeworking –
including non-manual and manual home-based workers – Phizacklea
and Wolkowitz decided to put a questionnaire in a large circulation,
national women's magazine. It was a simple way of distributing a
questionnaire at reasonable cost. They chose to run the questionnaire
in *Prima*, Britain's bestselling women's magazine which at the time of
the research (May 1990) had a monthly readership of over two
million. A total of 403 home-based workers returned the questionnaire (Phizacklea and Wolkowitz 1995: 39). Not surprisingly, 401
responses were from women, and two were from men who were
excluded from the subsequent analysis.

As Table 4.3 shows, their *Prima* sample comprised a group of
women with high household incomes compared with the readership
of *Prima* as a whole and with national population estimates. Just
under two-fifths (39.7 per cent) of their sample had a salary of less
than £15,000 per annum, compared with 47.7 per cent of the *Prima*
readership as a whole and 50 per cent of women nationally. Of this
sample, 22.1 per cent earned between £15,000 and £19,999, higher
than the *Prima* readership as a whole (15.1 per cent) and twice as
high as the national figure (10.9 per cent). Finally, a third of their
sample of women earned more than £20,000 a year, again higher
than all *Prima* readers (19.2 per cent) and, again, double the proportion of women (14.8 per cent) earning in this range according to
national population estimates (Phizacklea and Wolkowitz 1995: 40).
For reasons of time, Phizacklea and Wolkowitz were not able to draw
a sub-sample of women from the main sample to interview in-depth
even though some of the respondents supplied their names and
addresses. Even so, many of the women wrote letters alongside the
questionnaire which were a source of unexpected but rich data on the
advantages and disadvantages of homeworking (Phizacklea and
Wolkowitz 1995: 39).

Table 4.3 Annual household income of *Prima* homeworkers compared to *Prima* readership and (BMRB) UK population estimates (*Prima* Readership Survey Profiles and UK estimates BMRB, 1990)

Annual household income	*Prima* home-workers (per cent)	*Prima* readership (per cent)	National population estimate (per cent)
Not stated	5.2	17.6	23.9
£5,000 or less	5.2	12.1	19.2
£5–7,999	–	7.9	9.5
£5–9,999	12.9	–	–
£8–10,999	–	12.1	10.2
£10–14,999	21.6	–	–
£11–14,999	–	15.6	11.1
	34.5	35.6	30.8
£15–19,999	22.1	15.1	10.9
£20–24,999	13.9	10.4	7.0
£25,000+	19.1	8.8	7.8

Note: The income bands between £5–14,999 are not comparable across the table, we have bracketed these incomes.
Source: Phizacklea and Wolkowitz (1995: 40)

Phizacklea and Wolkowitz's choice of methods was much influenced by Christensen's research (1985, 1988, 1989) in the United States, carried out in 1984–5, which managed to incorporate non-manual and manual homeworkers. She published a questionnaire in the magazine *Family Circle*, which is read by nineteen million women across the United States. Although only 0.7 per cent of readers (7,000) replied to the questionnaire, she was successful in achieving a mix of professional employees, routine white-collar workers and skilled and unskilled manual homeworkers. At that time, Christensen rejected the notion that computer technology was the cause of homeworking since she found that only a minority actually used computers at home. The main motive for working at home was to combine family and work, and to make some money. Even so, she found that most women found this far from easy and there were considerable tensions in meeting the demands of each responsibility (Christensen 1985, 1989). Phizacklea and Wolkowitz were impressed by the coverage of Christensen's research (1995: 37–8). However, they also identified a number of limitations with her choice of methods. First, the sample is restricted to the readers of a magazine who are likely to be distinctive in some way. Second,

there is often a class difference in response rate to postal questionnaires. Third, an English language magazine is unlikely to be read by
non-English speakers. Fourth, it remains unknown how many
homeworkers do not return a questionnaire. Fifth, it may be that
dissatisfied homeworkers are more likely to complete a postal
questionnaire than more satisfied homeworkers (Phizacklea and
Wolkowitz 1995: 38). In combination, these five factors indicate
that this type of method may generate a biased sample of dissatisfied
white English-speaking middle-class homeworkers which, of course,
is not the category of people usually associated with either manufacturing or teleworking homework. Despite these limitations,
however, Phizacklea and Wolkowitz designed their research along
similar lines to challenge stereotypes about homeworking.

Phizacklea and Wolkowitz were, indeed, confronted by similar
drawbacks with their choice of method. First, they had a very limited
response to their questionnaire. As did Christensen, Phizacklea and
Wolkowitz had to make do with a very low response rate of 0.02 per
cent. It is not surprising that Phizacklea and Wolkowitz had a low
response given what we know about the proportion of homeworkers
in Britain. We do not know how many homeworkers saw the
questionnaire but failed to fill it in and return it by post. It is highly
likely that they tapped into a group of homeworkers who were
interested in the issues they raised, were not altogether happy about
their pay and conditions and were prepared to voice their dissatisfac-
tions and satisfactions with homework. Second, as Phizacklea and
Wolkowitz (1995: 39) readily acknowledged, their sampling frame –
Prima readers – is generally more affluent than the population at
large. *Prima* readers are underrepresented among women with an
annual household income of less than £10,000 (-9 per cent) and
overrepresented among those earning more than £20,000 (+4 per
cent). Their *Prima* respondents were even more of a skewed group in
that women respondents were underrepresented in low-income
households (-11 per cent) and overrepresented in high-income
groups (+19 per cent). Without doubt, the responding women
homeworkers formed a more affluent group, demonstrating the class
bias in response rates and the readership of the magazine. Both of
these limitations, however, are extremely difficult to circumvent, and
they highlight the limitations of relying on a postal questionnaire
and the use of a women's magazine – even one with a large national
circulation – in which to place the questionnaire.

It must be noted in their favour, however, that Phizacklea and Wolkowitz's choice of method was successful in tapping into a heterogeneous group of homeworkers. Their objective was to capture non-manual homeworkers who have frequently slipped through the net in previous research and their final sample embraced both non-manual and manual homeworkers. They found variations in pay across the occupational groups, although the majority (57 per cent) of the sample earned less than £3 an hour (including nearly a quarter who were clerical workers) (Phizacklea and Wolkowitz 1995: 87). Thus, even though the sample was skewed towards those with high household incomes, the research revealed that many of the women had low individual earnings as homeworkers. Phizacklea and Wolkowitz also found variations in the extent to which homeworking was a genuine choice or a choice borne out of constraint among the women homeworkers. Despite their skewed sample, therefore, the analysis of the results of the postal questionnaire produced some very interesting findings about the differences and the similarities in the terms and conditions of employment of a heterogeneous group of women homeworkers.

Locating teleworkers

Finally, Phizacklea and Wolkowitz adopted a case study approach to capture the much lauded 'teleworker' and the organisations who employ them. They drew on the assistance of a management consultant who advised organisations on the introduction of equal opportunities policies and 'teleworking' initiatives. Drawing on his contacts, they used a 'telephone snowball technique' which led them to identify 40 teleworking initiatives of which 30 were in the private sector and 10 were in the public sector (Phizacklea and Wolkowitz 1995: 43). All of the organisations involved were located in the South East (specifically around the M25 motorway) and had devised teleworking schemes to overcome the problem of recruiting and retaining highly qualified staff living in and around London. Phizacklea and Wolkowitz focused on six organisations in detail, which involved interviewing the people responsible for introducing homeworking initiatives (although all the information was provided by post in the case of London Borough). They included four firms in the private sector – the financial services sector of a big bank (Bank Ltd), an international credit card company

(Credit Co.), a legal bureau (Law Co.) and the regional headquarters of one of the major utilities (Utilities) – and two organisations in the public sector – a local authority in London (London Borough) and a county council in the south east (South County). Most of the women were highly qualified staff although London Borough employed routine clerical workers as homeworkers. While the focus of attention was on policies and practices in these organisations, Phizacklea and Wolkowitz also drew on the experiences of seven homeworkers who responded to an advert placed in the newsletter of the Working Mothers' Association, which is an offshoot of the National Childbirth Trust. These seven women were predominately middle-class professional homeworkers who used ICT in their work and they provided a useful source of information on the experience of teleworking (Phizacklea and Wolkowitz 1995: 42–3).

Phizacklea and Wolkowitz were interested in why organisations adopted teleworking schemes and the terms and conditions for the women teleworkers. Media interest in organisations has usually focused on a small number of high-profile companies such as Rank Xerox, which Phizacklea and Wolkowitz wanted to avoid. It was in this context that they sought the assistance of a management consultant with important contacts in the field. However, it is far from ideal to rely entirely on one person's contacts to generate a sample of organisations, especially if a national picture of teleworking is sought. We do not know, for example, how many of the 40 schemes which Phizacklea and Wolkowitz came across were confined to the initial contacts themselves or derived from those contacts. Moreover, all of the organisations were based around the South East. While there is plenty of evidence to suggest that homeworking is highly concentrated in this area, this is not to say that examples of homeworking cannot be found in other parts of the country. Other contacts may well have provided information on teleworking elsewhere which might have produced a different picture of the circumstances in which organisations have developed teleworking initiatives and the types of teleworkers they employ. Without the recruitment difficulties faced by London employers, for example, Phizacklea and Wolkowitz might have found other reasons why organisations were introducing teleworking initiatives. It may well have been interesting to explore whether other local authorities around the country were, like London Borough, introducing teleworking schemes in order to manage the routine administration associated with the introduction of the poll tax. Similarly, such research might well have identified more examples of low-level non-manual workers, as routine clerical work functions are rapidly changing in banks and elsewhere in the face of new technology (Halford *et al.* 1997). Much research is dependent on contacts of the kind used by Phizacklea and Wolkowitz but it is generally better to use a range of contacts to generate as diverse a picture of the topic in question as possible.

The information gleaned from the interviews about the particular circumstances in which the six organisations introduced teleworking initiatives is interesting and suggests that predictions about the growth of teleworking in the future sound somewhat exaggerated. The terms and conditions of employment of such teleworkers is less well documented in Phizacklea and Wolkowitz's book than the other aspects of their research. We know that all of the teleworkers employed by the case-study organisations were permanent staff and enjoyed the same pay and conditions as the on-site staff. Nevertheless, it is a shame that Phizacklea and Wolkowitz, for whatever reasons, did not have the opportunity to survey the teleworkers in their case-study organisations or at least interview a sub-sample of them. Such interviews may well have highlighted the variable experiences of high-level professional homeworkers and low-level routine workers. Instead, they had to rely on the responses of a small number of women from the advert which was placed in the newsletter of the Working Mothers' Association (and, to a lesser degree, their *Prima* respondents who used a computer in their home-based work). Not surprisingly, these women were highly qualified and experienced staff who enjoyed good incomes. They were clearly women who were in a position to exercise some choice and their preference to work at home was a way of avoiding career breaks, although there were costs in terms of training and promotion opportunities. Such women also enjoyed high levels of job autonomy as they did when they were officebound although, of course, they were still constrained by the demands of childcare and domestic responsibilities. Such women enjoy the 'best scenario' for homeworking. Phizacklea and Wolkowitz (1995: 122) also acknowledge that, 'Nevertheless, the material differences in income and autonomy between, for instance, the WMA respondents and the Council Tax workers in London Borough are huge.' It was a shame, therefore, that the opportunity was missed to explore the less favourable terms and conditions of employment of low-level non-manual teleworkers in more depth. Then again, it is not possible to do everything!

Conclusion

The difficulties of researching a seemingly invisible and often vulnerable workforce have been considered at length in this chapter. As we have seen, Phizacklea and Wolkowitz employed a variety of research methods to uncover the heterogeneity of homeworkers, ranging from the more glamorous teleworkers at one end of the spectrum to sweated labour in the clothing industry at the other. They encountered difficulties with each method of enquiry as they tried to locate ethnic minority homeworkers, obtain a national picture of home-based work and establish the extent and nature of teleworking. Be that as it may, Phizacklea and Wolkowitz's research tells us much about the nature of employment as well as forms of inequalities of race, gender and class in contemporary Britain. They note:

> Our investigations into homeworking show that these differences are imported into the home and reflected in differences in the situation of women working at home, with Asian homeworkers segregated into a narrower range of jobs and working very much longer hours to meet their household requirements. (Phizacklea and Wolkowitz 1995: 124–5)

They go on to conclude that:

> At the present time, racism and discrimination against ethnic minorities is a crucial aspect of the construction of the homeworking labour force... Some would argue that their situation has parallels with the expanding participation of women in causalized work at a global level, including North America and Australia as well as in the Third World, as all are affected by the spread of subcontracting and small batch production. (Phizacklea and Wolkowitz 1995: 132)

Without doubt, therefore, Phizacklea and Wolkowitz managed to capture the heterogeneity of the home-based workforce and, perhaps most powerfully of all, the different experiences of some white and ethnic minority women homeworkers.

Additional reading

Sheila Rowbotham is one of the major researchers on homeworking. She edited a book with Swasti Mitter, *Dignity and Daily Bread* (1994), which offers a global perspective on poor women's work. For an analysis of how social stratification affects other spheres of work, see Annie Phizacklea's *Unpacking The Fashion Industry* (1990). An excellent discussion of survey research, including postal questionnaires, can be found in D.A. De Vaus' *Surveys in Social Research* (1991). Ray Lee's *Doing Research on Sensitive Topics* (1993) includes a very useful discussion of the difficulties of sampling hidden populations.

Chapter 5

Housing: Saunders'
A Nation of Home Owners

Introduction

In the prologue to his book, *A Nation of Home Owners*, Peter Saunders provides a brief housing history of his parents and himself to demonstrate the growth of home ownership and the associated accumulation of wealth in the last 50 or more years. For both of the authors of this book, a similar story could be told of their parents' participation in the housing market. Owning their own home was the source of much personal satisfaction because they had 'bettered themselves' in comparison to their own parents. Saunders (1990: 3) acknowledges that his book is informed by a particular viewpoint which is 'generally favourable towards the spread of home ownership'. This view, he notes, is much at odds with the existing sociological literature on home ownership which has been dismissive of such bourgeois aspirations. Such views among the academic left, he argues, have become 'divorced from the lived reality of most people's daily existence' but are popular for reasons to do with a cultural lag (a persistent loathing of private landlordism), intellectual snobbery (a disdain for property ownership), a commitment to social engineering (a desire for a radical uniform 'mass') and the values of left academics (radical posturing against a bourgeois way of life). Against this background, Saunders sees his book:

> As a deliberate attempt to confront this left academic orthodoxy. It is not, I hope, a polemical confrontation, nor is it a theoretical one. Rather, I have selected what I take to be some of the key sociological questions

raised by the growth of home ownership in Britain and in each case I review evidence collected in my own research and in other studies to evaluate the claims which have been advanced in the academic literature. (1990: 7)

The central concern of *A Nation of Home Owners* is the phenomenal growth of home ownership over the course of the twentieth century in Britain. Saunders is not, however, interested in the causes of the growth of home ownership but its *consequences* for people's daily lives – be they home owners or not – and its wider impact on the character of British society. Saunders concentrates on the popularity of home ownership, the extent to which home ownership is a source of wealth, the political implications of widespread home ownership, the experience and meaning of home ownership and, finally, the implications for social inequalities in contemporary Britain. His overall argument is that the spread of home ownership has brought a variety of benefits to people of all social classes. Saunders acknowledges, at the same time, that a major social divide now exists between the majority of home owners and a minority of council tenants, and he evaluates a variety of policy options to alleviate the problems of polarisation and residualisation. A wide array of secondary sources, including government statistics and other academic surveys, is used in Saunders' research. His principal method of enquiry, however, is a local household survey of over 500 respondents in three predominately working-class towns: Burnley, Derby and Slough. The respondents were interviewed using a questionnaire including closed and open-ended questions. The results derive from an analysis and interpretation of the responses to the questions using a variety of statistical techniques and a liberal use of quotes from the respondents themselves. Saunders' published research has always included an explicit discussion of method as part of his commitment to link issues of theory and method. In *A Nation of Home Owners,* he provides a lot of information on how his sample was generated, the nature of his final sample, the conduct of the interviews and the analysis of the informants' responses. We are in a position, therefore, critically to evaluate his methods of research on all of these fronts.

As the reader will have already ascertained, Saunders is forthright in his criticism of left-wing orthodoxy within the social sciences, which he sees as predominantly anti-capitalist (see also Saunders 1995; Saunders and Harris 1994). He has become an *agent provocateur* on the (libertarian) right of the political spectrum, which is a lonely place for a social scientist. He remains, however, a highly respected sociologist for the way in which he challenges orthodoxy even though his belligerence is the source of discomfort and unease. His critical views of left orthodoxy can be seen in the next section which reviews previous literature and debate – including the development of Saunders' own ideas – on housing within urban studies. After a summary of the main substantive findings, attention focuses on three issues of method. First, the decision by Saunders to undertake a local rather than a national survey is considered with reference to issues of representativeness and reliability. Second, the influence of his viewpoint and the extent to which it is the source of bias is discussed in relation to his findings on the economic consequences – principally wealth accumulation – of home ownership. Third, his statistical analysis and interpretation of associations between tenure and cultural attitudes and behaviour are evaluated. His decision to conduct a local survey, to undertake the research himself and with colleagues and the low response rates in certain areas also raise issues – as with all random sample social surveys – about reliability and the extent to which he can generalise from his empirical findings. Deeply committed to home ownership, he overstates the extent to which everyone has benefited from the spread of home ownership and downplays the class differences in the accumulation of wealth in the housing market. Saunders' analysis does not examine whether variables other than housing tenure have an effect on cultural attitudes and practices and nor does he control for other variables when examining the effects of housing tenure. Thus, we do not know whether the associations he identifies are spurious or explanatory. Nevertheless, his research is a thoroughly stimulating and challenging sociological analysis of a current social issue.

Researching housing, stratification and consumption

Saunders (1979, 1986) has long been interested in the topic of housing, especially with reference to issues of consumption, stratification and politics within the field of urban sociology. Indeed, social inequalities – the causes and consequences of the differential allocation of resources – between and within urban and rural areas have been the dominant preoccupation of writers in the sub-discipline (see

Cooke 1989; Dickens 1990; Savage and Warde 1993). In the 1970s, urban sociologists such as Pahl (1975) and Rex and Moore (1967) focused on 'urban managerialism': namely, the way in which local notables influence the allocation of key resources such as housing, education and transport, and which groups win and lose in the distribution process. This perspective, however, was strongly challenged by the Althusserian Marxist Manuel Castells in his highly influential book *The Urban Question* (1977). He argued that it is important to link the nature of cities and towns to the broader character of capitalist society. The modern city is capitalist since it is the spatial dimension of 'collective consumption' – the consumption of services like education and transport collectively – which functions to ensure a productive labour force. Castells also argued that the provision of these services was the source of potential political conflict, inspiring protest groups and so forth to campaign for better facilities in the city. Castells was associated with the development of a more theoretically informed 'new urban sociology' among Marxists and Weberian sociologists – including Saunders (1981). Saunders, however, challenged the idea that urban protest movements had revolutionary potential. In his case study of urban politics in Croydon, for example, he found that the middle classes were very effective in protecting their own suburbs from further development and pushing for new housing schemes, transport improvements and whatever in working-class locales. Urban politics were as likely to be conservative as radical (see also Lash and Urry 1987).

Castells was widely criticised (Savage and Warde 1993) and he reformulated his ideas in subsequent publications (Castells 1983). That said, his concept of 'collective consumption' was taken up more widely as a way of analysing the political importance of state provision of goods and services at the local and national level. One of the earliest exponents of the politics of consumption was Dunleavy (1980; Dunleavy and Husbands 1985; see also Edgell and Duke 1991), who considered the effects of the expanded provision of services by the state on electoral politics and the social basis of political alignments. He distinguished between two types of consumption process: namely those which are largely private (such as housing and transport) and those which are largely publicly provided (such as education and health). Dunleavy argued these consumption processes were the basis of new sectoral cleavages which were undermining class alignments in British politics. More specifically, they had fragmented the working class and undermined its support for the Labour Party in the 1980s as more affluent working-class private consumers voted Conservative to protect and enhance their sectional interests. Dunleavy's arguments about new forms of structuration in British politics were heavily criticised by political scientists and sociologists (Franklin and Page 1984; Harrop 1980; Taylor-Gooby 1986; Warde *et al.* 1988) principally because he failed to explain how consumption locations shape voting behaviour. Saunders also became increasingly interested in collective consumption – especially private consumption – with reference to housing and stratification. He began to think about the consequences of home ownership for class divisions (Saunders 1984). As his political views changed, however, he became more critical of Dunleavy's Marxian perspective on collective consumption. His criticisms are developed most fully in *A Nation of Home Owners* (with reference to the debate on tenure and politics) where he derides Dunleavy for, among other things, ignoring the real economic interests which divide producers and consumers (Saunders 1990: 218).

It is against this background that Saunders undertook research on the consequences of home ownership in Britain. Saunders (1990: 15) notes that home ownership expanded from approximately 10 per cent of all households in 1914 to 65 per cent in 1986. It spread from the middle class to the working class to the extent, he argues, that class cleavages have blurred and the working class have been incorporated into the capitalist property system. While the growth of home ownership is evident in other nations – especially commonwealth countries – the rise in ownership has been especially rapid in Britain. Saunders (1990: 29) emphasises that these changes occurred 'without anybody actually planning or even anticipating them', and he challenges Marxist writers 'who have often insisted that owner-occupation was deliberately and intentionally fostered by governments or by capitalist interests in an attempt to bolster the bourgeois social order' for lacking the empirical evidence to support their claims. In an historical review, Saunders looks at the political, economic and cultural factors which contributed to the growth of home ownership. He charts the decline of the private sector as a result of wartime controls, the growing availability of mortgages to buy ever cheaper housing, demographic change, the rising income of the middle class in the 1930s and the working class in the 1950s, increasing government financial support for house purchase and popular values and expectations, all of which facilitated the unintended growth of home ownership in Britain (Saunders 1990: 36). Deriding Marxist denial of people's desire for ownership, Saunders (1990: 39) emphasises people's aspirations to own their own homes whether on the basis of calculated instrumentalism, or as a desire for its own sake, 'as an emotional expression of autonomy, security or personal identity'. To this end, he stresses that individualism – especially the desire for individual private property – is a key value within English culture which accounts for the popularity of home ownership in Britain. It is to the empirical findings of this study that we now turn.

A Nation of Home Owners

A Nation of Home Owners is a bulky book and not all of Saunders' empirical findings can be summarised here. He sought, first of all, to establish the popularity of owning over renting and the desire to own. The overwhelming majority (91 per cent) of his respondents expressed a preference for owner-occupation rather than council renting (Saunders 1990: 63–4). Saunders rejects left-wing thinking that the desire to own is the product of a dominant ideology or manipulated choices. Rather, he argues that natural inclinations – a territorial impulse or an instinct to possess – and social factors have influenced people's motivations to buy (Saunders 1990: 83). Saunders found that the most frequently cited reasons for his respondents' first house purchase were largely financial in terms of 'getting something for your money' (29 per cent) and 'investment' (20 per cent). A desire to own was another major reason expressed by just under one-fifth of the respondents (18 per cent). The perceived advantages of owner-occupation were also financial (38 per cent) although the most important advantage was the autonomy of 'doing what you like'. Moreover, just under one-third of home owners (29 per cent) could think of no disadvantages to owning their own homes. For Saunders, this was unequivocal evidence of the desire to own. In contrast, a large proportion (42 per cent) of council tenants could see no advantages to renting. The major disadvantages were 'lack of personal control' (24 per cent) and 'money down the drain' (21 per cent). Tenant dissatisfaction, therefore, was highly fuelled by what Saunders saw as the 'inability to influence decisions about where they live, what kind of house they live in, the deterioration of their accommodation' and 'the frustration of dependency' (Saunders

1990: 94). Indeed, Saunders went on to claim that tenant dissatisfaction has risen because as increasing numbers of households have moved into owner-occupation, 'so popular aspirations and expectations have been rising' (Saunders 1990: 94). The popularity of owning over renting, therefore, must be placed in this context.

Saunders also considered the extent to which home owners accumulate wealth from their housing. Drawing on the informants' housing histories, he found that the average sum accumulated across the three towns was £28,000 at 1986 prices (£20,000 after mortgage payments deductions). The sums are considerable – more than can be made in the labour market – which suggests that 'the spread of owner-occupation must have had a significant impact on the overall distribution of wealth in Britain' (Saunders 1990: 135). Examining the rates of return on housing investment in the three towns, Saunders found that the middle 80 per cent of home owners who had originally invested £500 or more of their own money had made nominal rates of return on their capital of between 4 per cent and 30 per cent per annum. Again, the return is higher than those offered by other types of investment. These findings led Saunders to reject the academic left's antipathy to mass home ownership. Gains made from the housing market increasingly enjoyed by the 'middle mass' are far from illusory. He also went on to reject the argument that gains made by some are at the expense of others since capital gains have derived from the increasing expense of housing. The increase in real house prices over time indicates that home owners will continue to gain. Finally, he argued that capital gains are realisable. He found, for example, that one-third of his sample had taken money out from over-mortgaging or remortgaging with the mean value of the total sum extracted amounting to over £10,000 at 1986 prices (Saunders 1990: 157). He also found that nearly one-third of home owners had received help from others when raising their initial deposit, while 28 per cent of children who had left home had been helped by their parents with their housing costs. Saunders concluded that new patterns of 'familial accumulation' are in evidence, as capital gains from the housing market are in this sense becoming cyclical, 'for each generation from here on will benefit from its parents while in turn benefiting its children' (Saunders 1990: 163).

Saunders found that home ownership does not make people more conservative in that working-class owners still have a high propensity to vote Labour. He also examined the effects of tenure on other forms of political mobilisation. To what extent does home ownership foster a commitment to the values of private property and undermine a commitment to collective provision? Examining his respondents' broader political values, he found that home owners support anti-collectivist measures on some items but not others. Home owners are more likely than tenants, for example, to support rate reductions (with its implications for poorer services) and welfare state expenditure generally. However, on more specific items, home owners and tenants alike support state provision. The majority of home owners (54 per cent) and council tenants (62 per cent) in the working class, for example, indicated that they were prepared to pay higher taxes to fund state expenditure on education (Saunders 1990: 253). Home owners, therefore, do not share a unified set of anti-collectivist political beliefs. Turning to housing policy, however, Saunders found that 'home owners form a distinct and crucial interest in the politics of housing at both local and national levels' (Saunders 1990: 255). Where a local organisation – such as a tenants' group – was available to join, only 10 per cent of tenants did so compared with 51 per cent of owners. Home ownership facilitates widespread participation in organisations representing householders' interest while council renting does not. Home owners are more likely to support mortgage interest tax relief than tenants (73 per cent compared with 63 per cent). Home owners, therefore, are an 'interest which cannot be challenged' and their power derives from politicians' anxieties concerning their possible reaction to, for example, the withdrawal of mortgage interest tax relief. The political affects of the growth of home ownership are most clearly evident in relation to housing policy issues at the national and local levels.

Saunders also explored whether ownership influences the way people experience their homes. He found that council tenants associate the home with the family, love and children more than home owners (43 per cent compared with 33 per cent) and also attached greater importance to belonging to a neighbourhood (21 per cent and 11 per cent). Owners, in contrast, placed greater emphasis on comfort and relaxation than council tenants (28 per cent compared with 14 per cent) and also personal possessions (11 per cent compared with 5 per cent) (Saunders 1990: 273). The meaning of the home, in other words, varied by tenure. However, Saunders rejected the view that home ownership has fostered a privatised lifestyle. While he found that council tenants are more involved in neighbourhood networks and provide more mutual support to neighbours than home owners, he also found that owner-occupiers are more involved in local organisations than council tenants. Over half (56 per cent) of home owners belonged to at least one local organisation compared with one-third (34 per cent) of council tenants (Saunders 1990: 287). Controlling for class and income differences, home owners also go out socially more than council tenants, suggesting that 'owner-occupation facilitates greater social engagement' (Saunders 1990: 290). He went on to argue that home ownership is tied up with feelings of psychological security and social well-being. Home owners, for example, were found to have a stronger attachment to the home than council tenants (64 per cent compared with 40 per cent). Home owners showed more pride in and commitment to their homes than council tenants (32 per cent compared with 14 per cent). Home ownership, therefore, generates a sense of ontological (psychological) security. Finally, Saunders rejected the feminist view that the home is not necessarily a haven to women as it is to men. He found that women associate the home with family, love and children as much as men (35 per cent and 37 per cent respectively) and the same applies to feelings of comfort and relaxation (23 per cent and 27 per cent respectively). Thus, 'the orthodox feminist image of the home as an oppressive institution simply does not square with what women themselves say and feel about it' (Saunders 1990: 309). The home, especially the owner-occupied home, is a haven for women and men alike.

In conclusion, Saunders identified a new division between the middle mass and the marginalised minority (or underclass) which is 'most vividly expressed through housing differences and is reproduced through tenure based inequalities' (Saunders 1990: 369). This underclass is concentrated in the least desirable parts of the council housing sector and also suffers other multiple deprivations. They are deprived of improving their position while home owners have the opportunity to increase their assets. Marginality, he argues, can only be overcome by allowing more tenants to become owners thereby escaping state dependency and becoming active citizens in a market system. Policies designed to help people buy their own homes should be extended and voucher schemes should be developed to help those who might have difficulty purchasing a house. The contradictory system of controls and subsidies should also be overhauled in preference for a tenure-neutral system of income support in which consumers can choose whether to rent or buy. Saunders concludes:

All that is required is a realistic social vision reinforced with firm political resolution. Failure to embrace this vision or to hold fast to this resolution will consign a minority of the British population to an unedifying and stigmatised state of dependency, and the cost of such failure in the years to come will be felt by us all. (1990: 371)

Saunders' book, perhaps not surprisingly, generated some strong feelings (see Byrne 1991; Hamnett 1991; Scase 1991). Hamnett (1991: 133), for example, described the book as 'one of the most important books on housing in the last few years' which 'presents a generally rigorous, comprehensive, scholarly, and well-documented analysis of debate on home ownership'. In opposition, Byrne (1991: 634) stated that Saunders' evidence 'was so flawed that if it had been presented as the basis of a "contribution to knowledge" in a PhD thesis, that thesis would very likely have been failed on technical grounds'. Against the backdrop of such contrasting reviews, how Saunders conducted his research will now be evaluated.

Local versus national survey

Saunders undertook a household survey in three English towns – Burnley, Derby and Slough – in 1986. Attention focused on home owners and council tenants since they are the major forms of housing tenure in Britain, representing the main private and public forms of housing consumption. The decision to focus on three towns rather than undertake a nationally representative survey was made in recognition of the influence of local variations – the diversity of histories, cultures and housing markets in Britain – which have influenced people's housing aspirations (Saunders 1990: 45). Two other factors influenced the choice of towns: the experience of industrialisation, and patterns of current economic prosperity and decline with their implications for the housing market.

Thus, Burnley was chosen as an old industrial town in long-term decline, Derby was chosen as a mature industrial town which had experienced recent economic recession and Slough was chosen as a new industrial town enjoying growth and prosperity (see Figure 5.1). Second, the towns were chosen because they contained high numbers of working-class inhabitants – characterised by working-class traditions, cultures and politics – so that the research would capture new generations of owner-occupiers with the growth of *mass* home ownership. Two of the towns – Derby and Slough – also had large Asian populations, allowing for an analysis of the extent to which members of an ethnic minority have gained in the housing market. Saunders concluded that 'these three towns represent ideal "testing grounds" for examining the impact, if any, of the growth of home ownership on working-class lifestyles, standards of living and political values' (Saunders 1990: 48).

Figure 5.1   The three towns survey study areas
(Saunders 1990: 46)

The final sample consisted of 522 individuals living in 450 households with the unit of analysis being the household rather than the individual. A target of 150 households was set for each town with a quota of 50 for three different types of housing areas: suburban houses at the higher end of the local price range (Type A), centrally located terraced households at the lower end of the price range of the housing market (Type B), and council estates including desirable and undesirable areas (Type C). A variety of neighbourhoods were included in each type: these were chosen from an inspection of small area census data and advice from local estate agents and local government housing officials. Clusters of roads were then selected under each quota and households selected randomly from the electoral register. Letters were sent to these households explaining the research and respondents subsequently were interviewed by Saunders and his associates. The interviews covered a range of topics including the respondents' past and present housing circumstances, leisure activities, household income and expenditure, and people's feelings about their house and home. Saunders identified three advantages of undertaking the research himself rather than employing a research organisation. First, he and his co-researchers were able to get a 'feel' for the data by talking to the informants in their own homes. Second, the researchers were trained social scientists, all with different views about home ownership in particular and varied political views in general, thereby avoiding the problem of bias. Third, they were able to include a large number of open-ended questions and to devote the time to taking notes verbatim. Saunders (1990: 383) concluded, 'what all this amounts to is that the findings we recorded probably have a higher degree of validity than that achieved in most surveys of this kind'.

A number of observations can be made about Saunders' choice of method. First, his decision to undertake a set of three local surveys rather than a nationally representative survey is worthy of comment. The sample size of 450 households is relatively small from which to generalise. A small sample presents two problems for statistical analysis of the data. First, the number of cases in cells for multivariate analysis can quickly drop, reducing the scope to examine the associations between several variables at once. Second, estimates from sample statistics to population parameters are imprecise, and apparently substantial differences between groups in the sample might not signal real differences across the population. Saunders acknowledges the difficulties which his decision presents for making generalisations from his findings, although he emphasises the advantage of being able to take account of the influence of specific local factors on housing experiences. However, Saunders does not fully explore the local dimensions of his survey (except in relation to capital gains), so arguably his choice of method is undermined by the use to which his data were subsequently put. In places, he effectively uses his local surveys as if they constituted a nationally representative survey and he often generalises from his empirical findings in three towns to British society as a whole. Be that as it may, it is a little surprising to find that Saunders did not explicitly choose the three towns for their different patterns and trends of home ownership. He could have chosen three towns with high, average, and low levels of home ownership but, instead, focused on one town with a higher than the national average level of home ownership (Burnley at 70 per cent) and two towns with below average levels of home ownership (58 per cent in Derby and 57 per cent in Slough). It is never made clear why home ownership might have a different significance in a declining region from one that is booming. Interestingly, in commenting on this chapter, Saunders acknowledged that the local focus was the result of compromises made in order to secure funding and liaison with other researchers undertaking four other projects at the University of Sussex. Had it not been part of a programme of research, he might not have devised the three towns survey as he did.

As Saunders readily concedes, the response rates were disappointing across the three towns and the three types of housing area. As Table 5.1 shows, the overall response rates ranged from 42 per cent in Slough to 61 per cent in Burnley, and within housing types from 33 per cent in Type C in Slough to 76 per cent in Type A in Burnley. Indeed, the research in Derby was also hampered by a spate of burglaries with the intruders claiming to be from the University of Sussex!

As Phizacklea and Wolkowitz were also aware (see Chapter 4), getting people's agreement to be interviewed is difficult in areas of high crime and vandalism. Saunders would have done well to draw on the advice of a survey research organisation who have to confront these problems frequently. Some organisations' interviewers are trained to avoid situations where they will meet with an outright rejection and to return on another occasion when cooperation might be more forthcoming. It is common practice to inform the local police that researchers are interviewing in an area to allay the fears of local residents. The crucial question which is left to be addressed is whether those who declined to be interviewed were in some way different – in their social characteristics or attitudes and behaviour – to those who were willing to be interviewed. Was it the poorer

members of Type B housing in the three towns who were less willing
to be interviewed than their more affluent counterparts in similar
housing? Were they from less desirable city-centre areas of the three
towns? Did this situation also apply in the council estates in Slough?
It may be, therefore, that Saunders generated a sample of home
owners who were very positive about their experiences of home
ownership because those with less positive views declined to be
interviewed. These issues apply to all random sample surveys which
achieve less than a 100 per cent response rate and doubts about
generalisability remain even when an 80 per cent response rate has
been achieved. Nevertheless, Saunders' low response rate raises
serious doubts about the representativeness and reliability of the local
survey data.

Table 5.1   Response rates by town and type of area sampled

| Town | Type of housing area | | | |
	Type A (per cent)	Type B (per cent)	Type C (per cent)	Total (per cent)
Slough	48	44	33	42
Derby	60	38	57	52
Burnley	76	40	66	61

Source: Saunders (1990: 379)

Analysis, bias and exaggeration

The effects of Saunders' opposition to left-wing views in sociology
can be seen in his analysis of the data and, in our view, the tendency
to exaggerate in the interpretation of the findings. Turning to his data
on home ownership as a form of wealth accumulation, for example, a
close evaluation indicates that the results do not substantiate his
argument that home owners have made *substantial* capital gains as
strongly as he asserts. He draws on a unique data set of detailed
information on individual housing histories which allows him to
measure real capital gains in a variety of ways. Saunders found that
the average gross capital gains of households was £28,089 (ranging
from £2,047 for the lowest 10 decile, through to £64,604 for the top
decile) and the average net capital gain was £19,697 (a loss of £1,925
for the lowest decile and a gain of £54,950 for the top decile) (see

Table 5.2). After allowing for inflation, the average real annual gross gain was £2,563 (a gain of £366 for the lowest decile and a gain of £5,477 for the top decile) while the average real annual net gain was £1,557 (a loss of £329 for the lowest 10 decile and a gain of £3,882 for the top 10 decile) (Saunders 1990: 134). Saunders describes these figures as 'astonishing' and indicative of the substantial amounts of money to be made in the housing market (which are often more substantial than savings from a lifetime's work) with widespread implications for the distribution of wealth within society as the middle mass has become more wealthy than in the past with the diffusion of capital in this way. In Saunders' presentation, there is a good mix of hyperbole and the findings on their own indicate that a much more cautious interpretation might have been more appropriate. Saunders' analysis of home owners' rates of return expressed on the basis of their original investments, for example, show that some people enjoyed considerable gains (the top decile) while the majority experienced far more modest gains, with the lowest decile even experiencing losses. Saunders, therefore, overstates his case about the growth of home ownership on the distribution of wealth in society.

Table 5.2   Capital gains and annual gains by home owners in the three towns survey

Measure of gain (£)

Decile	GCG	Real GCG	NCG	Real NCG	AGG	Real AGG	ANG	Real ANG
Lowest 10 per cent	2,216	2,047	−161	−1,295	441	366	−16	−329
20 per cent	7,844	7,525	2,164	1,420	845	810	409	272
30 per cent	12,061	11,282	2,164	1,420	1,196	1,172	676	627
40 per cent	17,239	17,453	10,303	9,523	1,603	1,538	940	913
50 per cent (median)	22,750	22,159	13,527	13,517	2,000	1,987	1,273	1,253
60 per cent	27,597	27,848	19,282	19,343	2,409	2,508	1,594	1,639
70 per cent	33,755	37,231	24,268	26,963	2,956	3,039	2,142	2,054
80 per cent	41,092	46,788	33,255	35,808	3,625	4,004	2,606	2,539
90 per cent	54,999	64,604	45,965	54,950	5,203	5,477	3,210	3,882
Mean	25,823	28,089	18,195	19,697	2,570	2,563	1,696	1,557
n=289								

Key to column headings: GCG = gross capital gain; NCG = net capital gain; AGG = annual gross gain; ANG = annual net gain.
Source: Saunders (1990: 134)

Looking at capital gains by social class, Saunders found that the vast majority of home owners across all classes have gained. The average real capital gain, for example, for members of the service class was £30,523, for the intermediate class £21,662 and for the working class, £6,734. It was only the bottom 10 per cent in each class which actually made losses (of £200, £5,180 and £2,407 respectively) and who were the most recent entrants into the housing market. Saunders accepts that there are clear class differences in terms of total gains since the differential between the service class and working class for the median real net capital gains is 54 per cent. However, he emphasises that the class differential is squeezed to 80 per cent in terms of the median real annual net gains. He eagerly concludes that, 'in relative terms, home ownership is reducing rather than reproducing or widening existing class inequalities'. Yet, his subsequent analysis shows that capital gains are more even, partly because members of the service class had owned their home on average for longer than members of the working class and partly because many working-class purchasers had made high gains as a result of buying their council houses at very favourable rates. The relationship between social class and capital gains, therefore, is influenced by such factors as the time spent in owner occupation by the different social classes and the different values of the houses they own. Saunders conducted a multiple regression analysis to disentangle these effects on capital gains and found 'the higher total gains accruing to the service class are mainly a product of the fact that people in that class have on average been in owner-occupation for longer than members of the service class'. Arguably, however, Saunders does not undermine the effects of class on capital gains but unpacks the processes by which class has the effect that it does on capital gains. It is the affluence of the middle classes, after all, which allows them to have owned their more valuable homes for longer than poorer members of the working class. Again, the claimed progressive evening-out effect of owner-occupation on class inequalities seems somewhat exaggerated by Saunders.

Saunders also shows that other groups usually identified as losers – council house buyers, owners of older, inner-city houses and home owners in declining regions – have also made gains, leading him to conclude that 'home ownership is widely regarded as a secure form of investment which demands little attention, entails little risk and offers long-term substantial gains' (Saunders 1990: 201). Overall, the evidence from the three towns survey allows Saunders to reject the antipathy among academics – especially left academics – and to undermine arguments that gains are illusory. In typical style, he concludes: 'that the evidence presented here would seem to undermine familiar fairy tale academic images of 'the masses" as a propertyless, powerless and dependent proletariat with nothing to lose but their chains' (Saunders 1990: 202). Rather, Saunders asserts that all home owners have made substantial gains from the housing market and the growth of home ownership is having – and will continue to have – major consequences for the distribution of life chances and wealth in British society. It has been argued here, however, that his interpretation of the empirical findings is exaggerated. It is undoubtedly true that the majority of home owners, including members of the working class, have made real gains out of the housing market (although a different view could certainly be taken about the claim that there have been few losers in the housing market from the vantage point of today). Nevertheless, the evidence also shows that the gains have not been substantial for everyone for they are unevenly spread down the class structure. The middle class and working class have gained but the former has gained a whole lot more than the latter (see also Hamnett 1995; Savage and Warde 1993). The claims of Saunders concerning the economic consequences of the growth of home ownership for the distribution of life chances and wealth in Britain are not, therefore, as well supported by the empirical evidence as he might have liked.

Associations and explanations

The attempt by Saunders to show that tenure is an important variable which shapes people's attitudes and behaviour is also problematic. As we have already seen, his research focuses on home owners (excluding owners of flats, maisonettes and so forth) and council tenants (excluding those in flats and other types of housing as well as private tenants) as the major forms of housing tenure in Britain, representing the main private and public forms of housing consumption. Saunders provides an interesting account of how he placed all of the respondents into class categories. Even though nearly half of his sample were economically inactive, Saunders placed 97 per cent of his sample into Registrar-General and Goldthorpe class categories by including housewives, the retired and unemployed according to their last job.

The consequences of this strategy was to increase the size of the intermediate classes – where women predominate – and the working class – where the retired and unemployed predominate. However, what is surprisingly absent from this discussion is a summary outline of the social characteristics of home owners and tenants (or, indeed, according to his three housing types). It would have been useful to have background information on the two groups in terms of sex, age, ethnicity, employment status and occupational class to get a feel for the two categories of people whose attitudes and behaviour Saunders subsequently compares and contrasts. Did the groups differ in terms of sex, age or ethnicity? Were the home owners more likely to be in employment than the council tenants as one would expect? Were the home owners a mixed group in terms of social class and were the tenants predominately working class? The reader is left with only a vague idea about the character of his large group of home owners and his smaller group of council tenants. We can only presume that the former group was quite heterogeneous in character while the latter was more homogenous in form. The inclusion of this background information would have been extremely useful when evaluating Saunders' findings about the effects of tenure on everyday attitudes and behaviour. Indeed, it can be argued that he should have controlled for these factors when comparing the attitudes of the two tenure groups.

Against this background, Saunders' analysis of people's experience of their homes conflates associations between two or more variables with a causal explanation of the relationship between them (see Table 5.3). Saunders argues that owners are more likely to identify their house as a home than are tenants, who place a greater stress on the people around them. He suggests these attitudinal differences are influenced by whether the respondents owned their home.

Noting that council house purchasers also view their houses as homes (even though the majority of them – 41 out of 45 – had lived in the same houses as council tenants), Saunders concluded that: 'What is clear… is that owners are more likely than tenants to express a sense of self and belonging through their houses, and that this difference is related to ownership rather than to the nature of the housing itself.' The data on the small number of council tenants, however, are not sufficient to discount the influence of the type of housing and nor are they sufficient to demonstrate the overriding importance of tenure on the meaning of the home. Indeed, it would not have been difficult for Saunders' to analyse the influence of housing types on the meaning of the home by exploring similarities and differences in attitudes between owners of Type A (affluent, suburban) housing and Type B (modest inner-city) properties and between Type C council houses in desirable and less desirable areas. Somewhat surprisingly, however, no such analysis of differences within tenure groups is forthcoming. Instead, Saunders overstates the differences between home owners and council tenants (and a recalculation of his figures to exclude council house buyers from owners paints a somewhat different picture) and he fails to adequately account for the differences between the two groups anyway. Arguably, the associations he finds between housing tenure and meanings attached to the home is, at worst, spurious and, at best, in need of better explanation.

Table 5.3   The meaning of home for owners and tenants

Home means	Council tenants		All owners[1]		Council buyers		Total	
	No.	%	No.	%	No.	%	No.	%
Family, love, children	48	43	111	33	12	27	159	36
Comfort, relaxation	16	14	95	28	16	36	111	25
Place you own or worked for	19	17	60	18	9	20	79	18
Belonging to a neighbourhood	24	21	37	11	5	11	61	14
Personal possessions	6	5	38	11	2	4	44	10
Long residence or memories	10	9	25	8	6	13	35	8
Privacy, a retreat, peace	4	4	12	4	2	4	16	4
Place of sanctuary or safety	2	2	14	4	1	2	16	4
Independence, being your own boss	2	2	12	4	5	11	14	3
Don't know	7	6	22	7	4	9	29	6

[1] Figures for all owners include council house buyers.
Source: Saunders (1990: 273)

Saunders' discussion of home ownership and privatism is also problematic for the same reasons (on privatism, see Devine 1992a and Pahl 1984). He found different patterns of neighbourhood relations between the two tenure groups. Council tenants, for example, were more likely than home owners to have at least some close friends in the neighbourhood. Saunders acknowledges that the findings are a function of length of residence rather than tenure *per se*. He also found that home owners are more involved in local organisations than tenants (56 per cent compared with 34 per cent). Half of all home owners who were eligible to join residents associates did so compared with only one in ten of council tenants. Moreover, one-third of home owners belonged to a trade union or other work-based association compared with 18 per cent of council tenants. Again, however, it is arguable whether tenure is the causal influence here or a proxy for other factors at work. Union membership, for example, is probably low among council tenants because more of them are unemployed or economically inactive than home owners. Labour market position rather than housing tenure, in other words, may be the more important determinant of union involvement. Interestingly, Saunders found that home owners go out more than tenants but that income differences between the two groups explain the pattern. Owners and tenants within the same income bands had similar levels of sociability indicating 'that it is people's financial situation and possibly their class culture, which shapes the extent to which they stay at home rather than their housing tenure as such' (Saunders 1990: 288). Others might argue that these factors explain a lot more besides! Saunders claims home ownership generates feelings of ontological or psychological security, as owners have a greater attachment to their homes than tenants (64 per cent compared with 40 per cent) and look after their homes better (32 per cent compared with 14 per cent). Again, however, his findings may be spurious associations rather than explanations since he did not explore the effect of other factors such as the states of the homes on their respondents' attitudes. Similarly, it may be income rather than housing tenure which allows people to maintain their houses and thereby feel pride in their homes.

Saunders' statistical analysis of the data, therefore, is not very secure. Convinced that tenure explains the meaning which people attach to their home and the extent to which their lifestyles are home and family centred, he emphasises differences and ignores any similarities between the two groups. In doing so, he also neglects differences in attitudes and behaviour within the two groups when it is not unreasonable to expect variations within the heterogeneous group of home owners. The one instance in which Saunders concedes this point is in his analysis of the political attitudes and behaviour of owners and tenants. Looking at the relationship between housing

tenure and political alignment, Saunders (1990: 232) confirmed the
long-established association between tenure and vote. The majority
of council tenants among his sample voted Labour (55 per cent
compared with 29 per cent per cent of mortgagees and 28 per cent of
outright owners). In controlling for class, however, the effect of
tenure on vote was not as convincingly established as Saunders had
hoped, playing only a minor role for the working class. While 59 per
cent of tenants voted Labour, nearly half (47 per cent) of working-
class home owners voted Labour as well. He conceded:

> This is partly because, while council tenants are overwhelmingly Labour,
> owner-occupiers are divided across all parties and it is partly because
> skilled and (to a lesser extent) semi-skilled manual working-class
> households remain solidly supportive of the Labour Party even if they
> own a house. (Saunders 1990: 233)

Saunders (1990: 233) concluded that the small tenure effect which
he found 'is almost stifled by the class-based pattern of party
allegiance'. The analysis of the empirical data, therefore, undermined
his original hypothesis. Arguably, the effect of tenure on other socio-
political attitudes and behaviour would be found to be very small
indeed if Saunders controlled for these factors that are likely to
influence them.

Conclusion

The spread of home ownership in Britain in the twentieth century
has had important implications for people's daily lives and for society
as a whole. It has given people a measure of security – financial and
emotional – which did not exist at the turn of the century. Home
ownership has been the source of wealth accumulation for the
majority of the population including a substantial section of the
working class, and the author of this chapter will be one such benefi-
ciary in years to come. In all these respects, therefore, Saunders is
entirely correct to highlight the advantages of home ownership. At
the same time, however, financial gains have not been equal and, not
surprisingly, members of the middle class have done rather better
than the working class in most parts of the country. The growth of
home ownership, therefore, has reinforced and even exacerbated class

inequalities rather than undermined them. Moreover, there are clear losers in the housing market as council tenants' lives have been increasingly blighted by declining housing stock and inadequate repairs which have turned council estates into 'sinks' for the socially excluded. Saunders is not unaware of these consequences of the growth of home ownership although the disadvantages of the spread of home ownership are rather downplayed in his book. Arguably, the social exclusion of council tenants is one of Britain's most pressing social problems. Saunders' policy recommendations focus on finding ways of shifting more people into home ownership. Facilitating such opportunities would be no bad thing. However, it must also be acknowledged that some people, for whatever reasons, will not be able to own their homes. Some vision is also required, therefore, to provide public housing to those who need it which allows them to lead as decent a life as the mass of home owners.

In the introduction, it was noted that Saunders is something of a lonely scholar in challenging left-wing and feminist orthodoxy and championing the cause of the libertarian right in the social sciences. Undoubtedly, he is firm about the shortcomings of other academics' views and the virtues of his own viewpoint. Saunders cannot be accused of bias in the sense of tampering or distorting the evidence. Indeed, he is one of the few sociologists openly to acknowledge when his theoretical position has changed or the empirical evidence has undermined his hypotheses. That said, Saunders' book is also marred by tirades against socialists and feminists whose work he characterises somewhat simplistically at times. Even favourable reviewers (Hamnett 1991: 133) have noted that the 'tendency to excessive polemic when he thinks he has the left on the ropes' is the central weakness of the book. Moreover, the effects of his viewpoint can be seen in his interpretation of the empirical findings since he exaggerates the consequences of growth of home ownership for people's daily lives and the character of society. This is rather a shame in an otherwise important study.

On a more positive note, one final point needs to be made. In his prologue, Saunders reflects on the sociological enterprise:

> For me, the attraction and promise of sociology has always been its capacity for illuminating aspects of our lives which we rarely stop to examine for ourselves. Personal experiences can be reinterpreted, and our understanding of them enriched, by setting them in a broader social

context which makes sense of why we do certain things, how other things happen to us and what the unforeseen consequences of our actions are likely to have been. (Saunders 1990: 4)

Although Saunders seems disheartened by much current sociology, most sociologists would be hard pressed to find a better description of the attractions and promises of the discipline.

Additional reading

A general overview of the sub-discipline, which includes a discussion of Saunders' contribution, can be found in Mike Savage and Alan Warde's book, *Urban Sociology, Capitalism and Modernity* (1993). The issue of social polarisation and deprived council estates is discussed in Anne Power's *Estates on the Edge* (1999). Catherine Marsh's *Exploring Data* (1988) provides a user-friendly introduction to quantitative data analysis. A more recent book on a similar theme is David Rose and Oriel Sullivan's *Introducing Data Analysis for Social Scientists* (2nd edn) (1996).

Chapter 6

Health: Wellings and Colleagues' *Sexual Behaviour in Britain*

Introduction

Sex is a topic which is virtually guaranteed to attract widespread attention. Indeed, from the expansive media coverage of the latest exploits of the rich and famous or the indiscretions of senior politicians, through to routine office gossip about who is sleeping with whom, one might reasonably conclude that the British probably spend far more time talking about sex than they do in actually *having* sex – however defined! Undoubtedly, much of this fascination can be attributed to prurience on the part of the British public (for which we are, of course, internationally renowned). It may equally be the case, however, that many people are merely eager to find a benchmark for their own behaviours and attitudes. A flip through the pages of the average glossy magazine does not exactly help in this regard, with the typical story lines of many publications – aimed at both men and women – doubtless leaving many readers feeling somewhat inadequate! It is in this context, then, that the specific fascination of the sex survey needs to be considered. It perhaps also helps to explain why many people seem to be quite happy to reveal their most intimate sexual attitudes and behaviours to a total stranger, whether that stranger be the features editor of *Cosmopolitan* magazine, or a door-to-door survey interviewer. Perhaps it is felt that the giving of such information is a price worth paying for being able to discover at the end of the day whether or not one's own attitudes and behaviours are statistically 'normal' or 'average'.

The National Survey of Sexual Attitudes and Lifestyles (NSSAL), carried out at the beginning of the 1990s by a team of researchers – Kaye Wellings, Julia Field, Anne Johnson, Jane Wadsworth and Sally Bradshaw – has provided ample opportunity for statistical inferences to be drawn, as it remains the largest national sex survey ever to be attempted. So, to put readers out of their misery right at the start of the chapter, the survey revealed that the average number of incidents of sexual contact in the four week period preceding the survey was a staggering… read the book in order to find out! Frivolity aside, there was a very serious rationale behind the study: the emergence of the human immunodeficiency virus (HIV) epidemic and the need to gather data that might help to assess and prevent its future spread. In particular, Wellings and her colleagues noted that existing studies had tended to focus on high risk groups and had been based on clinic and volunteer samples, resulting in a lack of knowledge concerning the sexual attitudes and behaviours of the broader population. In other words, it was crucial to find out whether or not people from high-risk groups differed significantly from the wider population.

It should be noted that, unlike the other studies discussed in this book, the NSSAL research team did not set out to develop a strongly theoretical perspective on the topic it sought to investigate; rather, the research arose from a very practical need for reliable data on sexual behaviour. Nonetheless, the research team sought to avoid a narrow biological perspective in favour of a more overtly social perspective (Wellings *et al.* 1994), and we have included the survey alongside other more theoretically orientated pieces of research because it raises a number of key issues of relevance to the survey tradition within the social sciences more generally. Moreover, to have completed a survey of 20,000 people on such a sensitive and personal topic remains a remarkable achievement.

This chapter will start by briefly considering the broader tradition of sex surveys from which the National Survey emerged. It will then provide an account of the main features of the National Survey's research design and some of its key findings. The bulk of the chapter will be given over to a consideration of three particular issues which arise from the survey's design and conduct: political intervention in social research; the difficulties of asking questions on sensitive topics; and the difficulties of adequately representing 'hidden populations'.

Researching sexual attitudes and behaviours

The National Survey of Sexual Attitudes and Lifestyles is part of a tradition of British national sex surveys stretching back to the 1940s. The sexual mores of the British public began to be put under the spotlight during this period as never before. In 1951, for example, Slater and Woodside published *Patterns of Marriage* , a study which claimed to be broadly representative of the national population despite being based on a sample of hospitalised soldiers, half of whom were in hospital suffering from 'war neurosis'. Fourteen years later *The Sexual, Marital and Family Relationships of the English Woman* was published (Chesser 1965), a study noted for its large coverage of just under 11,000 women recruited through their doctors. During the 1960s, research sponsored by the Health Education Council shed light on *The Sexual Behaviour of Young People* and *The Sexual Behaviour of Young Adults,* as a response to the apparent increase in sexual activity among younger generations (Schofield 1965 and 1968), while later work maintained the focus on young people by exploring attitudes to sex education and knowledge of birth control in the context of an increased incidence of teenage pregnancy (Farrell 1978).

All of these surveys were strongly influenced by the work of the American researcher Alfred Kinsey, whose two ground-breaking reports on male and female sexuality were published in 1948 and 1953 respectively. Of the first report it was said that it had 'done for sex what Christopher Columbus did for geography. It makes a successful scientific voyage to explore an unknown world' (Pomeroy 1972). Quite a claim! However, despite the fact that Kinsey's fieldwork was based on a form of intensive, informal interviewing, albeit in the framework of a series of standardised research questions, the reports tend to ignore the broader social context of people's sexual attitudes and behaviours in favour of an approach which emphasises the quantifiable. Indeed, Liz Stanley has pointed to the general failure of the sex survey tradition to move beyond the facts and figures, thus ignoring 'love, passion, desire, pleasure, disgust, distaste, hate, despair: powerful feelings indeed lie behind the statistical head counts of all sex surveys' (Stanley 1996: 6). She goes on to describe the sex survey tradition as 'something of a rogues gallery', remarkable more for empirical rigour than 'the sophistications of high theory' (Stanley 1996: 37).

In contrast, Stanley points to the existence of a parallel, albeit much neglected, tradition which places considerably greater emphasis on the meanings which individuals attach to the sexual activities in which they engage (or not, as the case may be), and stresses the grounded and changing nature of people's actions and attitudes. In *Sex Surveyed: 1949–94*, Stanley (1996) includes the full, hitherto unpublished, manuscript of the 'Little Kinsey' report, based on a survey which was conducted by Mass Observation in 1949. 'Little Kinsey', although clearly influenced by Alfred Kinsey's work, was based on a much broader range of methods and data sources. These included: a survey of 2,000 people interviewed in the street (with a large number of open-ended questions, the responses to which were noted verbatim by the researchers); a postal survey of 3,000 'opinion leaders' (clergy, teachers and doctors); written responses to open-ended questions from around 450 people on Mass Observation's National Panel; and material from a series of observation studies carried out slightly earlier than 1949 – studies of 'Churchtown' and 'Steeltown' (highlighting issues such as prostitution and sexual morality in two contrasting areas), of 'Worktown' and of Worktowners on holiday in 'Seatown', and observations of homosexual men. 'Little Kinsey' could, then, be regarded as a classic example of a study based on the triangulation of both methods and data sources.

A more recent, albeit somewhat controversial, example of research on sexual attitudes and behaviour which has sought to present a more complex picture of human sexuality is the work of Shere Hite (1976, 1981, 1987). Hite's work is based on written responses to an extremely detailed 'essay questionnaire', and while it attempts to quantify certain responses, it does so in order to contextualise the more complex range of written responses, which are prioritised in her work. Hite's work is also noteworthy for being conducted within an avowedly feminist framework, giving centrality to the voices of women. Nonetheless, it should be noted that her work has been widely criticised on the grounds of the self-selectivity of her sample and due to the leading nature of some of the questions asked in the essay questionnaire.

Most of these studies, whether they have emerged from the survey tradition or from a more qualitative stable, have responded to a perceived crisis or shift in sexual attitudes and behaviours. The earlier studies, for example, were prompted by the changing social mores which were ushered in by Britain's experience of war, while those of the 1960s and 70s generally reflect concerns over the consequences of sexual liberalisation on different subsections of the population (particularly, although not exclusively, on young people). The NSSAL was no exception to this trend, its main impetus being derived from the HIV epidemic. Accordingly, many of the questions contained within the survey were directed towards shedding light on behaviours and attitudes which had a direct bearing on future patterns of HIV transmission. However, the researchers also took advantage of the opportunity to ask a large sample about a much broader set of themes, including attitudes towards public and individual sexual morality. In addition, throughout their published reports, they have presented data on differences which exist according to a number of key variables, including age, gender, social class, level of education and marital status. This acknowledgement of difference is of crucial importance; as the researchers have argued, 'while the biological human sexual capacity is universal, its expression is influenced by socio-cultural forces. Sexuality is defined, regulated and given meaning through cultural norms... Biology explains little of the variation between population groups' (Wellings *et al.* 1994: 7).

Sexual Behaviour in Britain: *The National Survey of Sexual Attitudes and Lifestyles*

The National Survey of Sexual Attitudes and Lifestyles (NSSAL) was conducted between May 1990 and November 1991. It was funded by the Wellcome Trust, a major source of funding for medical research in Britain. Over the course of the fieldwork period, 18,876 people from a randomly selected group of households across Great Britain agreed to be interviewed about a wide range of sex-related issues, including their current, past and projected future sexual activity, their knowledge and use of contraception, their knowledge of HIV and AIDS, their attitudes to fidelity, marriage and homosexuality, and the importance of sexual activity to their sense of identity. Each interview was conducted face to face, and lasted between 40 minutes to an hour (depending on which parts of the questionnaire were relevant in each case).

The fieldwork for the survey was carried out only after an intensive period of piloting and a larger scale feasibility study had been carried out. This was conducted in order to finalise question wording and ordering, and to enable the researchers to make final decisions over the necessary sample size. One major issue of concern was the best way for the interviewers to introduce themselves to householders in order to maximise response rates. The initial moments of contact between an interviewer and a potential respondent are, of course, crucial to the success of a survey, perhaps no more so than in an investigation of sexual attitudes and behaviours. If refusals are due in part to the nature of the topic itself, rather than a general reluctance to participate in *any* survey, then this carries considerable implications for the representativeness of the sample. Consequently, a great deal of thought went into the initial moment of contact to ensure maximum cooperation. At each sampled household, the interviewer made an initial visit to provide residents with a set of briefing documents, explaining the purpose and rationale of the survey, and then called again to see if they were willing to participate. As a further measure to secure consent, it was made clear that potential respondents could choose to be interviewed by either a man or a woman, in case this was a factor affecting their decision whether or not to participate.

By the end of fieldwork, interviews had been secured with 18,876 individuals. Of the original 50,010 addresses selected from the Postcode Address File for inclusion in the sample, only 59.6 per cent of addresses (29,802) contained at least one person in the target age group of 16 to 59. Consequently, the effective response rate is calculated as a percentage of interviews secured from among the potentially eligible households. Figure 6.1 indicates how the final response rate of 63.3 per cent was calculated.

The two situations which produced the vast majority of failed contacts were an outright refusal by or on behalf of the person targeted for interview, and a refusal to give the interviewer the information on household composition which would allow him or her to select a household member for interview. These account for 31.1 per cent of the eligible sample. Wellings *et al.* (1994) note that some of the refusals were made indirectly but were nonetheless tantamount to an outright refusal. For example, people who made appointments only to subsequently break them would fall into this category. This is, of course, a good strategy for an individual to adopt if they do not wish to 'lose face' by appearing to be obstructive or awkward – or in this case, appearing to be prudish – or if they feel pressurised into participating, when for a whole range of reasons they would really rather not take part.

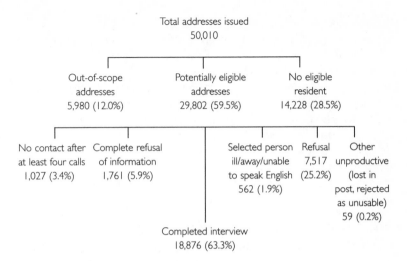

Figure 6.1   Calculation of final response rate to the National Survey
(Wellings *et al.* 1994)

As to the representativeness of the *achieved* sample, the researchers were satisfied that it reflected the broad demographic make-up of the wider population with respect to characteristics such as social class, marital status and ethnic group. They were, however, aware that the sample very slightly underrepresented men, and both men and women in the fifty-plus age group and, relatedly, slightly *over*-represented younger men and women. Difficulty in recruiting older people has been a relatively common phenomenon for survey researchers for some time (Hoinville and Jowell 1978: 137), while it has become increasingly difficult in recent years to recruit young males in sufficient numbers to produce unweighted samples which are representative of the broader population. Readers may recall that even the 1991 Census of Population, conducted in the middle of the NSSAL period of fieldwork, experienced considerable difficulty in enumerating young males, largely attributable to the poll tax effect which caused many of this group to go to ground during the census period (Dorling and Simpson 1994).

It is impossible to attempt to summarise the wide-ranging findings of the National Survey. There have been two full-length books arising from the research, each running to several hundred pages of text and tables of data, (Johnson *et al.* 1994; Wellings *et al.* 1994) while numerous research papers have been published in various specialist journals and periodicals. Many of the findings, as originally hoped, have had important implications for the provision of sex education and the promotion of safe sex, particularly among younger people. The research confirmed, for example, the continuing decline in the age at which young people first experience heterosexual intercourse, as well as the increasing proportion of young women who have intercourse before the age of 16, the age of heterosexual consent in Britain. The researchers also note that in some respects the old 'double standards' over the expression of male and female sexualities may be being eroded, with a growing convergence in the sexual behaviour of young men and women, although less so among young people from lower social classes. Educational attainment was also highlighted as an important factor in determining the likely sexual experience of young people. For example, while acknowledging the strong relationship between educational attainment and social class, it was found that non-graduate men were three times more likely to have had sex before the age of 16 than were graduates. A number of other findings from the research will be referred to in later sections in order to illustrate the particular issues of method we wish to highlight in this chapter.

Political intervention in social research

A key theme within this book is that social research is an inherently political act, in the broadest possible sense. In Chapter 2, for example, we looked at the impact on his research of Maírtín Mac an Ghaill's own personal values and beliefs. Similar themes emerged in Chapter 5, based on a discussion of Saunders' work. The original impetus for the NSSAL had a strongly political dimension yet, as we shall see, in its early days of development the Survey fell foul of government politicking at the highest level. Given the climate of the time this is perhaps not at all surprising: as Jeffrey Weeks has argued: 'By the end of the 1980s, to an unprecedented degree, sex had become a critical issue in British politics' (Weeks 1989: 292).

The need for a major survey on the general public's sexual attitudes and behaviours was first mooted in the mid-1980s, as the AIDS crisis continued to unfold in Britain. By 1987, a number of university-based researchers had entered into discussions with officials from the then Department of Health and Social Security and representatives of the Medical Research Council concerning the possibility of conducting a major survey. By the end of the year it was agreed that the proposed survey ought to go ahead, and that any government funding should be channelled through the Economic and Social Research Council (ESRC) and the Health Education Authority (HEA). The Department of Health had earlier been responsible for a major HIV health education campaign launched in the autumn of 1986, which had included high-profile advertising in the press, radio, television and cinema, as well as the production of a leaflet that was delivered to 23 million households. This campaigning was taken over by the HEA in July 1997. Such campaigning, with the aim of changing people's attitudes and behaviours, was seen as the only effective protection against the spread of HIV until such time as a cure could be found. It was argued that the proposed national sample survey would allow the HEA to assess the impact of its efforts and help it to target any future health education campaigns. Throughout 1988 researchers worked on the development of the survey, carrying out a pilot exercise in the autumn which, having achieved its target response rate of 65 per cent, was considered a success. As a result, approval was given in principle to go ahead with the study. The final go-ahead was expected to be confirmed in February 1989.

The broader political climate was not so sympathetic, however. Earlier education campaigns had been viewed by many HIV campaigners as 'too little, too late', and the reason why the campaign had not taken off earlier was largely attributed to what can only be described as a widespread 'moral panic' over the AIDS crisis. This moral panic was stoked by an all too willing media and given political authority by the Thatcher government's agenda for moral regeneration (Weeks 1989). The link in the public mind between HIV/AIDS and homosexuality only served to provide further fuel for the New Right's crusade against so-called permissive values. The late 1980s were, therefore, a period marked by strong anti-gay feeling, sentiments which directly fed off broader public concerns around HIV and AIDS. All the more reason for the government to sponsor a major survey of sexual attitudes and behaviour, one might think; but alas, no. With no decision over the future of the National Survey forthcoming by the expected date of February 1989, the start of fieldwork had to be delayed. By March it transpired that the final decision had been referred to Cabinet level, but still with no response forthcoming. By the end of the summer, a decision had still not been reached. As the research team noted, 'effectively, the survey had been put on ice without explanation' (Wellings *et al.* 1994: 11).

The bombshell finally came on 10 September 1989, with a headline in *The Sunday Times* proclaiming that 'Thatcher halts survey on sex'. By this indirect means the research team found out that a decision had been made at the highest level to withdraw the promised funding for the National Survey. By the end of September, the researchers were officially notified by the Department of Health that 'in all the circumstances it is not appropriate for the Government to *support* [the survey] and, more generally, that it would not be right for the Government to *sponsor* the survey' (Wellings *et al.* 1994: 11). In the event, the research was saved by the intervention of the Wellcome Trust. The Trust stepped in with a grant of £900,000 to finance a research team based at a number of universities and research hospitals, and including researchers from Social and Community Planning Research, a well-respected social research agency. Fifteen months later than originally planned, and in the face of the highest political opposition, the fieldwork for the National Survey finally began in May 1990.

The British government was not alone in its refusal to fund such research. Similar surveys have been sidelined, and in some cases banned, in a number of other western countries, including the United States, France, Switzerland, and even in Sweden, usually better known for its relaxed attitude to sexual matters (Wellings *et al.* 1994). The reported reasons for the British decision were as follows: the survey would be an invasion of public privacy; it was unlikely to produce valid results; and it was an improper use of public funds given that numerous other surveys had been, and were being, carried out (albeit on a considerably smaller scale). However, the news was greeted with disbelief and widespread concern among AIDS researchers, and was immediately branded a politically motivated decision. It is perhaps important to note in this context that the National Survey was being developed at precisely the same time that the 1988 Local Government Act was being debated and subsequently enacted. This Act contained the infamous Section 28 banning the 'promotion' of homosexuality by local authorities, including the outlawing in state schools of any teaching which promoted the acceptability of homosexuality as a 'pretended family relationship'. Weeks argues that the successful enactment of Section 28 was in part attributable to the feeling 'that in the age of AIDS, strongly linked as it had been in the media with gay lifestyles, few would oppose the provision' (Weeks 1989: 295). A similar argument could be advanced in considering why the government thought it could – and indeed did – get away with vetoing such an important survey.

The experiences of the National Survey illustrate two important points. First, in an age when many social researchers are increasingly reliant on various forms of government funding, the power of governments to withdraw funding can represent a serious threat to the pursuit of knowledge. Further, while government opposition to this particular study is undoubtedly an extreme example of political intervention, it nonetheless can – and does – operate more insidiously through the moulding, by governments, of the broader social science research agenda. For example, researchers seeking funding from the Economic and Social Research Council – one of the major funders of social research in the United Kingdom – are required to demonstrate the relevance of their research to a set of key themes and the priority given to the needs of user groups. Second, it highlights the political significance of all knowledge: knowledge is, indeed, power. Indeed, Wellings *et al.* (1994) have suggested that the government's decision was strongly influenced by this consideration. In particular they point to 'the power of statistical norms to change moral norms, and the difficulty of maintaining ethical values in the face of evidence that a considerable proportion of the populace feels or behaves differently' (Wellings *et al.* 1994: 14). This point can be illustrated by highlighting another of the findings from the National Survey. The survey found that fewer than 1 per cent of both men and women in the youngest age cohort (aged 16 to 24 at the time of the survey) were married at the time of their first experience of heterosexual intercourse. So, despite the best efforts of the clergy and some politicians to promote a *moral* norm of the sanctity of marriage as the only legitimate context for sexual relationships, premarital sex is clearly the *statistical* norm among the younger generation (and indeed, across the entire sample, only 8.2 per cent of men and 10.8 per cent of women felt that sex before marriage was 'always or mostly wrong'). Efforts to persuade young people of the validity of a moral norm such as this are likely to meet with considerable opposition in the face of such evidence.

Asking sensitive questions

It was revealed above that one of the three 'official' justifications for banning the survey was that the results from such a survey would anyway be invalid because of the implied unreliability of asking people to talk about such a sensitive topic. In the week that the study was finally published, *The Times* carried an article reinforcing this idea: 'Bedroom survey can't be trusted', it proclaimed with page three prominence (Laurance 1994). Ironically, *The Times* based this assertion on the findings of 40 in-depth interviews which were carried out in the developmental stage of the National Survey precisely in order to ascertain the limits of the survey's reliability. The article included some of the interview material from the pilot exercise to cast doubt over the validity of the survey's findings, even though the interview material was actually used to ensure that similar difficulties did not arise in the main phase of the survey.

The researchers were of course acutely aware of the potential difficulties of asking members of the public to talk about their sex lives to total strangers. This was the reason why they had decided to carry out pilot interviews prior to the final drafting of the question-naire. Specifically, the interviews were designed to find out the extent of sexual information which the public would be willing to disclose, whether there were any sources of obvious discomfort or embarrassment, what was the most commonly preferred terminology, and to ascertain the popular understandings of partic-ular sexual terms. Answers to these questions were vital in making the final, crucial decision over whether or not the survey would be conducted by face-to-face interview, telephone interview or by self-completion methods. Face-to-face interviews were eventually selected, albeit partly based on the use of a self-completion booklet, completed in the presence of the researcher. In part this decision was based on practical reasons, as it was felt that the required data were too complex to gather by any other means, and that the use of telephone interviews would lead to an in-built bias in the sample: some individuals, although forming a small minority, do not have access to a telephone, while the researchers also considered the possibility of bias arising from a potential eavesdropping effect. However, the overriding factor was the need to put people at their ease and the particular need to ensure that potential respondents fully understood the questions which they were asked. The physical presence of an interviewer meant that clarification could be easily sought if needed (or if the interviewer suspected that clarification was necessary).

The final questionnaire consisted of two main sections. First, a face-to-face section covered areas of a less personal nature – general health, family background, attitudes towards and experience of sex education, moving on to early sexual experiences: in other words, moving gradually from relatively neutral questions to more sensitive topics. The interviewers also used 'show cards' containing a range of potential answers for some of the more personal aspects of the face-to-face section (thus allowing the respondent to specify a code number or letter, rather than having to specify a more detailed response). Second, topics which had produced a higher degree of discomfort among respondents in the pilot interviews were covered in the self-completion questionnaire. These topics included the number of sexual partners a person had had, the incidence of sex with prostitutes, drug use, and the frequency of particular sexual behaviours. The self-completion questionnaire was personally sealed by the respondent and was identifiable only by a number. In some circumstances, though, the self-completion questionnaire had to be read out by the interviewer, mainly due to language or literacy problems.

Clearly, then, decisions concerning the ordering of the questionnaire and which parts were more sensitive than others were crucial to the final design of the survey. Equally crucial, though, were decisions over the actual phrasing of the questions to be included, regardless of their order. It is widely acknowledged that the validity of a survey can be strongly affected – whether for good or ill – by factors such as a person's ease with the language used in a questionnaire, their understanding of that language, as well as the specific wording of individual questions. It is of paramount importance, therefore, that the design of a questionnaire takes these factors into account and makes people feel comfortable about their involvement in the research. Consequently, the researchers were extremely keen to use forms of language with which the greatest number of respondents would be comfortable, and debated whether or not to use different versions of the questionnaire embracing different terminologies (as Kinsey had sought to do). In particular, the researchers had to decide whether to use various vernacular terms for sexual activities in preference to more 'clinical' language. Would they risk alienating large sections of their target population if they used the former, in which case would the more 'clinical' option be preferable? The consensus which emerged from the pilot interviews was that most people preferred more formal terms such as 'sexual intercourse', 'oral sex', 'penis' and 'vagina', rather than vernacular terms such as 'screwing' or 'fucking' or other euphemisms such as 'making love' or 'doing it'. However, while allowing the researchers to standardise on more formal language, it was still essential to discover what people understood these different terms to mean, and the qualitative pilot interviews revealed that individuals invariably had very different understandings of the same term. It was some of these differing understandings that were highlighted in *The Times* article mentioned above. It quoted, for instance, a 30-year-old single man who when asked what he understood by the term 'heterosexual' had replied: 'Well, it's all the same to me. Heterosexual, bisexual, they're all bloody queers' (quoted in Laurance 1994). Wellings *et al.* (1994) report other differences in understanding. The term 'sexual partner' – a rather fundamental concept in the research – was equally problematic, with some people in the feasibility study not counting their spouse as a sexual partner, even though they reported having had sexual contact with them in the previous seven days! The term 'having sex' was highlighted as most problematic of all, with many people defining it only as penetrative heterosexual intercourse, while others used the term to encompass a range of sexual activities. The subsequent questionnaire avoided the phrase entirely, instead using separate terms for each specific form of sexual activity. This also avoided the implicit exclusion of same-sex sexual activities from the term 'having sex', a major advance on many previous surveys. The final questionnaire used a standardised set of terms, with a glossary provided in the self-completion booklet. The word 'partners' for example was defined in terms of 'people who have had sex together just once, or a few times, or as regular partners, or as married partners', while the general term of 'any sexual contact or experience' was defined as 'a wider term (which) can include just kissing or cuddling, not necessarily leading to genital contact or intercourse' (Johnson *et al.* 1994: 349).

It is common practice in surveys of sensitive subjects to couch questions in a way that assumes that a person will probably have engaged in a particular activity rather than not. Thus, the wording implies that the interviewers expect, or at least won't be surprised by, an affirmative answer, placing the onus of denial on the interviewee.

The National Survey employed this method, asking for example 'how old were you when you first had sexual intercourse with someone of the opposite sex, or hasn't this happened?' or 'when, if ever, was the last occasion you...'. There was one important exception to this line of questioning within the Survey, though: rather than asking 'when, if ever...' with respect to same-sex sexual contact, the self-completion questionnaire asks of women 'Have you ever had ANY kind of sexual experience or sexual contact with a *female*', and of men 'Have you ever had ANY kind of sexual experience or sexual contact with a *male*' (emphases as in the original). The researchers had decided upon this terminology because the piloting had revealed that people tended to exclude very early same-sex experiences, but not very early opposite sex experiences, hence the phrasing and emphases were designed to encourage people to mention *all* forms of sexual experience. Nonetheless, there is a subtle difference in the implicit assumptions underlying the wording of each type of question, albeit unintentional. The implication of the wording of the same-sex questions is that such sexual contact is not going to be so widespread and that respondents must 'opt in' rather than 'opt out'. Statistically the first assumption may well be correct, but as Stanley (1996) has noted, the former style of questioning is 'leading' while the latter is 'prohibitive'. In other words, whereas respondents are given positive encouragement to 'admit' to heterosexual behaviours, that same encouragement is lacking with respect to homosexual behaviours. There is an implication that it is acceptable to assume individuals engage in heterosexual activity unless proved otherwise, whereas it is *not* acceptable to assume homosexual activity unless proved otherwise. This exception within the questionnaire has direct relevance to the next section of this chapter, which deals with the representativeness of some of the survey's central findings.

Researching 'hidden' populations

An earlier section commented briefly on the representativeness of the survey's final sample with respect to social characteristics such as class, ethnicity and gender. It was, of course, impossible for the researchers to know how representative the survey was in terms of its key variables, attitudes towards and involvement in a variety of sexual behaviours. A key objective of the survey was, after all, to establish an up-to-date benchmark (from which subsequent surveys could then benefit). However, on the grounds that their respondents' socio-demographic characteristics were broadly representative of the wider population, the researchers have claimed that their results are valid and reliable. Most of the findings that have been highlighted so far in this chapter have been about the sexual attitudes and behaviours of the heterosexual population, and the researchers are particularly confident that these findings stand up to scrutiny. Nonetheless, regardless of whether or not the survey's findings are representative of the heterosexual population, the survey has been criticised for its claims concerning the proportion of the population who have been or are involved in homosexual sexual activity. The results of the National Survey suggested that only 1 per cent of men and 0.3 per cent of women defined their past and current sexual experiences in general as 'mostly or only homosexual' in nature, with a further 0.3 per cent of men and 0.2 per cent of women defining their sexual experiences as 'both hetero- and homosexual'. Interestingly, a further 3.9 per cent of men and 2.2 per cent of women defined their experience as 'mostly heterosexual', suggesting some limited experience of homosexual activity. In total, then, the survey found that 5.2 per cent of men and 2.6 per cent of women had at least some experience of homosexual activity (taken from Table 5.1 in Wellings *et al.* 1994: reproduced here as Table 6.1).

Table 6.1   Reported incidence of homosexual and heterosexual attraction and experience

	Attraction			Experience		
	Men	%	Women	Men	%	Women
Only heterosexual	93.3		93.6	92.3		95.1
Mostly heterosexual	4.0		3.8	3.9		2.2
Both hetero- and homosexual	0.5		0.2	0.3		0.1
Mostly homosexual	0.5		0.2	0.6		0.2
Only homosexual	0.5		0.3	0.4		0.1
None	0.8		1.2	2.0		1.6
Refused	0.5		0.7	0.6		0.7
Base	8,384		10,492	8,384		10,492

Source: Wellings et al. (1994: 183)

This aspect of the survey attracted rather more publicity in the media than any other aspect, not least because the survey's findings were seen as being directly relevant to the Parliamentary debate on Edwina Currie MP's amendment to the Criminal Justice Bill in early 1994, which sought to reduce the age of consent for gay men from 21 to 16. Consequently, many on both sides of the debate attempted to use the survey to provide ammunition for their arguments, albeit often in rather illogical, naive and contradictory ways. Some who were against the proposed reduction argued, for example, that a change in legislation was unnecessary given that homosexuality was relatively rare, causing those in favour of the amendment to quite rightly point out that 'discrimination should be no more justifiable because there are fewer homosexuals' (*The Economist* 1994). Conversely, Stonewall, the lesbian and gay pressure group, highlighted the survey's findings that early homosexual experience did not necessarily lead to an adult homosexual orientation, presumably in an attempt to calm fears to this effect among the opposition (Wilkins 1994). Others, however, argued quite categorically that what they regarded as low rates of homosexuality revealed by the National Survey demonstrated the survey's lack of validity in this respect: in other words, they sought to cast doubt on the accuracy of its findings. Peter Tatchell of the pressure group Outrage, well known for arguing that the real incidence of homosexuality is nearer to one in ten of the adult population, argued for example that 'closet gays are very unlikely to admit their homosexuality to a total stranger who turns up on the doorstep' (Laurance 1994).

In their defence, the researchers have pointed out that the figures for homosexuality among men were actually higher than those found in any previous British survey, and were also comparable to the rates revealed by studies carried out at roughly the same time in a number of other countries (the Netherlands, Norway, Sweden and France), to which critics such as Peter Tatchell responded by arguing that while the National Survey may have produced a slightly more accurate figure than other surveys, it still failed to adequately represent the true incidence of gay and lesbian experience. The researchers were acutely aware of the difficulties of making accurate population counts with respect to homosexuality, and had sought to avoid bias where possible. In particular, as their use of a scale of experience suggests (see Table 6.1), the researchers rejected the notion that human sexuality could be neatly categorised into 'either/or' categories, and argued instead in favour of a continuum of sexual experience (particularly important in the context of health education: people may engage in same-sex activity, yet not necessarily regard themselves as predominantly homosexual, and vice versa). Consequently, the terms 'heterosexual' and 'homosexual' were not used within the questionnaire itself, avoiding the compartmentalising of respondents into 'either/or' categories. Rather, the questionnaire asked about sexual activities with same-sex and different sex partners, with the researchers arguing that the questionnaire did not therefore assume heterosexuality unless proved otherwise (despite the point made about this issue in the last section). It is also worth noting that the term 'homosexuality' was in part avoided because of the confusion about the meaning of the term which had been revealed in the pilot interviews, again noted earlier, but mainly because many men in the feasibility study who reported having had sex with men did not regard themselves as homosexual: the researchers were therefore concerned with reports of sexual *practices* rather than perceptions of sexual *identity*.

Before considering the particular criticisms which have been levelled at the survey with regard to its estimates of homosexuality, it is also important to note that the researchers in fact do *not*, as implied by some of their critics, view the figures revealed by the survey findings as the definitive statement on the incidence of homosexuality in modern Britain. In Wellings *et al.* (1994) they acknowledge that given ongoing social censure and widespread intolerance among certain sections of society concerning gay sex – including of course the illegal status of 'underage' gay men – the results should be viewed as *minimum* estimates only. Nonetheless, critics have argued that the researchers have grossly underestimated the strength of social taboos against the admission of homosexuality and the likely effects that this would have had on the validity of the survey's findings. Moreover, the survey method itself has been criticised on the grounds that the social dynamics of a highly structured interview are not best suited to encouraging people to 'come out' to a total stranger. Further, while a person may be 'out' in some, or even maybe in most, social contexts, this does not imply that they will necessarily be comfortable about revealing their sexuality in *all* contexts. As Stanley has argued, the survey 'makes the assumption that a two-hour interview with a stranger will successfully enable such consequential self-disclosure, an incredible failure to grasp the personal and political dynamics involved' (Stanley 1996: 51).

Stanley (1996) has argued that these criticisms are substantiated by the findings of 'Project Sigma', a research initiative which was conducted prior to the National Survey and which specifically asked nearly 500 self-identified gay men whether or not they would take part in the National Survey if they were included in the sample and, if so, whether they would be honest about their sexual orientation. Half of the respondents said that they would refuse to take part in the first place, while one-third said that they would cooperate but would not reveal that they were gay, leaving only one-sixth who would take part and actually reveal their homosexuality. Project Sigma's findings suggest that among *actual respondents* to the survey, the more accurate estimate for men whose sexual experiences in general was 'mostly or only homosexual' (taking this as a proxy for the group of men willing to identify themselves primarily, and openly, as homosexual, as opposed to bisexual) might be around 3 per cent of the sample, not 1 per cent as noted earlier: still, though, considerably less than one in ten.

The implications of the validity of the Project Sigma findings should also be considered in the light of the National Survey's overall response rate. As seen earlier in this chapter, by far the majority of the failed contacts were attributable either to an outright refusal to participate given by or on behalf of the person targeted for interview in a household, or to a refusal to give the interviewer the information on household composition which would have enabled an individual household member to be selected for interview. Together, these accounted for 31.1 per cent of the eligible sample. Given factors such as social censure, it might be assumed that homosexual men and women would be more likely to refuse than heterosexual men and women and would therefore account for a disproportionate number of refusals. If we assume along with Project Sigma that for every man in the National Survey's sample who described his sexual experiences as mostly or only homosexual there were a further three men who refused to take part in the survey at all – and if for the sake of argument we assume that this applied also to likely response rates among lesbians – this would still suggest that only 283 out of the 9,278 failed contacts were gay or lesbian. In other words, only 3 per cent of failed contacts could be attributable to the reasons given by Project Sigma (or 1 per cent of the potentially eligible sample). Yet again, then, Project Sigma's conclusions fail to account for the assumed underestimation within NSSAL, although, of course, these numbers would only be *minimum* numbers.

It is of course highly likely that the Project Sigma estimates of potential participation were themselves somewhat biased and accordingly provide underestimates of the true incidence of homosexuality. After all, Project Sigma's sample was based on a group of men prepared to be open about their homosexuality in order to be included in the project in the first place. Even Project Sigma would have had difficulty in tracing totally closeted gay men (and of course it had nothing to say about lesbians). This would imply that there was probably a far higher number of refusals in the National Survey on the grounds of gay men and lesbians not wanting to talk about their sexuality than suggested by Project Sigma – but it is impossible to calculate the actual numbers. This exposes the limits of any project which attempts to undertake population counts of essentially hidden populations, and mirrors the problems encountered by Phizacklea and Wolkowitz in attempting to locate Asian homeworkers, considered in Chapter 4. In the absence of physical characteristics which mark out members of certain groups in distinctive ways or of sampling frames which provide lists of individuals sharing a particular characteristic, it is almost impossible accurately to estimate the size of a hidden population (Lee 1993). Given the difficulties of estimating homosexuality in the broader population, one might be tempted to wonder why such estimates are seen as being so important. There can be no doubt that they *are* seen as vitally important: witness the scramble to make claims and counter-claims about the wisdom of lowering the age of gay consent on the basis of the NSSAL findings. Wellings and her research team, however, capture perfectly the significance of such estimates in an observation which was made no doubt in anticipation of the political waves that the survey's findings would make:

> According to some observers, one of the most important contributions a survey of sexual behaviour can make is to provide the empirical framework for a recognition of sexual diversity (Gagnon and Simon 1973). Statistical and moral deviance tend to be equated in this context. While deviation from a statistical norm might properly be termed *diversity*, relating to a continuum of behaviours in which no more value is attached to one point than another, deviation from a moral norm denotes *perversion* – a term heavily laden with opprobrium. Statistics

have political significance in so far as they have the potential to normalise particular practices. For this reason Kinsey's findings, indicating a larger than expected prevalence of same-gender sexual practice, were greeted enthusiastically by the gay community. (Wellings *et al.* 1994: 180–1, emphasis in original)

Conclusion

The National Survey of Sexual Attitudes and Lifestyles, despite the criticisms which have been advanced against it, represents a major achievement for the survey tradition in the social sciences. Almost from day one it was hampered by politicking at the highest level, with its development, fieldwork and eventual publication taking place alongside national arguments and debates about some of the most controversial moral concerns of successive Conservative governments. Nonetheless, given the considerable opposition to the Survey, it is highly laudable that the researchers survived these setbacks and went on to conduct the largest survey of sexual attitudes and behaviours ever undertaken in this country. Moreover, in view of the eagerness of Conservative politicians to ditch the survey, and their reasons for doing so, it is somewhat ironic to note their later willingness to quote (albeit rather selectively) from the Survey's results in support of some of their most cherished beliefs.

The aspect of the research which has attracted most criticism and which has, for some, represented the greatest disappointment of the survey has been its findings on the incidence of homosexual behaviours. In fairness to the researchers, considerable efforts were made to minimise sources of bias in this part of the research. However, the survey's imputed failure to have adequately represented the experiences of gay men and lesbians may say more about the limits of the survey tradition rather than the specific failings or omission of the National Survey itself. While some commentators have argued to the contrary, the claims of critics that the traditional survey approach is not conducive to encouraging people to be open about aspects of their personal lives which are overwhelmingly regarded within broader society as taboo would appear to have some substance.

Additional reading

Liz Stanley's *Sex Surveyed 1949–94* provides a highly readable and critical overview of the sex survey tradition (1996), while Jeffrey Weeks' fascinating *Sex, Politics and Society: The Regulation of Sexuality Since 1800* explores the changing nature of discourses surrounding issues of sex and sexuality in British society (1989). Hoinville and Jowell's *Survey Research Practice* (1978) and Moser and Kalton's *Survey Methods in Social Investigation* (1971) both discuss the difficulties of asking sensitive questions in survey research, as well as ways of boosting response rates.

Chapter 7

Crime: Hobbs'
Doing the Business

Introduction

This chapter focuses on an ethnographic study involving participant observation of the policed (petty criminals) and the police (the local CID) in the East End of London. The central argument of Dick Hobbs' book, *Doing the Business,* is that a unique working-class culture has developed in the East End of London and, contrary to police practice elsewhere, this distinctive culture also characterises the forms of social control in the locality. The book, Hobbs (1988: 1) argues, is 'about both formal and informal control strategies and the coercive regulatory power of the market place'. Although it may be shelved alongside the growing number of studies on the police, Hobbs is anxious to point out that it is not an analysis of policing in itself. It is not about the ordinary bobby on the beat but on detectives working in the Criminal Investigation Department (CID) of the Metropolitan Police. More importantly, he does not study them from within an organisation. Rather, the activities of the CID are studied from 'within the urban milieu' which Hobbs (1988: 2) describes as 'a view of policing largely from the point of view of the policed: policing from below'. The research, therefore, is simultaneously a study of the policed (petty criminals) and the police (CID detectives), both of whom are firmly located in the East End and its culture. It is a culture which celebrates entrepreneurship – an eye for the main chance in the business of buying and selling – and which itself can be situated in the economic relations of the locality. Like many good books, *Doing the Business* is hard to classify since it addresses issues to do with urban studies, economic sociology, class analysis and, of course, with the study of crime, deviancy and social control.

Hobbs was the winner of the British Sociological Association's Philip Abrams Memorial Prize for the best sociological book of 1988. He enjoyed critical acclaim from academics and non-academics alike. Indeed, the media were very taken with both Hobbs as an East Ender, with the accompanying cockney accent, and his research which seemingly involved drinking in pubs and engaging in criminal activities. Radio programmes, newspaper articles and so on followed. As Hobbs has recounted elsewhere (1993: 58): 'I was treated as light entertainment, my accent was always commented on, and before going on air, detailed biographical snippets were fed to the host and hostess.' Hobbs had seemingly captured the quirkiness of the East End which appears to have a special place in the heart of Britain or, at least, in the British media. While reading this book, for example, there was extensive coverage in the tabloids on Reggie Kray's marriage to a young woman (a graduate no less!) who was looking forward to his release from prison in 1998 (which was not to be). It provided another opportunity to recount the notorious activities of the Kray Twins in the East End of the Swinging Sixties. In actual fact, the ethnographic research which caught so much attention is but one part of Hobbs' work. A large part of *Doing the Business* consists of a series of chapters on the early development of the British police in which contemporary policing is located, the emergence of the post-war CID and how it achieved a cult status in its investigations in the 1960s and the history of the CID in the 1970s as its illegal practices and corruption clashed with the more formal policing of the uniformed Metropolitan Police. There is also a detailed history of the East End, its economic activities and the evolution of its culture which, Hobbs argues, 'appear to encapsulate many essential features which invite comparisons with the CID'. This historical context is, of course, what you would expect of a sociologist who is trying to make some large claims about the linkages between the culture of the East End and the everyday practices of the policed and the police. Context is everything.

Hobbs' research also involved a lot of drinking in pubs and some thieving, about which he is very witty. Not many sociologists face the dilemma of 'whether to write it up or bring it up'. That said, Hobbs is also very serious about how he conducted his research. He is highly reflexive in the way he tackles issues of method head on in the opening chapter of his book. He has also reflected on methods issues elsewhere (Hobbs 1993). In this chapter, Hobbs' work is located in the sub-field of crime and deviancy before the key substantive findings of his research are summarised. The rest of the chapter is then devoted to examining three issues of method. First, questions of biography and reflexivity are considered in relation to Hobbs' historical account of the police and the East End. Second, attention is given to issues of distance and ethics in relation to Hobbs' research with criminals. Third, issues of informal access and field relations with regard to Hobbs' study of the police are addressed. It is argued that Hobbs could have addressed some of the pitfalls of being an insider as an East Ender. Arguably, he proffers a less than critical account of malpractice within the Metropolitan CID than might have been the case if a non-local had researched the same topic. He stresses the distinctive sub-culture of the East End and ignores some of the similarities with other working-class cultures in Britain. He could also have confronted the problems for his research findings of being an outsider in relation to the non-uniformed police (CID). Relying on informal access to the CID and his subsequent relations with detectives may well have provided Hobbs with only a partial picture of police malpractice. How Hobbs corroborated material derived from various drinking sessions with material from other sources could have been discussed explicitly. Yet, it is hard not to conclude that only a cockney turned academic could have written such an interesting account of the East End, and the fact that Hobbs was very much part of the world he studied, undoubtedly, contributed to the richness of his ethnography.

Researching crime and social control

The sociology of crime and deviance has undergone significant changes as the boundaries of the sub-discipline have been redefined and widened over the last 30 years (Downes and Rock 1995; Maquire *et al.* 1994). In keeping with the dominant functionalist perspective in the 1950s and 60s, early criminology defined crime as a social problem and there was a consensus as what was deviant behaviour. The emergence of more critical currents – notably Marxism – in sociology from the late 1960s, however, led to new questions being asked about how crime is defined and labelled.

Deviancy was no longer taken as given but became a contested concept. The main proponents of the new Radical Criminology, as it became known, included Ian Taylor, Jock Young, Laurie Taylor and Phil Cohen (Taylor *et al.* 1973, 1975; Young 1971). Influenced by the Chicago School and the work of Becker (1963) and Matza (1964, 1969), they talked to drug takers, prisoners and so forth while others explored the culture of the so-called deviant – especially the juvenile delinquent (Brake 1980; Cohen 1971, 1972; Hall and Jefferson 1976; Hall *et al.* 1978; Hebdige 1979). Research on different types of criminals now has a long tradition, from the work of Ditton (1977) and Henry (1978) who focused on petty theft, to the research of Ruggiero and South (1994) who have studied the drug business. In the 1980s, however, when law and order became a major social and political issue, Taylor (1981) and Young (Matthews and Young 1986) acknowledged that crime is real and has real victims. This new perspective became known as Left Realism. Young, for example, focused his research in the inner city where the victims of crime are often members of the working class (Jones *et al.* 1986; Lea and Young 1984; see also MacGregor 1990 on crime and the city and Walklate 1991 on victimology). There has also been a growing interest in gender and crime (Smart 1977) and race and crime (Small 1983), reflecting their increasing importance in sociology.

Attention has been increasingly focused on issues of social control (which raises issues to do with power and politics (Box 1981, 1983; Pearson 1975)): especially the agents of social control and how they respond to crime (May 1990; Reiner 1996). With reference to the police, for example, attention has focused on the handling of events such as the inner-city riots of the early 1980s (Scarman 1981) and the miners' strike in the mid-1980s (Green 1990). There has been growing concern about the effectiveness of police practices in the face of rising crime and with sexism and racism in an overwhelmingly white, male police force (Holdaway 1991). That is, the police force is no longer viewed as an autonomous institution which operates fairly in the interests of all. Rather, it has been recognised that policing is a highly political issue. The police and police practice – how they interact with criminals, how they make decisions and so on – have been far from easy to research. The best study of the police is Holdaway's (1983) *Inside the British Police* which was based on a participant observation study from within the institution. Holdaway, who was a police officer for 11 years, was particularly interested in the occupational culture of the police which he found was based on secrecy and interdependence. The police seek to own and control the 'ground' in which they work which is often perceived as on the verge of disorder. This notion reinforces a notion of police work as both dangerous and exciting (Holdaway 1983: 36–7). Police practice is influenced by who they deal with so black people were seen as trouble and dealt with heavily. The way in which suspects are dealt with reinforces the notion of control, hedonism, action and challenge (Holdaway 1983: 100). Overall, Holdaway emphasised the way in which policing, like crime, is socially constructed and, indeed, that police activities play a substantial role in constructing crime.

It is within this context that Hobbs' work needs to be located. That said, it is extremely difficult to do so because he does not really engage with the literature on crime and deviance to any great extent. Those searching in his book for the standard review of the literature will do so in vain! Indeed, Hobbs distances himself from the crime and deviance tradition and especially from Left Realism. He acknowledges that crime is a real social problem especially for members of the working class in the inner cities. They are frequently the greatest victims of crime. Hobbs (1988: 13) also applauds the 'gradual recognition that the relationship between victim and offender is somewhat more intimate than had previously been articulated'. However, he is concerned that the new focus on intraclass crime will lead to an increasing preoccupation with control and containment as have previous studies of crime. Hobbs (1988: 13) emphasises that not all working-class crime has working-class victims since 'They also nick from those who have'. He also emphasises that, 'on occasions, these opportunities can enhance rather than encumber inner-city life'. There is a vitality to working-class crime which is often ignored by Left Realism. Working-class crime, in other words, can be seen more positively as a solution to social problems although he warns against the dangers of romanticising working-class crime. As has already been noted, Hobbs also distances himself from earlier studies on the occupational culture of the police – such as Holdaway's previously discussed research – which have tended to focus on uniformed police practices from an organisational perspective or from within institutions. Rather, Hobbs' research focuses on non-uniformed detectives *in situ* in the East End. The remit of his research on detectives

belonging to the CID, therefore, is wider than the standard participant observation studies of the police officer in the local station.
Against this background, it is the issues of method raised by the
unique nature of Hobbs' study – standing as it does outside the crime
and deviance tradition – that are to be discussed in the remainder of
the chapter.

Doing the Business

Hobbs (1988: 17) argues that there was a gradual movement away
from early forms of localised social control to the centralisation of
power in London from the nineteenth century onwards. The
'congenital disorder' of the capital, where the working classes were
not confined by factory discipline but remained independent casual
workers, witnessed the emergence of an early police force in London.
The overarching ethos of the 'new policing' was the non-military
prevention of crime, albeit controlled by the state, which was
quickly endorsed by the propertied middle classes. The emergence of
the uniformed bobby preoccupied with preventing crime was
accompanied by the development of a separate branch of plain
clothes officers concerned with detecting crime. The contrast
between the constraints on police work and the autonomy of
detective activities was the source of much conflict. Despite scandals
and corruption, the CID enjoyed the upper hand as the mystique
around the rogue detective grew (Hobbs 1988: 44). In the 1960s,
the CID continued to enjoy its cult status as a result of the investigations of three high-profile cases: The Great Train Robbery, and the
respective criminal activities of the Richardson Brothers and the
Kray Twins. The crimes included violent robbery, gangland torture
and shootings and, in the case of the Kray Twins 'everything
including the hint of police corruption, murder, homosexuality,
madness, show business personalities, politicians and the aristocracy'
(Hobbs 1988: 61). CID investigations were heralded as the triumph
of good over evil as convictions were secured. However, methods of
detection were far from rigorous in that detectives were lackadaisical
in the presentation of evidence, suspects were arrested and detained
without bail and dubious characters were used as witnesses who were
granted immunity and financial inducements. As corruption
increasingly became an issue in the 1970s, the appointment of

Robert Mark – who was strongly committed to eradicating malpractice – as Commissioner of the Metropolitan Police, led to even more
strained relations between the uniformed and non-uniformed
branches of the police service (Hobbs 1988: 83).

The central thesis of Hobbs' research is that the police practices of
the CID are especially distinctive in East London where the police
have adopted the culture of the East End. This emphasises independence, tough masculinity, a traditional deviant identity and an
entrepreneurial ability. Hobbs locates this culture in the unique pre-
industrial history and development of an essentially (one-class)
working-class city. The East End, Hobbs argues, first served the city
with an array of goods and services whose production – sometimes
distasteful – was located outside the city walls (see Figure 7.1). It was
separate from the city while also sharing the profit motive of city
institutions. Street trading was followed by the development of the
docks, shipbuilding, brewing, baking, fishing and consumer trades as
well as various workshop trades which were practised, of course, by
the range of immigrants – Huguenots, Jews, Irish and others – who
flooded into the area from the seventeenth century onwards. Without
the discipline of the factory system, the pre-industrial culture of
trading continued and an 'entrepreneurial style' prevailed (Hobbs
1988: 101). Consequently, the East End was seen as a deviant area.
This perception of the locale – and its attitudes to property –
prevailed since the docks provided plenty of opportunities for the
buying and selling of stolen goods. Even with its split from the city
and the decline of the docks, the casual worker has had to survive
economically by 'ducking and diving' in the face of low wages and
seasonal work. Market forces, in other words, have strengthened the
pre-industrial economy of the East End. Hobbs concludes:

> The resultant culture is essentially entrepreneurial in that the peculiar
> economic structure of East London has required generation upon
> generation of individuals to acquire and internalise the essential charac-
> teristics of the business entrepreneur, while continuing to operate at the
> very rump of capitalism. (1988: 118)

This historical context, therefore, accounts for the 'trading culture'
which is the 'distinctive style of the locals'.

Figure 7.1 The East End of London

It is against this historical background that Hobbs' participant observation study needs to be viewed. He draws on the experiences of his criminal respondents – Mick, Ken, Bill, Paul, Terry, Graham and Charlie – to show how they inherited the entrepreneurial spirit of their forebears. While they enjoyed the youthful fashion of the 1950s and 60s, they also adopted the autonomy, independence and entrepreneurial skills of their fathers. As Charlie explained:

> Us kids, we always earned money. We were always out after any way of earning... I used to help the toffee-apples man... then when the carters came back we'd take the 'orses back to the stables. Then there was tobacco company. It was when the big strike was on. I was only a tot, and they would throw out the big barrels... we'd smash 'em up bundle 'em up, and sell 'em for firewood. If you got a shilling, well a shilling was worth pounds. (Hobbs: 1988: 137–8)

Turning to the present day, Hobbs examined the range of entrepreneurial activities in which other informants – Keith, Nob and George, Jack and Tom, Chester, Terry, Bob and Danny – were engaged by means of an entrepreneurial scale (see Figure 7.2).

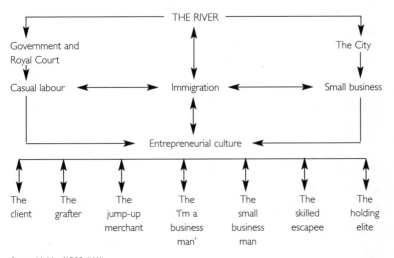

Source: Hobbs (1988: 141)

Figure 7.2   An entrepreneurial scale

Many of the deals described were struck in a pub and it is here that Hobbs conducted much of his research. At one end of the spectrum, Hobbs describes the story of Keith who started 'doing the business' following his wife's death, subsequent depression and unemployment. He allowed local thieves to use his garage to store stolen goods (subsequently re-stolen), stole some scaffolding at the behest of a local criminal (re-erected under the eye of the police) and acted as a driver for another (and was sacked for pretending it was his business). Thus, he 'not only proved himself to be incompetent and unreliable but more importantly he had failed to trade successfully' (Hobbs 1988: 146). He returned to the legitimate world of work. At the other extreme, Hobbs describes the activities of Danny, a highly skilled print craftsman and trade union official. Living in an exclusive area of Essex, he works officially only three days and the remaining time is spent wheeling and dealing including the 'almost routine trade in stolen goods' to build his house extension (Hobbs 1988: 180). There are varying degrees of competence, therefore, in that some are engaged successfully in illegal activities and others not. Some take risks while others are secure.

This entrepreneurial spirit, Hobbs (1988: 183) argues, pervades the everyday practices of the local CID and separates them from the uniformed branch. His observations of CID activities in the courts led him to describe the way in which the ethic of business collaboration prevails over the bartering of information in search of a good result. The detectives' performance is like that of a game in which they exude competence and confidence especially in comparison to the stilted performance of the uniformed police (Hobbs 1988: 192). Hobbs also found that officers were expert in reconstructing their activities on paper and the construction of events also took the form of business negotiation over information between officers (Hobbs 1988: 195). However, Hobbs argues that a considerable amount of CID time is spent drinking in pubs as a way of nurturing contacts and it is in this arena that detectives quickly find themselves adopting the business ethic. Hobbs recounts a story of how a detective positively assisted a criminal who had stolen an antique book by establishing it was not on any list of stolen goods before the criminal sought to sell it. As Hobbs explained:

I have no way of knowing what kind of checks Doug (the detective) made, but options exist for officers, if they have adequate descriptive detail, to draw upon collated information regarding both crime and stolen goods. On his return, Doug appeared pleased to announce that (for reasons unknown to me), the book was not on any list. Max (the seller) was pleased, Peter (the thief) was wary but the details of the deal were agreed, and Doug seemed almost sanctified at being able to make people happy. (1988: 203)

However, turning a blind eye to some trading activities was more usual. For these and other criminal activities, information was gleaned either directly or indirectly from CID contacts. Detective practices, therefore, took on an entrepreneurial form of 'trade-offs' and 'fit-ups' (Hobbs 1988: 211). This was informal community policing in the East End of London.

Hobbs' *Doing the Business* enjoyed widespread interest both inside and outside the academy. Hobbs was congratulated, for example, for producing a stimulating book 'in danger of resurrecting the good name of ethnography'. The same reviewer noted, 'the historical and ethnographic account of the culture of the East End is extremely effective, cogent, closely observed and replete with illuminating detail' (Hughes 1990: 536). Interestingly, Hobbs' criminal contacts thought it was 'crap' because it focused on the amateur criminal rather than on 'the more serious end of the crime spectrum' (Hobbs: 1995). In the remaining discussion, three issues of method and their implications for the substantial findings of the research will be considered in turn.

First, we will consider Hobbs' biography and its implications for his historical account of the development of the police, both uniformed and non-uniformed, and his economic and social history of the East End; second, his activities with the policed (as he called criminals) and the ethics of researching them; and third, field relations with the police which led him to conclude that detective practices are shaped by the culture of the East End. It will be argued that Hobbs proffers a less than critical view of the local CID and a somewhat romantic perspective on the distinctiveness of the East End of London which raises doubts about his central thesis on the symbiotic relations between East End criminals and the East End CID.

Biography, reflexivity and history

Before commenting on Hobbs' research, it is worth noting that he was very much part of the world he studied. Hobbs originally came from the East End, moved away, and then returned before embarking upon his ethnographic research. As he readily acknowledges, his biography is crucial for understanding why he did the research and how he did it. Hobbs was born and bred in the East End, and on leaving school was employed in various low-level jobs. For reasons which remain unclear, he left home to work in northern England in similar jobs including, as in the East End, a spell as a dustman. He found that London dustmen were invariably involved in other activities – legal and illegal – once the shift was finished, while dustmen in the North usually retired to the pub, the allotment or to their homes and families. It was these contrasting experiences which led Hobbs to 'become aware of both the diverse nature of working-class culture and particularly the uniqueness of East London' (Hobbs 1988: 3): not all members of the working class were 'ducking and diving and wheeling and dealing', or 'opportunistic and alert to the main chance' (Hobbs 1988: 3). Hobbs started night classes which were followed by a four-year teacher-training course at a northern college. He subsequently returned to the East End but now as an upwardly mobile teacher. While his new status cut him off from his former trading networks, he gained access to the local entrepreneurial culture in his role as a coach for a youth football team. His experience, however, led him to question the activities of East Enders 'as anything but normal' and his 'own involvements were now novelties' (Hobbs 1988: 4). Hobbs then gave up teaching to return to full-time study and, without funding, he became 'just another East-Ender scraping a living from the area's ever declining economy' (Hobbs 1988: 4). Hobbs, therefore, was very much an insider but had outsider status as well.

Hobbs, however, saw himself as an insider. Answering Becker's (1963, 1967) famous question, 'whose side are we on?', he clearly aligned himself with the people of the East End, be they the policed or the police (Hobbs 1988: 16). Being an East Ender undoubtedly had advantages. He enjoyed considerable contact with local criminals who were prepared to recount stories of their thieving, and his informal contact with the police facilitated much observation of their trading activities. His accent, style and local knowledge helped his insider role as participant observer. However, there are disadvantages to being an insider, including the difficulties of maintaining distance from a familiar milieu. In Hobbs' case, this problem can be seen in the historical context he provides for his ethnographic research. In his description of the tense relationship between the uniformed police and the plain-clothed detective, the reader is left with the view that Hobbs is not unimpressed with the irregular practices of the CID and the elite status they enjoy. This view is subsequently confirmed in Hobbs' account of increasing concern about illegal practices of the London CID in the late 1960s and the appointment of Robert Mark as Commissioner in the Metropolitan Police, a man who was intent on stamping out seemingly widespread corruption. There is almost a tirade against Mark's attempts to stamp out malpractice by disciplining CID officers and the introduction of more formal practices of police interrogation. Hobbs, for example, denigrates Mark's limited experience of street policing in Leicester and the fact that he was neither ex-Hendon nor a Met man (Hobbs 1988: 64–6). This makes for some uncomfortable reading for the sociologist used to challenging the informal malpractices of insider groups over, for example, sexual and racial discrimination. There is no doubt as to whose side Hobbs is on, for the ducking and diving activities of the local CID are much preferred to the new powers of the more formally organised uniformed branch under Robert Mark. Hobbs, therefore, proffers a less than critical view of the irregular practices of the East End CID.

Hobbs' account of the distinctiveness of East End culture in terms of the primacy attached to entrepreneurship is also affected by a lack of distance. Recognising that working-class cultures are not all of a piece, Hobbs argues that East End culture is unique. He provides an excellent summary of the economic development of the East End, the importance of the docks in providing opportunities for the handling of stolen goods and how the East End has long been known as a deviant area. Hobbs presents a powerful account of the links between the economic circumstances of a locale and the subsequent cultural attitudes and behaviour which it has generated. It is highly plausible to argue that the presence of the docks created the opportunities for thieving which were not available elsewhere and that the local population exploited the opportunities to the full. Nevertheless, Hobbs would have found 'an eye for the main chance' also prevailed among the dockers of Liverpool or Cardiff. Indeed, other research has shown how fiddling, on the border of criminality, is common in occupations where the opportunities to pilfer with relative ease exist. Hobbs is familiar with both Ditton's (1977) research on pilfering on bread rounds and Henry's (1978) work on fiddling and the informal economy. This research suggests that thieving of this kind is pervasive in certain occupations and it is probably to be found in most workplaces as well as other areas of life to a greater or lesser degree. In other words, entrepreneurial practices are not unique to the East End (and, of course, there are predictably plenty of East Enders who do not engage in criminal activities). Sociologists have long struggled with the issue of how to define subcultures and they have tended to overstate differences and downplay similarities (Valentine 1969). Arguably, Hobbs does the same, since the East End is at the same time both remarkably unique and unremarkably similar to elsewhere. While acknowledging that all working-class cultures are unique, Hobbs celebrates the particular uniqueness of the East End and downplays some of the similarities shared by all working-class cultures across Britain.

Morals, ethics and criminality

As we saw earlier, Hobbs was engaged in a variety of entrepreneurial activities in his pre-academic life. Once associated with the academy, he continued to exploit the networks and relationships which he had previously enjoyed. Since his criminal contacts were, like himself, white working-class men, he did not have too much trouble blending into the scene. Hobbs describes how he had to be extremely flexible about doing his research and be prepared to engage in criminal activities whatever time of day. Thus, the research demanded:

> A willingness to abide by the ethics of the researched culture and not the normal ethical constraints of sociological research... Consequently, I was willing to skirt the boundaries of criminality on several occasions, and I considered it crucial to be willingly involved in 'normal' business transitions, legal or otherwise. I was pursuing an interactive, inductive study of an entrepreneurial culture, and in order to so I had to display entrepreneurial skills myself. (1988: 7)

His participant observation of various escapades of thieving gave richness and depth to his data which he would not have got otherwise and, indeed, not to have participated would have brought an abrupt end to his research. As it was, the criminals with whom Hobbs was involved were largely petty criminals whose activities were often bungled and somewhat farcical. Hobbs (1988: 9–10) recounts some stories with considerable wit. At the same time, he acknowledges that there were difficult ethical issues which had to be confronted while doing his research. There were occasions when contentious issues were discussed and he had to keep his mouth shut in order to acquire information. There was no easy way to achieve distance from contacts who were frequently his family and friends – not least when arrests, beating, and a murder were involved. This aspect of the research required a huge amount of emotional investment and 'he trusted those he spoke to and had that trust reciprocated tenfold' (Hobbs 1988: 10–11). Finally, he admits that he found racist talk unpalatable and in objecting to it found that important information was lost. For Hobbs (1988: 12), 'racism marked the parameters of [his] involvement in the cultural milieu'.

Hobbs' reflexivity regarding the ethical dilemmas of engaging in criminal activities and associating with criminals is laudable. However, he also makes light of two important ethical issues when further discussion would not have gone amiss. First, engaging in criminal activities certainly poses ethical problems for social scientists. Hobbs points to the fact that his informants were far from professional criminals engaged in crimes involving high stakes. While he is very funny in his reportage of various criminal activities, reference to arrest, beating and murder suggest that some events were far from jolly. While no one appears to have been injured, his account raises important hypothetical questions. What if someone had been hurt? What if the police had arrived at the scene of a crime and tried to arrest those involved? Should a researcher describe himself or herself as a criminal or a sociologist? Would the police understand the distinction between observing criminality and engaging in criminal behaviour? What would have been the implications for fellow sociologists if a researcher had been charged with criminal offences? Finally, what of the victims of crime? Do those who have property and valuables deserve less sympathy than those who do not? Do they deserve to be robbed? This list of hypothetical questions is far from exhaustive and highlights some of the difficulties of being involved in crime. They raise the fundamental question of where the sociologist should draw the line in relation to criminal activity. Is it always a personal matter which varies according to what individual sociologists find acceptable, or not? Of course, addressing the ethics of research, especially after the event, has the problem of becoming a retrospective justification of decisions made in the field. Hobbs' work shows how ethical codes are difficult to operationalise in the to and fro of ethnographic research, especially when decisions have to be made on the spot. Nevertheless, the ethical issues and the consequences of one course of action rather than another are serious ones, and further reflection by Hobbs would have been useful.

Second, what of his association with (albeit petty) criminals? Many of them, as we know, were family and friends from Hobbs' early life whom he trusted. One of the advantages of this situation, presumably, is that Hobbs was not taken for a ride, which may well have been the case with other petty criminals. Even so, knowing that Hobbs was researching their activities, some of the criminals must have been tempted to embellish their past criminal capers. Hobbs refers to some of the tensions he experienced in the relationships with the policed especially in relation to racism. However, he does not consider some of the tensions which the criminals may also have felt towards him and his research. It may well have influenced how they behaved towards Hobbs. Interestingly, Hobbs (Hobbs and May 1993) reflected on this later. The fact that his research involved long drinking sessions, for example, confused some of his informants who clearly felt uncomfortable with Hobbs and his research. As he explained:

> This led to some problematic confrontations with individuals who were even more confused about what research actually constituted than myself. One particularly helpful informant, who lived nearby, observed me staggering home in the early hours and confronted me the next day with: 'I see you were doing some of that research last night then'. From then on he was uncooperative. Research and sociology were obviously excuses for getting drunk and on state money at that. For others, however, my willingness to drink beer made me safe, one of them, whereas my former neighbour thought I should be somehow different, conforming to a different set of norms. (1993: 48)

Hobbs concedes that the informants with whom he had started his research had gone by the time it was completed, although a new group of informants had emerged over time. Of course, relationships change over the duration of a research project and early informants are often lost. Nevertheless, how did Hobbs attract other participants over time? As an overt researcher with his criminal informants, did he attract a certain type of petty criminal over the duration of his research and what are the implications of this for his claims to authenticity? Deception is a difficult issue to confront but Hobbs could have dealt with the issue of maintaining good relation with contacts, attending to some people's interests at the expense of others, and so forth, in more detail.

Informal access, relations and rapport

In relation to the non-uniformed, Hobbs was faced with the more familiar problems of gaining access and establishing good relations with his CID informants. Again, however, he was fortuitous in that the pub he frequented was also used by a number of detectives. Moreover, he was approached to coach another football team which he did willingly when he discovered that one of the parents was a detective. Simon was his 'principal police informant' who gave him 'formal and informal interviews, access to documents, introductions to individuals and setting which would not have been possible otherwise' (Hobbs 1988: 5). Access to the CID, therefore, was by informal means. Again, he was involved in both overt research in CID offices and overt/covert research in pubs, clubs and parties. In some instances, he was an 'outsider' but he found that:

> Police contacts often accepted that I was an outsider and were pleased to inform me about 'real' police work, while I assumed an open-mouthed expression of wonderment as they told me about 'real' villains on their manor, men who I know had trouble holding up their trousers'. (1988: 6)

Some senior policemen, for example, were prepared to be formally interviewed in their homes which allowed Hobbs to ask about points of law and institutional structure which could not systematically be covered using covert techniques in the boozy ambience of the pub (Hobbs 1988: 7). In the pubs and clubs, he was as unobtrusive in speech and style as possible and was often regarded as being 'one of the chaps'. Much information on the occupational culture of the CID was gleaned from his conversations with detectives in these different settings, as well of his observations of detectives in the courts and, more importantly, court canteens. Hobbs' relationship with his CID informants differed from that with his criminal informants since his emotional investment in the detectives was negligible. They were frequently sexist and racist. Thus, the degree to which the detectives exposed their views and the nature of their work to him depended on his ability to strike up a rapport with the individuals concerned.

There are two issues of method in need of further consideration here: namely, the issue of informal access to the CID and relations and rapport with his detective informants. Hobbs acknowledges that informal access to the police provided only a partial view of their work. However, he argues that the time spent in pubs and clubs was far from wasted since this is where much detective work is done. While Hobbs asserts this to be the case, the reader is not in the position to judge the truth of his claim. Evidence from a study undertaken by the Policy Studies Institute suggests that 17 per cent of a CID officer's working day is spent outside the office with much of this time spent in pubs. While this report's authors (Smith and Gray 1983) felt this figure was an underestimate, Hobbs feels sure that it is a *gross* underestimate. However, even if, say, three times as much time was spent in the pub (that is, 51 per cent of the working day), it would still leave detectives with half of their working time elsewhere, unobserved by Hobbs. Of course, some officers might spend more time in pubs and clubs but if it was these with whom Hobbs spent his time, they are probably not a representative group of all East End CID detectives.

Hobbs might also have given some explicit attention in his work to the problems of doing research in the boozy atmosphere of the pubs and clubs. After all, he does not disguise the fact that both he and his informants engaged in heavy drinking sessions. It is not unreasonable to wonder if there was some trading of stories, boasting and exaggeration. They key question is how did Hobbs check and corroborate what he heard and remembered? Who did he turn to and were they impartial informants in relation to the police? In these circumstances, it is a shame that Hobbs did not have more formal access to the local CID to see how they operated in the more mundane office situation and how they went about detective work outside the confines of the pub. It would have been interesting, for example, to compare and contrast police practices in different settings. No doubt, however, having *formal* access would have meant the loss of *informal* access. Given Hobbs' reliance on the informal, however, a more explicit discussion of how material gleaned from the pubs and clubs was corroborated to avoid police deception would have been informative.

Finally, Hobbs' relationships with CID officers needs further elucidation. As noted earlier, Hobbs was extremely fortuitous in meeting his main contact, Simon, via the pub and his football coaching. As is so often the case, participant observers are dependent on their first key informant who often dictates the nature of wider access to his or her colleagues. It would have been interesting to know more about the process by which further contacts were made. Was

Hobbs confined to a few of Simon's drinking pals who engaged in some dubious malpractices or was he able to cast his net further to get a variety of different contacts within the local CID? Did he talk to any local CID officers who were *not* engaged in wheeling and dealing? If he did, what are the implications for his thesis that the spirit of entrepreneurship pervades the cultural practices of the local CID? It might be that what Hobbs found was some localised wheeling and dealing among a closed group of drinking pals from the local CID (from which he never broke free) – and no more. Furthermore, Hobbs concedes that he was perceived as an outsider by the local CID and that he did not have the level of rapport which he enjoyed with his criminal contacts. Despite his outsider status, Hobbs felt his relationships with the local CID were good. Again, however, the quality of these relations and their implications for the quality of the data needs to be considered. As Hobbs found, the police are as likely as his criminal informants to regale any listener with stories of real crime and real villains. As Holdaway (1983) also found, there is a widely held view among the police that beyond the confines of the police station is a world of chaos which they need to be active in controlling. One is left wondering how far Hobbs was able to get beyond the hyperbole of police stories – especially in relation to irregular practices – and obtain a clear view of the occupational culture of the local CID. Certainly, the ethnography of the CID was not as rich in detail as the material on criminals in the East End.

Conclusion

This chapter has focused on a study based on participant observation and some of the methodological difficulties associated with research of this kind. Hobbs clearly enjoyed many advantages of being an insider (of sorts). He did not, for example, have the usual problems of establishing access and generating a rapport with his criminal informants. That said, there are important ethical implications to be confronted in research of this kind. The problem of being duped is one example. Some of the pitfalls of being an insider, therefore, could have been more explicitly acknowledged and their effects on the quality of the findings more thoroughly analysed. The difficulties of being an outsider in relation to the police were also evident in Hobbs' research. Confined to informal access, it was unclear whether Hobbs went beyond a particular group of detectives who wheeled and dealed in a specific pub. This raises the issue of corroborating material. Again, the methodological issues of this aspect of the research should have been discussed more fully. Overall, Hobbs' material on the East End is far richer than the ethnography of the police (which he readily acknowledges). Hobbs was highly reflexive about himself and his research and, as a consequence, his book is a joy to read. It has been suggested that a fuller discussion of the ethics of research and how they influenced his substantive findings would not have gone amiss. Whether to have done so would have detracted from such an entertaining read is quite another matter.

Additional reading

The revised second edition of *Understanding Deviance* by David Downes and Paul Rock (1993) provides an excellent introduction to the sub-field of crime, deviance and social control, while Simon Holdaway's *The Racialisation of British Policing* (1996) examines new issues in the study of social control. Geoffrey Pearson's (1993) discussion of field relations and distance is very illuminating. It is the preface to Hobbs and May's edited collection, *Interpreting the Field* (1993), in which Hobbs also has a chapter. For a broader discussion of ethical issues and the research process, see Martin Bulmer's *Social Research Ethics* (1982).

Chapter 8

Class: Gregson and Lowe's *Servicing the Middle Classes*

Introduction

One of the major changes in the British class structure over the twentieth century has been the expansion of the middle classes as a result of the growth of professional, managerial and high-level administrative occupations (Butler and Savage 1995; Savage *et al.* 1992). The number of people employed in these jobs increased from approximately 12 per cent of the labour force in 1951 to about 27 per cent by 1985 (Marshall *et al.* 1988; Routh 1987). Previously, these well-remunerated, high-status and often powerful positions were the preserve of men. There has, however, been an increase in the number of women entering middle-class occupations, although they have gained access to only some (often caring) professions (Crompton and Sanderson 1990; Devine 1992a) and remain a minority in (top) managerial jobs (Savage 1992; Wajcman 1996). More often than not, these women have been married to middle-class men and together these couples constitute work-rich dual career families (Bonney 1988a, b; Pahl 1984, 1988). These households, Gregson and Lowe argue, face 'a crisis in social reproduction'. Their response is to employ waged domestic labour: namely, women in lower middle-class and working-class positions – sometimes from 'work-poor' families where neither partner is in formal employment – who undertake routine domestic and childcare tasks on their behalf. The growth of waged domestic labour raises broad issues about the

149

relationship between class and gender inequalities on the one hand and changing class divisions on the other, factors which are producing increasing social polarisation in contemporary Britain.

This chapter focuses on Nicky Gregson and Michelle Lowe's book, *Servicing the Middle Classes*, which was published in 1994. They examine the resurgence of national and local demand in waged domestic labour and the supply of nannies and cleaners. They also explore the nature of nanny and cleaner employment with reference to ideologies of motherhood and domesticity. As geographers, Gregson and Lowe choose two case study areas – Newcastle and Reading – to explore spatial differences in the demand and supply of waged domestic labour. First, they established the pattern of national and local demand by analysing advertisement data from the national magazine *The Lady,* and from local newspapers – *The Newcastle Evening Chronicle* and *The Reading Chronicle* – published in their two case study areas. Second, they conducted a survey in Newcastle and Reading of middle-class households in which both partners worked full time as a way of establishing the incidence of waged domestic labour. Third, they conducted in-depth interviews with a small number of nannies and cleaners and their employers in the two locales to uncover the nature of their employment. Gregson and Lowe also collected a lot of contextual evidence as part of their pilot work and by talking to personnel in nanny agencies, college tutors on childcare courses as well as a host of middle-class households, nannies and cleaners who were not formally part of the research. The wide range of both quantitative and qualitative methods used is very impressive. Most important, Gregson and Lowe's study allows us to explore how different methods of research can produce different substantive findings, the extent to which the findings of one method corroborate the findings of another mode of enquiry, and the ways in which similarities and differences in results can be explained.

Gregson and Lowe's work is located within debates on the relationship between class and gender. These debates have often became rather narrow in focus as participants wrangle over whether the family or the individual should be the unit of analysis in survey research. In contrast, Gregson and Lowe's study of waged domestic labour in middle-class households adopts a refreshingly different way of addressing the issues of how classes are segmented by gender and how women are divided by class. A summary of the key substantive findings of their research is presented first of all. Three issues of method are then raised around, first, the use of advertisement data for establishing trends and patterns in the demand for waged domestic labour; second, the findings of the workplace survey and the need for comparative controls; and third, the use of intensive interviews for revealing tensions and conflicts between employers and employees. It will be argued that the advertisement data are not a reliable base for estimating national or even local demand because the sources from which they are derived have a small and particular readership. Indeed, the workplace survey shows that the use of waged domestic labour in middle-class households is not extensive and it is the cleaner rather than the nanny that is the most popular form of waged domestic labour. Finally, it will be suggested that the employer–employee relationship (especially in the case of the nanny) is characterised not only by trust and consensus but also by tensions and conflict, yet these are not systematically explored by Gregson and Lowe. These comments suggest that the crisis in social reproduction of domestic labour in households is not as great as they claim. That said, their research raises important issues about the relationship between class and gender and their work is undoubtedly one of the more novel pieces of work to explore these issues in recent years.

Researching class and gender

The debate about the interrelationship between class and gender has been the most contentious within class analysis over the last 30 years (see Abbott and Sapsford 1986; Crompton and Mann 1986; Devine 1997; Marshall *et al.* 1988). The debate has narrowed from a concern with the contribution to the life chances of families of women's increasing participation in the labour market towards a preoccupation with the question of whether the family or the individual should be the unit of analysis in survey research (Crompton and Harris 1998). Throughout the 1980s, for example, there was a protracted debate between Goldthorpe (1983, 1987) who defended the conventional view (of using the male head of household as a proxy for the class position of the family), Heath and Britten (1984) who championed the joint approach (taking wives' characteristics into account in the study of class), and Stanworth (1984) who proffered the individual approach (of collecting information separately on men's and women's class positions). The individual approach was subsequently employed by Marshall and his colleagues in their survey of the British class structure. They suggested that 'social classes are neither families nor individuals but individuals in families' (Marshall *et al.* 1988: 85). They found a 'high degree of class segmentation by sex'. Men dominate the higher echelons of the middle class (in management and the professions) and the working class (especially skilled manual work), while women are concentrated in the intermediate classes (routine white-collar work) and the working class (especially semi- and unskilled manual work) (ibid: 74). They also found that sex has a profound effect on patterns of social mobility in that women of middle-class origin are far more likely to be downwardly mobile than their male counterparts, while the chances of women entering the middle class from the working class are far less favourable than men of working-class origin (ibid: 76–7). The class structure, therefore, is highly gendered as a result of the sex segregated social division of labour.

More recently, however, there is evidence to show that more women have begun to enter the higher echelons of the middle class (Allen 1988; Crompton and Sanderson 1990; Greed 1991). Crompton and Sanderson's research, for example, found that women are entering the professions (such as accountancy and pharmacy) following their acquisition of high-level educational qualifications. They argued that, 'education may be assuming an important role in breaking down occupational segregation for a growing number of women' (Crompton and Sanderson 1990: 558). Professional practices of social closure have been undermined by the 'liberal feminist strategy' of pulling the 'qualifications lever'. Moreover, in a climate in which feminism has been influential, it is no longer possible to exclude women from professional occupations by formal discriminatory practices. However, women's entry into high-level jobs has been accompanied by the growth of a secondary labour market of women practitioners who remain in the lower echelons of the professions. Women still face barriers which men find easier to surmount – such as the demand for continuous work experience and geographical mobility – in their progress through the internal labour markets of organisations (Crompton and Sanderson: 70–1). Childcare and domestic responsibilities are a constraint on women's participation in the labour market especially in professional occupations which have working practices that are not compatible with these responsibilities. Crompton and Sanderson (1990: 58) speculated that this tension 'may be a source of pressure for change in the division of labour in both the narrower and broader senses'. Gregson and Lowe (1993), however, argue that the domestic division of labour – whereby women take primary responsibility for childcare and household tasks and men help them to a greater or (mainly) lesser degree – is highly resilient to change. It is in this context that the demand for waged domestic labour by middle-class households has grown and, as we shall see, has been supplied by women of lower middle-class and working-class origins.

Gregson and Lowe's research is an important contribution to our understanding of the relationship between class and gender, looking first at the ways in which class is segmented by sex and the sexes divided by class. They note the increasingly heterogeneity of women's employment (Brannen 1989; Hakim 1996; McCran *et al.* 1996; McRae 1993) and its implications for class divisions. That is, women do not share a subordinate class position but occupy a range of advantaged and disadvantaged position within the occupational class structure. They are as divided by class as men. Second, they address the issue of class formation (Crompton 1995; Witz 1995) by examining the ways in which different classes are segmented by sex. Rather than just describe the gendered character of different classes, they offer an explanation of the way in which women come to occupy different class positions. They highlight the polarisation in the life chances and lifestyles of middle-class and working-class households in the 1980s: as the middle class became increasingly burdened by paid work, the working class was increasingly without it. The implications of the changing nature of paid work on households in different class positions, therefore, is addressed (Pahl 1988; Saunders 1990). Finally, they demonstrate the way in which paid work in the formal sector and unpaid work in the informal sector are highly interconnected in that the organisation of one affects the organisation of the other in both simple and complex ways (Morris 1985; Wheelock 1990; see also Gregson and Lowe 1993). One of the virtues of their research, therefore, is the way in which it connects a wide range of contemporary issues within British society.

Servicing the Middle Classes

Turning to Gregson and Lowe's substantive findings, their analysis of adverts in *The Lady* showed a national resurgence in demand for privately hired waged domestic labour, which had increased from an estimated low of 9,608 in 1982 to a high of 17,496 in 1989 (Gregson and Lowe 1994: 13) (see Table 8.1). The nanny – whose primary responsibility is to look after young children – enjoyed the greatest demand (27 per cent of all adverts for waged domestic labour) and its importance relative to other forms of waged domestic labour grew throughout the 1980s.

Local demand for domestic labour as revealed by adverts in local papers also increased from 4.9 per cent of all adverts in the North East in 1982 to a high of 16 per cent in 1989, and from 5.9 per cent in the South East in 1982 to a high of 13.2 per cent in 1986. Demand for the care of young children represented the largest category of adverts in both Newcastle (47 per cent of all relevant adverts) and Reading (48 per cent) (Gregson and Lowe 1994: 16). Advertising data from *The Lady* revealed that demand for waged labour was concentrated in the affluent south; namely, London, Surrey and Berkshire. Demand was highest in London with households accounting for 52 per cent of all recorded adverts. Households in south-west London had the highest levels of demand, particularly for nannies among young middle-class families, followed by households in north west London, which had the highest demand for housekeepers in London. A spatial concentration of the demand for waged domestic labour was also found in the middle-class areas of Gosforth and Jesmond in Newcastle in the North East and, to a lesser degree, in Reading, Cavendish and Earley in the South East.

Table 8.1 Recorded and estimated advertised demand for waged domestic labour in Britain, July 1981–91

Advertisement	July 1981	1982	1983	1984	1985	1986	1987	1988	1989	1990	June 1991
Recorded	577	1,201	1,374	1,709	1,742	1,992	1,949	2,176	2,187	1,848	649
Estimated Totals	*	9,608	10,992	13,672	13,936	15,376	15,592	17,408	17,496	14,784	*

Total recorded advertisements: 17,334.
Estimated UK total, 1981–91: 138,672.
Source: The Lady (12.5 per cent sample)
Note: *Estimates have not been produced for 1981 and 1991, given the half-year samples.
Source: Gregson and Lowe (1994: Table 2.1, p. 12)

Finally, their local workplace surveys in Newcastle and Reading showed that between 30 and 40 per cent of middle-class households employed waged domestic labour, about 40 per cent of them employed a nanny to care for young children and 67 per cent employed a cleaner. They concluded that waged domestic labour is a 'vital facet of daily social reproduction among the middle classes of contemporary Britain' (ibid: 50) (see Figure 8.1).

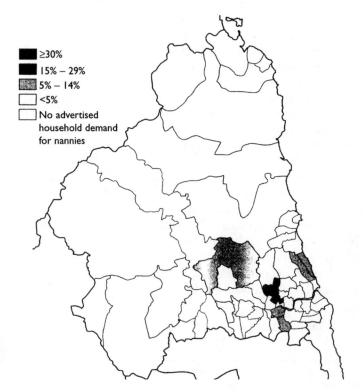

Figure 8.1   Advertised demand for nannies in the North East, 1981–91
(Newcastle Evening Chronicle, Gregson and Lowe 1994: 36)

Gregson and Lowe unpacked the demand for and supply of labour by examining the context in which waged domestic labour was employed by middle-class households and the circumstances in which women become nannies and cleaners. They found that the cleaner was employed to undertake a highly labour intensive activity thereby increasing the leisure time of middle-class couples. Moreover, those couples who exhibited a traditional domestic division of labour were more likely to employ a cleaner compared with those who fully shared domestic labour (85 per cent compared with 7 per cent) (Gregson and Lowe 1994: 99; see also Gregson and Lowe 1993). In the absence of a national childcare system, Gregson and Lowe found a preference for nannies as a convenient form of exclusive care for children in the parental home which was flexible and often cheaper than other forms of care. The nanny 'closely approximated with dominant social conventions' about motherhood (Gregson and Lowe 1994: 118). Turning to issues of supply, Gregson and Lowe found that cleaners were predominately older working-class women with little education. Of the twenty cleaners they interviewed, twelve (60 per cent) were 51 or older and nineteen (95 per cent) of them had left school with no formal qualifications. Many of the women had been made redundant from manufacturing industry and they were caring for relatives or dependent on benefits (Gregson and Lowe 1994: 126) (see Table 8.2). In contrast, nannies were younger, lower middle-class women who still lived at home. Of medium academic achievement, most had left school at 16 with some qualifications and the majority (74 per cent) were qualified, having taken childcare and related training courses (see Table 8.3). Faced with limited options in the labour market, becoming a nanny was especially attractive for those young women who had traditional identities and aspiration. Waged domestic labour was, then, clearly 'mediated by class and lifecycle effects' (ibid: 122).

Table 8.2   Labour force characteristics of cleaners

Age				
	North East		South East	
Categories	Numbers	Percentage	Numbers	Percentage
<40	–	–	3	30
41–50	4	40	1	10
51–60	3	30	–	–
61–70	2	20	4	40
>70	1	10	2	20

Source: Fieldwork interview data

Marital status

Categories	North East		South East	
	Numbers	Percentage	Numbers	Percentage
Single	–	–	–	–
Married	7	70	7	70
Separated/divorced	2	20	1	10
Widowed	1	10	2	20

Source: Fieldwork interview data

Social class

(a) Husband (by last/current occupation)

Categories	North East		South East	
	Numbers	Percentage	Numbers	Percentage
I	–	–	–	–
II	–	–	1	10
IIIN	–	–	–	–
IIIM	–	–	7	70
IV	9	90	–	–
V	1	10	2	20

Source: Fieldwork interview data

(b) Father (by last occupation)

Categories	North East		South East	
	Numbers	Percentage	Numbers	Percentage
I	–	–	1	10
II	1	10	–	–
IIIN	–	–	–	–
IIIM	–	–	5	50
IV	9	90	3	30
V	–	–	1	10

Source: Fieldwork interview data

(c) Self (by last previous occupation)

Categories	North East		South East	
	Numbers	Percentage	Numbers	Percentage
I	–	–	–	–
II	–	–	1	10
IIIN	–	–	–	–
IIIM	–	–	1	10
IV	3	30	4	40
V	7	70	4	40

Source: Fieldwork interview data

Educational qualifications

(a) School leaving age

Categories	North East		South East	
	Numbers	Percentage	Numbers	Percentage
14+	4	40	5	50
15+	6	60	2	20
16+	–	–	3	30

Source: Fieldwork interview data

(b) Highest educational qualification on leaving school

Categories	North East		South East	
	Numbers	Percentage	Numbers	Percentage
School certificates	–	–	–	–
O levels	–	–	1	10
None	10	100	9	90

Source: Fieldwork interview data

Length of time employed as a cleaner*

Categories	North East		South East	
	Numbers	Percentage	Numbers	Percentage
<6 months	–	–	–	–
6 months–1 year	–	–	2	20
1–2 years	2	20	–	–
2–4 years	3	30	1	10
>5 years	5	50	7	70

Source: Fieldwork interview data
*This period may include employment in more than one job.
Source: Gregson and Lowe (1994: 288–90)

Table 8.3   Labour force characteristics of nannies

Age

	North East		South East	
Categories	Numbers	Percentage	Numbers	Percentage
17 and under	–	–	–	–
18–20	8	40	5	21
21–23	8	32	11	46
24–26	6	24	7	28
Over 27	3	12	2	8

Source: Fieldwork interview data

Marital status

	North East		South East	
Categories	Numbers	Percentage	Numbers	Percentage
Single	21	84	18	72
Married	3	12	7	28
Separated/divorced	1	4	–	–

Source: Fieldwork interview data

Residential details

	North East		South East	
Categories	Numbers	Percentage	Numbers	Percentage
Parental home	13	60	0	38
Married/cohabiting	7	28	11	44
'Live-in' in employers' home	1	4	3	20
Single parent household	1	4	–	–
Single person household	1	4	–	–

Source: Fieldwork interview data

Social class of parental household

(a) North East

Social class of father	I	II	IIIN	IIIM	IV	V	Out of labour force
I (Professional)	–	–	1 (4%)	–	–	–	–
II (Intermediate)	–	1 (4%)	6(24%)	2(8%)	1(4%)	–	2(8%)
IIIN (Skilled, non-manual)	–	–	1 (4%)	–	–	–	–
IIIM (Skilled, manual)	–	–	3(12%)	1(4%)	1(4%)	–	1(4%)
IV (Semi-skilled)	–	–	–	–	–	–	–
V (Unskilled)	–	–	–	–	–	–	–
Out of labour force/unknown	–	–	1 (4%)	–	2(8%)	–	2(8%)

(b) South East

Social class of father	I	II	IIIN	IIIM	IV	V	Out of labour force
I (Professional)	2(8%)	1(4%)	–	–	–	–	3(12%)
II (Intermediate)	–	1(4%)	–	–	1 (4%)	–	1 (4%)
IIIN (Skilled, non-manual)	–	–	–	–	–	–	–
IIIM (Skilled, manual)	–	–	–	–	3(12%)	–	4(16%)
IV (Semi-skilled)	–	1(4%)	–	–	4(16%)	–	1 (4%)
V (Unskilled)	–	–	–	–	–	–	–
Out of labour force/unknown	–	–	–	–	2 (8%)	–	1 (4%)

Source: Fieldwork interview data

Educational qualifications

(a) School leaving age

Categories	North East		South East	
	Numbers	Percentage	Numbers	Percentage
16+	24	96	23	92
18+	1	4	2	8

Source: Fieldwork interview data

(b) Highest educational qualification on leaving school

Categories	North East		South East	
	Numbers	Percentage	Numbers	Percentage
CSEs	18	72	5	20
O levels	6	24	17	68
A levels	–	–	2	8
None	1	4	1	4

Source: Fieldwork interview data

Childcare and related training

Categories	North East		South East	
	Numbers	Percentage	Numbers	Percentage
NNEB (i) state	12	48	12	48
(ii) private	–	–	2	8
PCSC	7	28	4	16
None	6	24	7	28

Source: Fieldwork interview data

Length of time employed as a nanny*

Categories	North East		South East	
	Numbers	Percentage	Numbers	Percentage
<6 months	1	4	–	–
6 months –1 year	3	12	2	8
1–2 years	3	12	3	12
2–4 years	16	64	15	60
>5 years	2	8	5	20

Source: Fieldwork interview data
Note: *This period may include employment in more than one job.
Source: Gregson and Lowe (1994: 286–8)

Finally, Gregson and Lowe found different forms of organisation of work and social relations between employers, nannies and cleaners, 'reflecting the form of labour substitution involved in both cases, as well as the varying ideological constructs which suffuse and shape both forms of domestic labour'. Nanny employment is characterised by two major contradictions. First, the nanny is supposed to be a professional but is also a mother substitute and, second, the nanny is a paid employee, yet relations with the employing family can be characterised in terms of surrogate kinship ties. Thus, despite being a professional, the nanny is frequently expected to implement the parents' views of appropriate childcare, not her own. Thus, nannies are low-paid workers (earning an average of £3,840 per annum in the North East and an average of £5,760 per annum in the South East), often without formal contracts of employment and limited perks, yet employers regarded their nannies as kin, not least because they had close relationships with their children. Interestingly, however, this view was only partially shared by nannies, who were not entirely happy with their levels of pay and abuse over housework chores. In contrast, the relationship between employers and their cleaners was straightforward, albeit highly gendered (Gregson and Lowe 1994: 207). The cleaners were also low-paid workers (earning an average of £1,084 per annum in the North East and £940 per annum in the South East) and invariably paid cash in hand although they enjoyed a lot of flexibility in terms of hours and autonomy in the organisation of their work. This autonomy was very important for maintaining the cleaners' self-worth and identity (Gregson and Lowe: 216). Relations with employers were more distant for cleaners who often worked alone, although there were instances where the cleaner was a surrogate grandmother or aunt to young children (Gregson and Lowe: 223). In sum, there were different relations between employers, nannies and cleaners, with varying degrees of consensus and conflict, and trust and distrust, which were subject to constant negotiation.

Gregson and Lowe conclude that there has been a major change in the relationship between class and social reproduction in Britain:

> Employer–employee relations have been established between the middle class and working class around domestic labour. New social relations grounded in both false kinship and wage labour have manifested themselves. Above all, fundamental class differences have been reasserted. No longer exclusively unwaged, domestic labour (at least certain aspects of this) within the homes of the middle classes is increasingly being performed by one (and frequently more than one) waged woman, as well as by the unwaged labour of female partners (and sometimes male partners). And in its cleaning form, this waged domestic labour is being performed by working-class women. (Gregson and Lowe 1994: 231–2)

The consequence of these changes is that middle-class women have extracted themselves from the conduct of some domestic work (although not the responsibility for it) while lower middle-class and working-class women are more closely associated with these forms of work. Gregson and Lowe express their dissatisfaction with the resurgence of class divisions among women. There are possibilities for a united feminist strategy which could involve collective action to challenge the nature of employment for middle-class households and their domestic labour, although the evidence suggests that middle-class men and women are finding individual solutions for themselves. Thus, 'the relations of gender inequality constructed through domestic labour will, once more, become entwined with divisions of class and identity among women' (Gregson and Lowe 1994: 241). In the remaining discussion, three issues of method and their implications for the substantive findings of the research will be discussed. They are, first, the use of adverts to establish trends and patterns in the demand for waged domestic labour; second, the findings of the workplace survey and the need for comparative controls; and third, the use of intensive interviews to reveal tensions and conflict. We shall see that the consequences of these issues for Gregson and Lowes' substantive findings raise doubts about the authors' claim that there is a crisis in social reproduction in middle-class families.

Newspapers and adverts

Gregson and Lowe established the demand for waged domestic labour by studying advertisements from *The Lady* for a national picture, and the *Newcastle Evening Chronicle* and the *Reading Chronicle* for a local picture. Given that official statistics do not provide sufficient information on the different categories of waged domestic labour or the setting in which it is employed, Gregson and Lowe concluded that advertisement data were 'the most *reliable* measure of contemporary demand'. The data from local newspapers were collected each week on the day that the jobs page appeared, thereby constituting a 100 per cent sample of adverts between July 1981 and June 1991. The sheer volume of adverts in *The Lady*, however, demanded different methods of collection. All advertisements in the first week of alternate months in that period were recorded so that the 'data constituted a 12.5 per cent sample of the data source but not of all advertisements.' (Gregson and Lowe 1994: 10–11). Gregson and Lowe 'cleaned' the data by eliminating agencies from their totals so that they included adverts placed by individual households. The local adverts were coded according to geographical location using addresses and telephone numbers with varying degrees of success (it was possible to code 90 per cent of adverts in the North East in this manner, and 77 per cent in the South East). Adverts in *The Lady* were easily coded into counties or grouped into postal districts in London with the assistance of postcodes. Two further types of 'cleaning' were undertaken. First, any consecutive adverts from the local newspapers were eliminated to avoid double counting. Second, the category of waged domestic labour in each advert was checked and reclassified if necessary in two ways. Adverts which requested domestic help but specified childcare and involved more than 15 hours' work were reallocated to 'mother's help' category. Otherwise, they were allocated to a cleaner category. Second, adverts which did not specify exactly what was required were allocated to the categories of nannies, mother's help or nannies/mother's help accordingly.

Interestingly, the three sets of advertisement data showed an increase in demand for waged domestic labour throughout the 1980s, demand being greatest for the care of young pre-school age children and for general housework. However, the reliability of this data is questionable. In 1997, the Audit Bureau of Circulation estimated that *The Lady*, for example, had a circulation of 55,911. Its sales are concentrated overwhelmingly in London and the South East, and it is read predominately by women aged 45 and over (71 per cent of the readership), who are to be found mostly in social groupings ABC (61 per cent). The magazine, then, has a very small circulation figure and its readership consists largely of older, middle-class women who live in the Home Counties. Gregson and Lowe were well aware that the magazine has a small circulation and a limited readership. They suggest, however, that pilot interviews indicated that it is used more widely than the figures suggest. If this is the case – and the argument is highly plausible – it is a shame that its wide use was not established more firmly. Similarly, Gregson and Lowe acknowledge that the *Newcastle Evening Chronicle* and the *Reading Chronicle* were circulated in only small parts of their case study areas. There was a spatial bias rather than a comprehensive coverage of adverts in the locales under investigation. A full record of local newspaper-advertised demand would have required Gregson and Lowe to check all the papers in each of the two regions and to have amalgamated and cross-checked the data. Given the limitations of advert data, however, they were unconvinced that the exercise would be worthwhile. This is not an unreasonable conclusion. However, it would have been useful if Gregson and Lowe had explained their choice of local newspapers, the circulation of the papers and the spread of the readership across their two locales. Both the national magazine and local newspaper data showed an upward trend in demand for labour, but the reliability of these data as a basis for estimating the changing extent of the demand for waged domestic labour is questionable.

The use of advertisement data to ascertain the pattern of demand for waged domestic labour – the varied types of labour – is also problematic. The national and local data showed that the nanny was the most frequent category of domestic labour sought through magazine and newspaper adverts in the 1980s. However, advertising is only one source of recruitment and placing an advert in *The Lady* is a popular way of hiring as Gregson and Lowe found. The type of data they used may well have exaggerated the increased popularity of the nanny over other forms of waged domestic labour. Of course, it could be argued that advertising is not the only means of recruiting a nanny. Indeed, Gregson and Lowe subsequently found in their case study research that nannies are frequently recruited on the completion of their NNEB courses by employers who have made informal enquiries with course tutors. In this respect, Gregson and Lowe could claim that they have probably underestimated rather than overestimated the demand for this form of waged domestic labour. However, the point is that waged domestic labour is often recruited through informal channels and networks of social contacts or other means. As we shall see, Gregson and Lowe's own survey of demand in Newcastle and Reading found that cleaners were the category of waged domestic labour most in demand and that demand for the nanny was small in comparison. They suggest that the lack of visibility of adverts for cleaners is the result of the undeclared nature of this work (Gregson and Lowe 1994: 298). Advertising is only one of several ways of recruiting waged domestic labour, and it is associated with the recruitment of particular categories of labour. As a consequence, there are serious doubts about the reliability of Gregson and Lowe's estimates of the demand for domestic labour – both its trends and its patterns – given that they are based solely on national and local advertisement data.

Overall, Gregson and Lowe found an increase in demand for waged domestic labour in their advertisement data although we cannot be sure that there was a genuine increase in demand beyond their source of information. While the advertisement data might have shown an increase in the demand for nannies in particular, the reliance on adverts casts some doubt as to whether there was a genuine increase in popularity for the nanny over other forms of waged domestic labour in the 1980s. Given their national source – *The Lady* – was biased towards the affluent south, it is hardly surprising that they found that household demand for waged domestic labour was concentrated in London, the south and the south east. This spatial variation may well be accurate in relation to advertised demand in *The Lady*. What the information does not tell us, however, is the spatial variation in the demand for waged domestic labour recruited by other means in the rest of the country. Finally, the concentration of demand for waged domestic labour in middle-class enclaves of the north west and the south west of London might be a feature of Gregson and Lowe's reliance on *The Lady* while the concentration of advertised demand in particular middle-class areas of the North East and South East of England might be a reflection of the coverage of the local newspapers in the two localities which they used. Now, it is extremely difficult to get a picture for the demand and supply of work which is often unofficial and not captured in official statistics on paid work. In these circumstances, Gregson and Lowe are to be commended for their imaginative use of advertisement data as one means of tapping into this issue. The issue of the reliability of these data as a basis for estimating overall demand, however, suggests that their findings have to be treated with some caution. As we shall see, their survey of dual-career middle-class households provides a somewhat different picture of the demand for waged domestic labour, and one which might be more accurate than that provided by their advertisement data.

Associations and comparisons

Gregson and Lowe conducted a workplace survey to establish the incidence of demand for waged domestic labour and its association with the middle class in Newcastle and Reading. A pilot survey of 50 households (generated via employment agencies) revealed that waged domestic labour was associated with households in which both partners worked full time in professional and managerial occupations. The full survey consisted of a postal questionnaire distributed to 1,140 couples in Newcastle and 977 in Reading which yielded responses from 542 middle-class dual career partnerships (268 in the North East and 274 in the South East). The sample was generated by approaching workplaces known to employ women in professional and managerial jobs including health, local government and education in the public sector, and financial services, professional services, literary and artistic professions and retail management in the private sector. It was not a random sample. The survey was administered by personnel departments through payroll numbers after some discussion of the grades of employee to which they should be sent. The number of questionnaires administered in each organisation was determined by personnel estimates and the level of cooperation achieved within each organisation. The sample, therefore, was not a quota sample. Gregson and Lowe found that the majority of their responding couples were both employed in either senior national or local government positions (38 per cent in the North East and 26 per cent in the South East) or in education, welfare and health (19 per cent in the North East and 25 per cent in the South East). Otherwise, they found a high incidence of women in these positions who had partners in technical and scientific occupations (23 per cent in the North East and 21 per cent in the South East). Given the gender segregation of the labour market, it was not surprising to find that women were concentrated in the education, welfare and health professions while men were concentrated in the scientific and technical professions (Gregson and Lowe 1994: 285).

The results of the survey showed that 36 per cent of households with both partners in middle-class occupations in the North East employed waged domestic labour (97 out of 268 households) while the equivalent percentage in the South East was 33 per cent (91 out of 274 households). Around one-fifth of households in each locality employed more than one person (18 per cent and 22 per cent respectively in the North East and South East). The incidence of waged domestic labour was remarkably similar across the two case study areas (see Table 8.4), with the cleaner being the most popular form of waged domestic labour. In Newcastle, 73 per cent of employer households had a cleaner while 76 per cent had a cleaner in Reading. Only 16 per cent of employer households had a nanny in the North East while 21 per cent did so in the South East.

Gregson and Lowe (1994: 41) argued that the figures underestimated the incidence of nanny employment since nannies are invariably employed to care for pre-school-age children. When they considered the presence of young children, they found that the percentage of nanny employment in the survey increased substantially. Just under one-third of households employing domestic labour in the North East had at least one pre-school-aged child, and 47 per cent of these households employed a nanny. Similarly, just under half

Table 8.4   Incidence of employment of categories of
waged domestic labour in case study areas

Categories	North East		South East	
	Numbers employed	Percentage of households employing these categories	Numbers employed	Percentage of households employing these categories
Cleaners	67	72.8	67	76.1
Nanny	15	16.3	18	20.5
Gardener	14	15.2	12	13.6
Mother's help	4	4.3	1	1.1
Au pair	1	1.1	4	4.5
Other	2	2.2	2	2.2
Total	103		104	

Source: Workplace survey data
Note: Percentages are calculated from 92 households in the North East and 88 households in the South East due to incomplete returns.
Source: Gregson and Lowe (1994: 41)

of the households employing waged domestic labour in the South East had at least one pre-school-aged child, and 37 per cent of these households employed a nanny. Gregson and Lowe concluded:

> Such findings lead us to suggest that approaching three quarters of all dual career households employing waged domestic labour employ a cleaner and that between a third and a half of such households with pre-school-age children employ a nanny. They also suggest that the cleaner and the nanny are the major forms of waged domestic labour used by the middle classes in contemporary Britain. (1994: 42)

Gregson and Lowe make only limited use of the workplace survey in their book. Yet, the way in which the research was conducted and the findings which emerged from the survey are very revealing. On the basis of their pilot work (the precise results of which are not provided), a decision was made to survey households in which both partners work full time in middle-class occupations. Thus, their survey focused on the incidence of waged domestic labour not in the middle class as a whole but in a particular sub-section of the middle class where 'the crisis in daily social reproduction' might be expected to be more intense. Their findings cast doubt on this conclusion, however, in that they found that just over one-third (35 per cent) of these households employed waged domestic labour. Put another way, this means that just under two-thirds (65 per cent) did not employ waged domestic labour. The employment of waged domestic labour was a distinctly minority activity within dual-career families implying that the large majority of the middle class do not face a crisis in social reproduction or, if they do, they do not manage it by employing domestic labour. Furthermore, contrary to the picture derived from the advertisement data, it was undoubtedly cleaners rather than nannies who were the most popular form of waged domestic labour among Gregson and Lowe's survey respondents. They seek to overcome this discrepancy in their findings by pointing to the incidence of demand for nannies among dual-earner couples with pre-school-aged children. Yet, even within this sub-section of the middle class, only a minority had a nanny. The key finding to emerge from the workplace survey is that the middle class do not, on the whole, use waged domestic labour, and this finding undermines the claim that the middle class faces a crisis of social reproduction.

This is not to suggest that the incidence of waged domestic labour has no consequences for class relations and gender relations in contemporary Britain. After all, a quarter of the households in both areas employed a cleaner. Rather, the findings do not illuminate the question of why some dual-career middle-class households employ waged domestic labour and why others do not. It is rather a shame that Gregson and Lowe did not address this question via the workplace survey data. We do not know about the nature of the data they collected because the questionnaire was not reproduced in the book. Nevertheless, a simple analysis of the data which they appear to have collected might have shown, for example, that women with two or more children or women without kin in close proximity were more likely to employ waged domestic labour than other women with only one child or with kin close to hand. Likewise, an analysis of the occupational data might have shown that women in managerial occupations are more likely to employ waged domestic labour than women in professional jobs such as teaching where there is some complementarity between paid work and domestic responsibilities. Similarly, it might have been women's level of income or their partner's income which facilitated the employment of waged domestic labour or not as the case may be. The workplace data might have shown interesting patterns of use of waged domestic labour within the middle classes thereby suggesting explanations of why some households employ cleaners and nannies and others do not. In this way, Gregson and Lowe might have been able to specify why some sections of the middle class use waged domestic labour and to tease out the precise implications of the relationship of class and gender in contemporary Britain.

Revealing tensions

Gregson and Lowe conducted intensive interviews with employers (men and/or women in middle-class households) and employees (nannies and cleaners) in each area. A total of 139 interviews were completed (29 employers, 25 nannies and ten cleaners in the North East and 40 employers, 25 nannies and ten cleaners in the South East). Within each locale, they were also able to achieve ten matched pairs of employers and their nannies and five matched pairs of employers and their cleaners. The sample of employers and nannies was generated through snowballing techniques. Originally, the intention was to interview 25 employers of nannies and 25 employers of cleaners but since some of their sample of middle-class households employed both categories of waged domestic labour, the number of interviews with employers was reduced while still meeting their initial targets. Gregson and Lowe (1994: 295) had also intended to interview 25 cleaners in each region. However, they found it difficult to locate willing participants because they worked alone and those cleaners who were supplementing their incomes from benefit were suspicious that the interviewers might be Department of Social Security 'snoopers'. Finding cleaners, therefore, was slow and difficult and only achieved with the employers' help. Given these difficulties, and the fact that they found considerable consistency in the interviews which they had conducted, they revised the number of interviews with cleaners downwards. The interviews with employers were conducted in their homes. In Reading, partners elected to be interviewed together while in Newcastle only the women were interviewed. All the interviews with nannies and cleaners were conducted in their employers' homes and in their employers' absence. The interviews were semi-structured and lasted between 1 and 2 hours. They were subsequently transcribed, coded and analysed manually by the research team (Gregson and Lowe 1994: 295).

The authors make extensive use of the interview material to develop their arguments about the reasons why middle-class households employ particular types of waged domestic labour and why particular groups of women become cleaners and nannies. Indeed, the way in which they 'unpacked' demand and supply is one of the strongest features of their research. It is somewhat disappointing, though, that they do not provide some biographical details on their middle-class households and thereby give the context in which these families employed waged domestic labour. It would have been useful, for example, to have had some information on the men's and women's occupations and salaries and the number and ages of any children. Similarly, details on the type of waged domestic labour which they employed would also have given a better 'feel' for the circumstances in which nannies and/or cleaners were employed by them. It would have been useful if Gregson and Lowe had specified the number of households which had time/space difficulties, those who attached importance to quality time and those with childcare responsibilities as a way of identifying the relative importance of different factors which propelled the households to employ waged domestic labour. After all, this type of information is put to excellent use when discussing the supply of cleaners and nannies. From biographical information, for example, they were able to show that cleaners are predominately working-class women with little education behind them, and were able to identify a number of reasons why they had become cleaners. In contrast, they showed that nannies are predominately from lower middle-class backgrounds of average academic ability who enrolled on childcare courses which propelled them into nanny employment. The information collected though their qualitative interviews, therefore, was very important for the development of their argument about the class character of waged domestic labour.

It is in their exploration of the social relations between middle-class employers and their domestic employees that Gregson and Lowe draw on their interview material exclusively. In relation to nannies, they argue that there are two major contradictions in their employment. First, the nanny is expected to be a childcare professional yet she is often treated as a mother substitute. Second, the nanny is a paid employee although relations with her employer may be characterised by what Gregson and Lowe describe as 'false kinship' relations. The authors acknowledge some of the tensions in the social relations between middle-class employers and their domestic employees. However, they do not explore these tensions in any systematic way and there is a tendency to give greater space to the employers' accounts of the relationship than to the employees' perceptions of the relationship. The employers' views about childcare, their children's educational development and their concern that their children may not be sufficiently stimulated by the nanny, for example, are discussed at length. In contrast, the nannies' views on childcare, their evaluation of their employers' views on childcare and any sense of loss of autonomy are not explored in as much detail. Similarly, Gregson and Lowe found that middle-class employers characterised their relations with their nannies as close and not dissimilar to kin relations. The nannies, however, aired their grievances about the poor level of pay and the tendency among some employers to expect them to complete housework tasks as well. This is not to suggest that Gregson and Lowe accepted their employers' accounts on face value. They devote considerable attention, for example, to relating the employers' perceptions of the nanny as a substitute mother back to the dominant ideology on motherhood. Nevertheless, it is a shame that they did not consider the issues of trust and consensus, and grievance and conflict among the employers and employees in greater depth.

Overall, Gregson and Lowe make good use of their qualitative material. It is used, most powerfully, to develop their arguments about the class character of the demand for and supply of waged domestic labour. That is, they demonstrate how qualitative material is not merely useful for illustrative purposes but can be used very effectively in the development of an argument or explanation. They also show how qualitative interviewing offers informants the opportunity to talk freely about their experiences from their point of view. The different preoccupations of the employing households and the employee nannies is a case in point. However, they could have teased out some of the tensions in the social relations between the two parties to a greater degree than they did. Similarly, they could have compared and contrasted the views, opinions, and feelings of the middle-class women and their nannies in a more systematic way. There was considerable potential to do this, for example, among their matched pairs of employing households and nannies and/or cleaners By discussing particular issues with both employers and employees, they could have captured both sides of the story of the nature of nanny and cleaner employment in contemporary Britain.

Conclusion

This chapter has focused on some of the difficulties of establishing the demand for waged domestic labour. Gregson and Lowe's sources – the national and local advertisement data – were not without their limitations. While there may have been an increase in demand in the 1980s, they probably overestimate the extent of that demand, especially in relation to nannies. After all, their workplace survey showed that only one-third of dual career households employ waged domestic labour (usually a cleaner) although among such households with pre-school-aged children nearly half did so. These findings beg the question of what the other half did. Did these households rely on partners and kin? Why were they able to do so while other households had to employ waged domestic labour? Neither should it be forgotten that while the majority of women in middle-class jobs nowadays return to work full time following the birth of a child and are far more likely to do so than other women, a sizeable minority of women do not return to work immediately or, to a much lesser extent, return to part-time employment. Just as middle-class women have the economic resources to buy waged domestic labour, so they are also in a position of relative financial security not to have to return to paid employment if they want to look after their children themselves. When this broader picture is taken into account, social reproduction within middle-class households does not appear to be in crisis. There is an array of factors which affect whether households employ waged domestic labour and the type of labour they employ, and an analysis of these issues may well produce a more nuanced picture of the relationship between class and gender than Gregson and Lowe offer. Much to their credit, Gregson and Lowe's research points the way forward as to how some of these issues could be examined further.

In sum, Gregson and Lowe's research is an important contribution to our understanding of the relationship between class and gender. They demonstrate the ways in which women are divided by class, and how their life chances – especially in the labour market – are very different, as is their capacity to pay for waged domestic labour. The strongest element of the study is the way in which they unpack supply and examine the circumstances in which predominately older working-class women with little or no education become cleaners and young lower-middle-class women of average academic achievement become nannies. Moreover, they focus not only on the individual circumstances in which these women became waged domestic labourers but also locate them firmly in the unfavourable economic climate of unemployment, which has fallen most heavily on working-class households, and the restricted job opportunities for young women with few educational credentials. In this respect, they illustrate how the quality of life enjoyed by middle-class and working-class households has polarised over the 1980s and 90s. In doing so, they also show how people with particular characteristics are associated with specific places in the occupational order (and thereby the class structure), which explains how classes are segmented by sex. These findings were derived from the qualitative interviews with the cleaners and nannies by looking at the social characteristics of the women involved and the circumstances in which they became waged domestic labourers. The analysis was simple yet highly revealing and demonstrates the value of detailed case studies of occupations and their incumbents within class analysis.

Additional reading

Rosemary Crompton is a leading scholar on gender and class stratification. On issues of gender, and especially the entry of women into the professions, see her excellent introduction, *Women and Work in Modern Britain* (1997). The new edition of her book, *Class and Stratification* (1998) discusses the theoretical debates on the relationship between class and gender. On case studies, see Robert Yin's now classic *Case Study Research* (1994). For a detailed discussion of in-depth interviewing, see Jennifer Mason's *Qualitative Researching* (1996).

Chapter 9

Politics: Roseneil's *Disarming Patriarchy*

Introduction

It is hard to convey to those too young to remember, the genuine sense of fear which gripped Britain in the early 1980s, as nuclear stockpiling by the United States and the Soviet Union escalated and the possibility of mass destruction became all too real. Growing up only twenty miles from the Greenham Common United States Air Force (USAF) base brought this alarmingly close to home to one of the authors of this book, who became one of the many thousands who joined the Campaign for Nuclear Disarmament and other anti-nuclear groups at this time as part of a dramatic resurgence of the peace movement. Living through this period proved to be even more of a life-changing experience for the researcher whose work forms the focus of this chapter, and Sasha Roseneil's *Disarming Patriarchy* (1995) is a fascinating chronicle of the experiences which she and thousands of others shared as 'Greenham women' during the early 1980s. Unlike the other studies examined in this book, *Disarming Patriarchy* is as much about Roseneil's own memories of the social setting she is researching as it is about those of the 35 women whom she interviewed as part of her study. As such, her research provides an intriguing example of a form of 'insider research' and highlights the impact that a researcher's own beliefs and experiences will have on the conduct of their work. It is also a study which is self-consciously located within the feminist research tradition and which was carried out in accordance with a set of clearly defined ethical principles.

Researching social movements

Disarming Patriarchy is a study which can be located within the broader literature on social movements and, more recently, *new* social movements. Much of this literature is theoretically orientated, addressing itself to the macro-level contexts within which social movements develop. Writers such as Alain Touraine, for example, have highlighted the link between the rise of new social movements and 'post-industrial society' (Touraine 1981, 1983), while others have highlighted the changing (middle-class) composition of new social movements in comparison with 'old' social movements based around working class solidarity (Offe 1985). Others again have focused much more on developing a micro-level analysis and have studied the processes by which social movements are mobilised (Jenkins 1983; Oberschall 1973). There has been much less of a focus on how people 'do' social movements: in other words, relatively little is known about the actual activities people involve themselves in as members of social movements or what those activities might mean to them both as individuals and as members of broader social groupings. Similarly, while some studies have addressed themselves to the political consequences of social movements, little is known about the *personal* consequences of such involvement. Hence, theoretical accounts of social movements, whether old or new, proliferate, while empirical studies of the day-to-day activities of particular social movements are few and far between.

It is often argued that the women's liberation movement is a classic example of a new social movement, although to claim that feminism is somehow new is to ignore or play down the movement's deep historical roots. Roseneil also highlights the difficulties of unproblematically trying to fit feminism into new social movement theory:

> Although the women's movement is cited as a key new social movement by a number of writers... and gender is sometimes referred to as an analytic category... no real attempt has been made to integrate gender into the theory of the new social movements approach... Greenham must be studied as a *women's* movement; the specificity of women's social position and history is of vital importance in understanding why, at a particular historical moment, it arose. (Roseneil 1995: 15 – emphasis in original)

Moreover, Roseneil places stress on the importance of studying women as *active agents*, taking control of their own actions, and resisting oppression. As she notes in the book's introduction, there has been a tendency within feminist sociology towards 'exposing, naming and analysing the structural oppression of women' (Roseneil 1995: 1), at the expense of research on situations where women are empowered and are actively working towards changing their own, as well as others, lives. There are, for example, relatively few academic studies of the contemporary women's movement or of specific feminist campaigns. Exceptions include Rowbotham's (1989) overview of feminist campaigning since 1960, Lovenduski and Randall's (1993) examination of contemporary feminist politics and Green's (1997) study of radical lesbian feminist politics in London during the 1980s. Roseneil sees her own research, therefore, as part of a corrective to this more general neglect within feminist scholarship. Roseneil's study also contributes to a relatively small sociological literature on the campaigning activities of various wings of the peace movement. Parkin (1968), for example, wrote about the activities of the membership of the Campaign for Nuclear Disarmament during the 1960s, while Byrne (1988) conducted a similar exercise during the 1980s. Roseneil similarly points to a relative silence among feminist scholars in relation to the activities of Greenham women, the exceptions being Young (1990) and Liddington (1989).

Disarming Patriarchy

Disarming Patriarchy is a book which arises from the author's first-hand experience of being a 'Greenham Woman'. Greenham Common, near Newbury, Berkshire, was one of the British sites chosen by the United States' government for the deployment of its nuclear-capability Cruise missiles during the 1980s. Not surprisingly, and even before the weapons arrived, Greenham Common became one of the focal points for the re-emerging peace movement. Unlike other key sites of protest, however – such as the nuclear bases at Faslane, Molesworth and Upper Heyford – Greenham was to become the centre specifically for *women-only* protests against the nuclear threat (and militarism more generally), and came to represent the peace movement's most radical wing. Roseneil, in common with other writers, traces the origins of the women's peace camp to the

1981 'Women for Life on Earth Peace March' between Cardiff and Greenham, following which many women decided to stay on at the camp as a permanent protest. In December 1982, Greenham Common was the focus for an 'Embrace the Base' demonstration, at which thousands of women gathered to form a human chain around the perimeter of the base and to voice their opposition to the imminent siting of Cruise missiles in the UK. This was also the occasion of Sasha Roseneil's first visit to Greenham, an occasion which made an indelible impression on the then 16 year old's life. Return visits followed, and in December 1983 Roseneil abandoned her A level studies to join the camp full time.

Disarming Patriarchy takes Roseneil back to her Greenham days in an attempt to explore 'the sociological significance of Greenham on both a micro-level, to the tens of thousands whose lives were changed by the experience of involvement, and on a macro-level, to the social structures and institutions of a hetero-patriarchal society' (Roseneil 1993: 177). She argues that her book is perhaps unique on two counts: in being a work of serious scholarship, written by someone who was personally present, and in providing a broad overview of the dynamics of the camp's development over time, rather than providing just a snapshot of camp life. Roseneil describes her research strategy as 'retrospective auto-ethnography', an approach which led her to use a variety of different methods and data sources. These included her own memories of Greenham; the memories of 35 other women who had been involved at Greenham, either as permanent or semi-permanent campers or as regular visitors; and documentary analysis of a wide range of primary sources, ranging from personal journals (both her own and those of other Greenham women), newspaper and magazine articles written about the camp, and newsletters and pamphlets produced by women involved in the peace movement both at Greenham and further afield.

Various sections of the book focus on different aspects of life at Greenham Common, looking both at the 'internal mode of action' – daily life within the camp and its dominant ethos – and the 'external mode of action', Greenham's public face and its actions in the public sphere. The book also explores the reactions to the camp of different sections of society, in particular those of various arms of the state and of the media, as well as the ways in which individual Greenham women responded to their experiences of involvement, and the impact it had on their own sense of identity. *Disarming Patriarchy* works at a number of levels, then; not only does it provide a scholarly analysis of the significance of Greenham Common within the broader context of work on women's agency and resistance but, in so doing, it makes an important contribution to a social history of the women's movement.

In an account of her methodology, Roseneil talks of camp life as 'exhilarating, liberating and great fun' (Roseneil 1993: 187). Indeed, tales of outwitting the authorities, the excitement of large scale demonstrations and moonlit incursions into the USAF base, the nightly exchange of stories around the campfire – not to mention Blue Gate's 'passion bender' – lend the camp an aura of romanticism in stark contrast to another side of camp life: the harsh realities of physical and verbal harassment from the authorities, sleepless nights in soggy sleeping bags, and regular episodes of arrest, court appearances and, often, imprisonment. However, Roseneil herself warns against the beatification of 'Greenham Woman', and as a counter to these tales of self-sacrifice and heroism the book also contains some candid insights into intracamp conflict, a point which will be discussed further later.

Throughout the book, Roseneil attempts to create linkages between the micro-politics of camp life and the macro-politics of its broader social and political context. The emphasis is very much on 'human actors... located within specific social and historical circumstances' (Roseneil 1995: 59). In focusing on the micro-political sphere, Roseneil concludes that 'Greenham was a place of transformations and transgressions' and that 'through Greenham, women created for themselves new forms of consciousness and new identities... women reflexively produced themselves as changed in significant ways, and sensed themselves, often for the first time, as possessing agency' (ibid: 163). At the macro-level, Greenham represented a major challenge to 'contemporary constructions of womanhood' (ibid: 171) and 'leaves a history of resistance in the late twentieth century which demonstrates women's agency and offers hope of the ultimate disarmament of patriarchy' (Roseneil 1995: 172). These are big themes, yet themes which Roseneil seeks to ground within her empirical research.

In this final case study chapter, we explore two sets of methodological issues which are raised by Roseneil's work. First, we return to a consideration of the implications of feminist methodology for the conduct of research and in this light critically examine Roseneil's claim to transparency and reflexivity within the research process. This section also explores the appropriateness of Roseneil's claim that her research is an example of retrospective ethnography. Second, this chapter will explore the relevance of informed consent to retrospective research of this kind, and at the same time consider the impact of bias and self-censorship on the process of publication and dissemination.

Dislocated ethnography and reflexive practice

Roseneil's use of the term 'retrospective auto-ethnography' to describe her work implies that she has not relied merely upon the experiences of others in reconstructing the events of Greenham, but has also relied on her own memories of being a Greenham woman. It is not particularly unusual for sociologists to research a setting of which they have had some first-hand experience; indeed, Lofland and Lofland have even argued that 'much of the best work in sociology and other social sciences… is probably grounded in the remote and/or current biographies of its creators' (Lofland and Lofland 1985: 8). Hobbs' research on the police and the policed in the East End of London (described in Chapter 7) is a case in point, as it grew out of his broader personal knowledge of the locality. What distinguishes Roseneil's work from Hobbs', however, is that the personal interest and involvement with the *specific* group being investigated predated any intention to carry out research on that group. Thus, while Hobbs' direct knowledge and experience of the police and the policed only developed as a direct consequence of his decision, as a trained researcher, to investigate East End criminal activity, Roseneil's involvement at Greenham pre-dated any training and experience as a researcher. As Roseneil herself comments, when she made her first visit to Greenham in December 1982: 'I had no idea that a year later I would be living there, let alone that six years on I'd be writing a PhD thesis about the place' (Roseneil 1993: 177).

Following her initial visit in December 1982, Roseneil visited the camp regularly before moving to Greenham on a permanent basis in December 1983. She stopped living at Greenham in October of the following year, although she remained a frequent occasional visitor to the camp for another 7 years, sometimes staying for up to a week at a time. In conventional ethnographic terms, this represents a considerable period of immersion 'in the field', and one assumes that these first-hand experiences provided the bulk of her knowledge of how Greenham operated. In addition to drawing on her own experience, though, Roseneil conducted a series of in-depth interviews with 35 other women who had been involved at Greenham, whether as permanent campers, as regular 'stayers' (weekend campers, for example), or as regular day visitors. Ten of these women were already known to Roseneil, mostly from her own time as a camper, and one can perhaps assume that they would – at least in part – have discussed events which they had jointly experienced. This combination of methods is very common to ethnography: direct observation enhanced by interviews with other group members, with both observer and interviewees experiencing essentially the same set of events and activities within the same time frame. The remaining 25 women had not been known to Roseneil previously, and were contacted through 'snowballing'; that is, the original ten women referred Roseneil on to other women who had been involved at Greenham. In the majority of these interviews, then, the women concerned would have been discussing events which were *not* directly experienced by Roseneil, either because the women were based at different gates or because they were involved at a different period of time from Roseneil.

This sense of slippage, however, perhaps renders the term 'retrospective auto-ethnography' slightly inaccurate. Roseneil's methods clearly extend beyond drawing exclusively on her own autobiographical experiences. Indeed, it is by going beyond her own experiences that she was able to build up a more dynamic, longitudinal picture of Greenham, even though the bulk of the interview data, from which this broader picture is drawn, cannot be verified by her own observations. All the data are undoubtedly 'retrospective' in as much as all the research participants, Roseneil included, are drawing upon events which occurred some time in the past, but the extent to which this approach can be described as both strictly autobiographical and ethnographic at the same time is perhaps doubtful. These comments are not made in criticism of the methodology *per se*, but of the appropriateness of the terminology. Perhaps a term such as 'dislocated ethnography' would be more accurate, in order to indicate the varying degree of overlap within the research between different women's experiences at different points of time, and the extent to which those experiences were shared or not by Roseneil.

Roseneil's research would inevitably have been very different if she had not experienced Greenham for herself. Indeed, she has presented a convincing argument that the research would not have been possible *at all* if she had not had this shared experience with other Greenham women:

> Greenham was an intense, 'life-changing' experience which many of my interviewees said they would never have agreed to talk about to someone who hadn't shared it... I am convinced that the degree of intimacy between myself and the women I interviewed was the product of our shared experiences, and was only possible because they knew I was a Greenham woman and a feminist first, both temporally and in allegiance, and a sociologist second. (Roseneil 1993: 191)

Moreover, it is unlikely that Roseneil would even have considered writing about Greenham in the first place if it had not played such an integral part within her own life story, given her stated commitment to conducting research which is informed by personal experience. This commitment is brought out within the introductory chapter of *Disarming Patriarchy*, where she makes it clear that the book is heavily influenced by her own experiences. For a much fuller discussion of her own relationship to and involvement in the peace camp at Greenham, however, she refers readers to an earlier paper (Roseneil 1993), a shortened version of which – if not the whole thing – could usefully have been included as part of the methodological appendix to *Disarming Patriarchy*.

The paper in question – 'Greenham revisited: Researching myself and my sisters' (Roseneil 1993) – provides a detailed account of Roseneil's reasons for becoming involved in the peace movement and of the feminist principles underpinning her work. In the first part of the paper, she outlines what are commonly regarded as 'the three guiding principles of feminist methodology' (p. 178) – a focus on women's experiences, conducting research *for* women, and a location of the researcher on the same critical plane as the researched. *Disarming Patriarchy* meets all three of these criteria. It is quite clearly a piece of research which focuses on women's experiences, while Roseneil also sees the work very much as 'research for women', providing a contribution both to greater knowledge of a critical phase in the history of the women's movement and, more generally, to a greater understanding of women's agency. The third principle is borne out in Roseneil's commitment to reflexivity within the research process:

Feminist research rejects the self-obscuring and alienating methodologies which are rooted in the knower–known, subject–object dichotomies of traditional positivist epistemology. In contrast, feminist methodology aims to highlight and examine the role of the researcher, and demands that research work be unalienated labour (Reinharz 1984; Stanley 1990). Based on an epistemology that considers all knowledge to be socially constructed, it begins with the acknowledgement that the identity of the researcher matters. (Roseneil 1993: 180)

Reinharz (1992) has argued that this deliberate situating of the feminist social scientist within her own research is not just an important principle of feminist approaches to methodology, but may indeed be a distinguishing feature of the approach, acting as a corrective to the 'pseudo-objectivity' of much mainstream research. One of the best known examples of this commitment to research reflexivity, and a book long considered a feminist classic, is Helen Roberts' *Doing Feminist Research* (1981). In this influential collection, eight women (and one man) provided personal accounts of their own research, each highlighting the relevance to the social research process of the feminist slogan 'the personal is political'. In the case of Roseneil's own research, she too has written a fascinating and startlingly honest autobiographical account of her own positioning *vis-à-vis* Greenham Common, described in the following terms by Roseneil herself:

To traditional methodologists what follows may seem, at best, irrelevant, a self-indulgent excursion into adolescent *angst*; at worst, it will be seen as indicative of complete failure at the enterprise of social–scientific research. (Roseneil 1993: 182)

Roseneil goes on to provide two parallel accounts of her growing involvement in Greenham Common. The first of these – an everyday tale of the growing political awareness of a 'Jewish vegetarian daughter of socialist acupuncturists' – she describes as the 'public' account, which she argues would be recognisable to those who knew her during this period. The second account, though, is 'one that was intensely private at the time' and relates to her growing awareness of her lesbian sexuality, a sexuality which received resounding affirmation at Greenham, in contrast to her experiences of 'coming out' at school: 'Greenham offered me a way of committing myself fully to opposing nuclear weapons, and the possibility that it was all right to be a lesbian, that I could be happy with who I was. At Greenham I could integrate my "political-self" and my "lesbian-self"' (Roseneil 1993: 186). Greenham also proved to be the means of integrating her 'academic-self', and Roseneil eventually left Greenham in order to study sociology: 'Writing my thesis on Greenham has been, in part, an attempt to finally reunite those three parts of myself that I had believed were irreconcilable. The project has been the antithesis of alienated labour, a labour of love' (ibid: 186).

In Roseneil's methodological account of her research, then, she provides a highly personalised and reflexive account of her involvement at Greenham. It is clear that the events she describes in this paper were all experienced at first hand: she was there, she was an active participant, and we see the camp through her eyes. However, and surprisingly given the transparency of the earlier piece, when reading *Disarming Patriarchy* it is less clear through whose eyes we are actually viewing the camp at any given time, in as much as it is unclear how much of the narrative was experienced *directly* by Roseneil. This is largely because she resorts to writing in the third person for most of the book, with the exception of the introductory chapter. Admittedly, she does state that during her months living at the camp she had 'the full gamut of "Greenham experiences"' (Roseneil 1993: 186), and that 'my memories and reconstructions of experiences of Greenham have been plundered continually in the course of the formal research process' (Roseneil 1995: 7). However, it would still be useful to know which parts of the account are autobiographical and based solely on her own experience, which parts are also backed up by the accounts of others, and which are based purely on other women's perspectives or on documentary sources.

Why is this so important? After all, Roseneil nonetheless builds up a convincingly comprehensive picture of camp life, and in many respects, then, it could be argued that it is irrelevant whether Roseneil is describing her own, others', or shared experiences. Further, when commenting on the draft of this chapter, Roseneil questioned the practicality of the kind of extensive footnoting that such a task would imply: 'What I tried to do was to weave a readable account of Greenham from a wide range of sources, and I felt that attempting to show exactly what the source of everything I said was would be impossible' (personal communication). This is a point which we accept, yet we would nonetheless argue that Roseneil's precise location within the account *does* become important when her descriptions are also accompanied by value judgements and used to support a particular line of argument. That Roseneil makes deliberate value judgements in her research is beyond question; indeed, in common with Mac an Ghaill (Chapter 2), it is an intentional characteristic of her research strategy:

> The research is certainly 'passionate' and politically engaged; as a Greenham woman myself, I am as passionate and politically-engaged as the women I have interviewed. I have no qualms about rejecting 'value-neutrality' and taking sides. (Roseneil 1993: 79)

This approach arises from Roseneil's commitment to a version of feminist standpoint epistemology known as 'feminist fractured foundationalist epistemology' (Stanley and Wise 1990). Standpoint epistemology in general terms is based on a critique of the 'male epistemological stance' (MacKinnon 1982) of much mainstream (or 'malestream') social science, whereby the hallowed principle of objectivity is exposed as both gendered and partial and as serving male interests. Feminist standpoint epistemology, as we noted briefly in Chapter 2, is based on the idea that women possess a more complete and less distorted knowledge of the social world by virtue of their experience of male oppression (Harding 1986, 1987). Fractured foundationalism takes this position a stage further and acknowledges the *multiplicity* of viewpoints among women. Accordingly, it 'recognises the contingency of all claims to truth and their inevitable partiality and situatedness' (Roseneil 1995: 8). Thus Roseneil, in common with many feminist researchers, rejects a version of objectivity which ignores the importance and validity of personal experience and which seeks to marginalise the values held by individual researchers.

Roseneil's research is heavily influenced by feminist values and, more specifically, the values of the Greenham peace camp; indeed, 'the ethics and politics that guided my research originated more in Greenham's values and politics than the sociological literature on ethics' (Roseneil 1993: 203). She thus takes sides *with* Greenham women *against* the values of militarism and patriarchal state violence. This much is clear and indisputable. But within the parameters of the research, how partial is Roseneil in her retelling of particular events and the details of camp life? For example, Roseneil provides a fascinating insight into the very different reputations attached to each of the camps set up at Greenham Common's perimeter gates, and argues that the existence of these different camps helped in the management of difference. Blue Gate, for example, had a reputation for being rather anarchic and disorganised (as one of the women interviewed by Roseneil described it, it was 'the Scallies' Gate… the Piss Artists' Gate and the Frivolous Gate… the Young Gate and the Lesbian Gate, the Working Class Gate'). Yellow Gate, in contrast, was perceived as 'grown up' and 'serious', Orange Gate had a reputation for being a religiously orientated gate (it was much frequented by Quaker women, for example), while Green Gate was seen as the cosmic gate, concerned with exploring feminist spirituality in its wider sense. Perhaps the most intriguing reputation was attached to Violet Gate, renowned for 'being obsessed with eating'. But at which gate, or gates, was Roseneil based for most of her time as a camper?

The answer to this question, surprisingly, is provided in neither the book nor in Roseneil's reflexive account of the research, and although one might be able to make an educated guess it would have been extremely useful to know for certain in view of her comments about tensions between the different gates. In particular, Roseneil is quite critical of some of the women at Yellow Gate (the main gate), pointing to disagreements over the allocation of money – initially the responsibility of Yellow Gate – and over the superior status often ascribed to Yellow Gate women by outsiders. If Roseneil's account of both conflicts is accurate, these criticisms would appear to be fair. However, without knowing Roseneil's own relationship to Yellow Gate it is difficult to assess to what extent her comments might be affected by her own understanding of how each gate operated, and whether her comments reflect a sense of prior allegiance to one gate over another. So, in view of her clear and incontrovertible alignment with Greenham *qua* Greenham, Roseneil's opacity concerning her *intra*camp loyalties represents a disappointing omission.

There is a final twist to this point, however, as in personal correspondence with Roseneil she expressed herself rather surprised that she had not anywhere revealed the identity of the gate at which she was based. Further, it transpired that our own educated guess was in fact incorrect: we had assumed that Roseneil was based at Blue Gate, possibly after a short spell living at Yellow Gate, when in fact she was at Green Gate all along! She then asks: 'Knowing this, do you think it significantly affected my account of intergate conflict? Perhaps if I had lived at Yellow Gate my perspective would have been different, but I do feel that I transcended gate loyalties, through interviewing women from a range of gates' (personal communication). So, Roseneil's prior allegiance would have been to Green Gate – a gate which did not appear to suffer at the expense of the fortunes of Yellow Gate any more or less than any other gate. Ultimately, we have to take Roseneil at her word when she says that her own loyalties were put into the background when writing about this aspect of camp life, although knowing what we now know there is little reason to suspect that she wrote the book from a position of any obvious bias. Knowing that she was at Green Gate also helps to answer the question of how much of the book is based on her own, as opposed to other people's, memories: from the appendix, we know that only eight of the 35 women interviewed by Roseneil were also at Green Gate. We can therefore reasonably conclude that most recollections of life at other gates are based largely on interview material rather than first-hand knowledge.

Disarming honesty: 'telling it like it is'

One of the issues which has to be faced when conducting research based on observation is whether or not it should be done overtly or covertly. This was a discussion touched upon in Chapter 7, where Hobbs adopted the role of a covert participant observer, with all the attendant ethical difficulties. In Roseneil's case, however, she had no inkling at the time of her participation that she would eventually make use of her experiences for research purposes. That she undoubtedly mulled over Greenham's significance in her own life at the time and that she also kept a diary of her experiences at the peace camp is fortuitous, but was by no means a deliberate research strategy. Indeed, as already noted, Roseneil had had no formal sociological training prior to or during her time as a camper at Greenham.

Even if she had been a trained researcher at that time and had wanted to conduct research on Greenham, one gets the impression that an overt attempt to do so would have been frowned upon by many Greenham women, or at best tolerated but not actively encouraged. As Roseneil reminds readers, living at Greenham Common during the early years of the camp was not unlike living in a goldfish bowl, with a constant stream of visitors arriving 'to see what it was like'. Some of these visitors would be women who might later become campers or stayers, who would arrive at Greenham with legitimate questions to ask about camp life, even if those questions might seem a little naive or predictable. Not infrequently, visitors would turn out to be undercover journalists, often with a prurient interest in camp life, and many were all too willing to write a negative story about activities at Greenham. Roseneil also mentions visits by more academic researchers of various kinds, referring to the frequent occasions when she would be greeted first thing in the morning by 'a questionnaire-toting undergraduate' (Roseneil 1993: 190). The constant battery of questions asked of Greenham women is captured wonderfully in the lyrics of one of the camp songs which Roseneil reproduces both in her book and in the 1993 article, and which is reproduced here as Figure 9.1.

> What are the questions visitors will ask us
> At the Peace Camp, Newbury, Berkshire?
> I'll tell you now of some that I know,
> And the rest, you'll surely ask them.
> 'Are there many of you here?'
> 'Is it cold, and are you queer?'
> 'Where do you get your water from?'
> 'Would you die for the cause?'
> 'Do you shit in the gorse?'
> At the Peace Camp, Newbury, Berkshire.
>
> What are the questions the media will ask us
> At the Peace Camp, Newbury, Berkshire?
> I'll tell you now of some that I know,
> And the rest, you'll read them later.
> 'Why do you make this sacrifice?'
> 'Can I talk to someone nice?'
> 'How does it feel now you have failed?'
> 'Can you pose by the gate?'
> 'Hurry up, it's getting late.'
> At the Peace Camp, Newbury, Berkshire.

Figure 9.1 'At the Peace Camp, Newbury, Berkshire' (to the tune of 'English Country Garden') (Roseneil 1995: 9–10)

Regardless of her intent at the time, Roseneil subsequently has made extensive use of her own experiences of life at Greenham and, by implication, the experiences of the women she was living with during this period. For many researchers, this could be interpreted as a flouting of the principle of informed consent, a principle which is given a high profile in the ethical guidelines of most professional research associations. The guidelines of the British Sociological Association note, for example, that:

> As far as possible sociological research should be based on the freely given informed consent of those studied. This implies a responsibility on the sociologist to explain as fully as possible, and in terms meaningful to participants, what the research is about, who is undertaking and financing it, why it is being undertaken, and how it is to be disseminated.(British Sociological Association 1993: 2)

But how relevant are these guidelines to Roseneil's research which, due to circumstances outside of her control, is arguably beyond the bounds of usual concerns about consent? According to Homan, these guidelines remain highly relevant:

> There is… a well-studied continuum of participant research from the covert and witting observer, to the unconscious observer and retrospective recorder, whose principal reason for not seeking consent was that he or she did not know at the time that observations would later be rendered as data…. Whether sociological sense is made of experience by those who were there at the time and have turned sociologist or by professional researchers to whom they present their memories does not alter the ethical implication that a situation that was closed or private may be open or disclosed. (Homan 1991: 63)

But was Greenham a closed or private world in this sense? It could be argued that there was nothing particularly 'private' about the Greenham peace camp. Indeed, its very existence was concerned with the cultivation of a high level of visibility in the media and in the public consciousness more generally, in order to galvanise opposition to the nuclear threat. Throughout its life, the camp actively courted publicity through its many high-profile actions, such as cutting the fence, invading the base, dancing on the missile bunkers and blockading the Cruise missile carriers whenever they attempted to leave the base. The camp was in the public eye, and was therefore the legitimate focus of research and investigation. However, Homan points out that even within the most public of spaces individuals and groups often create, and expect to be able to protect, *private* space. Goffman (1969) described this phenomenon in terms of 'front' and 'back' region behaviour and, while individuals may be more than happy for front region behaviour to come under public scrutiny, back region behaviour is not intended for public gaze. Roseneil uses a similar concept when she talks of the external and internal modes of action at Greenham; while it might be considered entirely legitimate to write freely about the public face of Greenham, other aspects of camp life were not intended for public consumption. This was not because the camp had anything to hide, but because the women felt that they deserved some degree of privacy given the high degree of surveillance to which they were otherwise subjected. Nonetheless, Roseneil directs as much attention towards these aspects of camp life as she does to the external modes of action – and indeed, therein lies much of the fascination of the book.

The public/private dichotomy and the validity of drawing upon experience of both sides of camp life for research purposes without consent is further complicated by Roseneil's commitment to what she calls the ethos of Greenham, 'a powerful moral discourse about the practising of feminism that shaped and constructed life at Greenham' (Roseneil 1995: 61). Despite individual differences between women, one is nonetheless struck when reading *Disarming Patriarchy* by the strong sense of loyalty and solidarity between the women involved. It is hard not to believe that many of the women who lived with Roseneil and shared camp life with her would feel somewhat aggrieved if they were to discover that she had published a 'no holds barred' account of life at Greenham. By the same token, given the importance of the notion that the personal is political, it could be argued that one cannot fully understand the workings of Greenham's external mode of action without also gaining an understanding of its internal mode of action.

A further element of the Greenham ethos was a rejection of hierarchical organisation at the camp and a suspicion of the motives of any woman who claimed to be a Greenham 'expert'. This status was often thrust upon individual women by the media on the basis of the length of time they had been involved in the camp, but was nonetheless the source of ongoing conflict. Given Roseneil's shared commitment to these values, what are we to make of her desire to write a book about Greenham? As Roseneil herself writes: 'The anti-hierarchical impulse of Greenham actually made me very dubious about doing research on Greenham at all. Greenham women, myself included, have always been very critical of anyone setting themselves up as an expert on the camp' (Roseneil 1993: 203). This is precisely what Roseneil does, however, by writing a book about Greenham. Thus it could be argued that Roseneil's research, at the point at which she went public with her findings, did not after all represent a straightforward reconciliation of her 'academic-self' and her 'political-self', but rather acted as a source of *conflict* between these two aspects of her identity. Given her own qualms, then, how does she justify her decision to write about Greenham?

In order to answer this question it is first important to consider Roseneil's initial rationale for writing the book. Above and beyond her personal motivation for conducting research on Greenham, Roseneil has also highlighted a number of other considerations. First, she is concerned with using the experience of Greenham as the basis for celebrating and theorising women's agency and activism, a theme which has received much less attention within feminist scholarship than the theorising of women's oppression. Second, and building upon this first point, she is concerned with using Greenham as a means of developing a feminist perspective on social movement theory. Third, her work seeks to challenge inaccurate representations of Greenham, including those advanced by feminists who have been critical of some aspects of Greenham. In particular, she points to work which has been critical of Greenham's assumed maternalistic – and hence essentialist – agenda, arguing that the assumption that protest mobilised around the duty of women as mothers to protect life owed rather more to media representation than it did to the reality of many women's motivation for involvement. Each of these strands represents an important reason for conducting research on Greenham, despite the ethical difficulties raised by the specific circumstances of the research.

In Roseneil's defence, it has to be said that once she had made the decision to make Greenham the focus of her doctoral studies, from then on she was totally honest about her dual role as both researcher and peace activist in any further contacts she had with the camp or with individual Greenham women. Indeed, she writes that on subsequent visits to Greenham she tried to tell as many women as possible about her intentions, and presumably they would have told her if they had any particular worries about her research plans. The question of the lack of informed consent to draw upon events with which Roseneil had been personally involved may also contribute to the relative invisibility of Roseneil within the main text. In other words, if we could specifically place Roseneil as being personally present at certain key incidents, then it might be possible for other Greenham women to recognise either themselves or women who had been close to them within the account. Thus, her visibility might have been a deliberately protective strategy. It should also be noted that all 35 women subsequently interviewed by Roseneil quite obviously participated in her research with full knowledge of her research intentions, so by no means all of the data used by Roseneil are affected by the consent issue.

Regardless of whether consent had, or even should have, been obtained, there are a further set of issues which relate to the dissemination of Roseneil's work and the potentially negative consequences of publication. In writing about publication of results, Homan has argued that 'at this stage it is common for researchers to be troubled with feelings of guilt that they have betrayed their subjects' (Homan 1991: 154). It is, of course, important to distinguish between a sense of betrayal arising from *inaccurate* reporting (particularly when the inaccuracy is deliberate) and a sense of betrayal arising from what might be seen as an accurate yet *unnecessary* washing of dirty linen in public, even though the distinction may be lost on those who feel betrayed. Deliberately misleading reporting was something with which Greenham women were all too familiar, as highlighted by the following extract from an account of Greenham written by a freelance writer:

> I told Pat (a Greenham woman) that I was writing an article about the peace camp and she was neither interested nor scornful. She said that many people had written about the Greenham women, that they were mostly lies and she felt it was a waste of time to read them. I could understand that it would be rather futile for Pat to sit on Greenham Common reading lies about the Greenham women. (Blackwood 1984: 13)

Greenham women were, then, used to inaccurate accounts being written about their lives and the activities of the camp, particularly within the pages of the tabloid press. In contrast, Roseneil was seeking to provide a faithful portrayal of life at Greenham, yet nonetheless felt that in so doing she might be betraying the spirit of Greenham. Many researchers share similar misgivings at the point at which they 'go public', such that there is often a strong temptation to engage in some form of self-censorship of research findings. Indeed, in some cases, a researcher may even decide either to delay publication or not to publish their findings at all (see, for example, Finch 1984). The temptation to censor one's own work will often arise – as in Roseneil's case – out of a sense of personal loyalty towards those being studied, while for other researchers the main motivation may be a desire to maintain involvement in the research site and consequently not to jeopardise one's field relations. Either way, there can often be strong pressures to 'tone down' one's findings in order to minimise feelings of upset and to offset unwanted publicity: thus a *faithful* representation of a social setting may not necessarily be equated with an *acceptable* representation (Homan 1991).

Despite her expressed misgivings and the temptation to water down her findings, Roseneil argues that she opted for a faithful, as opposed to acceptable, representation of life at Greenham Common: 'As far as criticising Greenham is concerned, having overcome the initial barrier of anxiety about undertaking the research… I have been determined to tell "the truth" about Greenham as I have seen it' (Roseneil 1993: 192). 'The truth' which Roseneil reveals includes tales of major conflict over the allocation of financial resources; of tensions between campers at Greenham and the wider women's peace network (Greenham women were often accused of being arrogant and adopting a superior attitude towards women involved in less high-profile activities); of disagreements between the different gates at Greenham; of a 'Leninist entryist' attempt by women from the King's Cross Women's Centre/Wages for Housework Campaign to take over the camp by appealing to anti-racist discourse; and conflicts over unilateral announcements of major actions by individual gates (Yellow Gate, for example, issued an extremely controversial – not to mention hopelessly unrealistic – call for ten million women to gather at Greenham for a ten-day period in September 1984). Each of these (and similar) events are, as far as the reader can tell, reported honestly and straightforwardly by Roseneil, and one can only agree with her conclusion:

> Greenham was far from being a harmonious, tranquil idyll, in which some innate womanly peacefulness reigned supreme. A community of strong-minded women, who grew stronger over time, there were many

differences of opinion, often vociferously expressed. Conflict sometimes rocked the camp, and arguments about money, hierarchy, class and, to some extent, race, created real divisions. (Roseneil 1995: 172)

However, two related observations arise from a detailed reading of the book and Roseneil's methodological paper. First, despite the honesty of the account she provides (and it should be remembered that the accounts of conflict are not the whole story, but part of a broader and more positive account of Greenham's successes and triumphs), on a handful of occasions Roseneil has a tendency to put a gloss on the accounts of conflict by including the occasional qualifying statement. For example, she writes in Chapter 5 that: 'Without downplaying its significance, particularly to women who felt personally attacked, excluded or ignored, it is important to recognise that conflict can be constructive and can result in positive change' (Roseneil 1995: 72). Similarly, in writing about the conflict over the Ten Days' Action – a debate which 'crystallised many of the conflicts which already existed within Greenham' (ibid: 104) – she makes the point that the debate was also 'one of the strengths of Greenham's structure', and that 'even though the positions taken up by the various groups of women were contradictory… Greenham as a collective identity and a movement was supple enough to accommodate them all' (ibid). Neither these nor similar comments attempt to play down the conflicts which occurred at Greenham, yet Roseneil appears to feel the need to remind us that conflict is not unusual within a social movement. Surely this is an obvious point, and certainly not one that in any way diminishes the significance of the peace camp. On certain occasions, then, Roseneil's startling honesty suffers a crisis of confidence; she loses her nerve, and falls back on superfluous reassurances that 'all was well' *despite* conflict.

The second observation relates to what may possibly be a glossing over of the extent of difference in one important respect, namely the different positions taken up by Greenham women in relation to both feminism and lesbianism. Chapter 8 of *Disarming Patriarchy* focuses on changes in consciousness and identity which Greenham wrought in women's lives, paying particular attention to the liberating experience of living in a women-only environment and, more specifically, of living within an environment in which, in a complete reversal of the world outside Greenham Common, heterosexuality was rendered strange. At no point in this chapter do we hear any voices of dissent;

all the women who are quoted, whether lesbians or heterosexuals, and in many cases despite initial misgivings and uncertainties, had only positive things to say about feminism and lesbianism. However, in her methodological paper, Roseneil includes evidence to suggest that while this may undoubtedly have been the majority view, this was *not* a universally held view. In a discussion of her interview strategy, Roseneil refers to two 'difficult' interviews, which were both marked by 'a low level of "rapport" and personal engagement with the women concerned' (Roseneil 1993: 199). These interviews clearly stood in stark contrast to most of the other interviews, which Roseneil describes as being based upon 'intense, passionate connections', in which women 'were prepared to expose their thoughts and feelings quite boldly' (Roseneil 1993: 198). The sticking point proved, significantly, to be a rejection of Roseneil's own political standpoint and view of Greenham: the two women 'were anti-feminist, anti-lesbian, and... thought of going to Greenham as a sacrifice rather than as an enjoyable, exciting political action' (ibid: 200). She writes of feeling under personal attack from both of these women, of feeling 'intimidated and upset' by their hostility towards her. Both these women clearly had a lot to say about feminism and lesbianism, yet their voices are nowhere to be heard within the main text of *Disarming Patriarchy*. Thus tensions and conflicts between women sharing a broadly pro-feminist, pro-lesbian position are admitted, yet tensions and conflicts between these women and women who were hostile to the feminist project of Greenham are largely played down. Given Roseneil's honesty concerning other areas of conflict at Greenham this is an odd omission; and once aware of the omission, it reads as if Roseneil is toeing a party line on this point, even if she demonstrates disarming honesty elsewhere in her book. Again, this is a point which Roseneil has subsequently conceded in connection with *Disarming Patriarchy*, although she also points out that these issues *are* dealt with in a forthcoming book which looks specifically at queer feminism at Greenham (Roseneil 1999).

Conclusion

Disarming Patriarchy was initially bought and read by one of the authors of this book out of personal interest, and was read cover to cover within a very short space of time: above and beyond its merits as a piece of research, then, it is undoubtedly a 'good read'. Much of its fascination (for this reader, at least) arises from the sense that Roseneil is 'spilling the beans' on Greenham, and its authority is unequivocally derived from Roseneil's 'insider' status. Roseneil's undisputed status as an insider has also given rise, however, to a number of issues relating to the way in which she positions herself within the text. In this chapter, therefore, we have examined questions relating to the feminist epistemological underpinnings of her research and to Roseneil's relative invisibility within the main text, in contrast to her high visibility within her reflexive account (Roseneil 1993); and we have explored the relevance of informed consent to retrospective research, as well as issues of bias and self-censorship within the process of publication and dissemination. The weaknesses of Roseneil's research arise largely from occasional moments of disingenuousness and lack of opacity; and we are only really made aware of these because of her extraordinary transparency, honesty and reflexiveness within the broader research process. Thus, these occasional weaknesses are rendered all the more surprising and disappointing.

For the most part, though, *Disarming Patriarchy* is an extremely thorough piece of research. It provides a detailed account of a highly significant phase in the history of the women's movement in Britain and, more generally, contributes to our understanding of women's agency within patriarchal society. Moreover, the reader is left with the impression that the undertaking of this particular piece of research was an extremely important process for Roseneil in gaining a richer understanding of *her own* agency. Such a chasing of personal demons (or angels?) may well be a characteristic, to a lesser or greater extent, of all of the studies explored in this book, yet this is a theme which comes much closer to the surface within Roseneil's research, which she aptly describes as 'unalienated labour' and 'a labour of love'. The result is a deeply personal account of Greenham, upon which we, the readers, are allowed to eavesdrop. We are in strong agreement with Roseneil, then, when she writes: 'I can but advocate that more sociologists look to their own unique life-histories and experiences for the inspiration of their research' (Roseneil 1993: 205).

Additional reading

For more on the politics of women's protest at Greenham Common see Sasha Roseneil's latest book, *Common Women, Uncommon Practices: The Queer Feminism of Greenham* (1999). For more on feminist epistemology, see Liz Stanley and Sue Wise's *Breaking Out Again* (1992), an updated version of their classic *Breaking Out* (1983). Martin Hammersley and Paul Atkinson's *Ethnography: Principles in Practice* remains an important introduction to ethnographic research (1983), while Dick Hobbs and Tim May's edited collection *Interpreting the Field: Accounts of Ethnography* (1993) contains a broad range of reflexive accounts by ethnographic researchers, Sasha Roseneil included.

Chapter 10

Conclusion

In this book we have provided a showcase for eight recent pieces of sociological research, all of which we believe are exemplary in their attention to methodological detail and in the contributions they make to the sub-disciplines they each represent. In exploring each of these studies we have, inevitably, drawn attention to their weaknesses as well as their strengths, highlighting the extent to which even the best examples of research are typically open to methodological criticism and improvement. This should not come as a surprise; and indeed, when the authors of each of the eight books were asked by us to comment on 'their' chapters, most acknowledged that our critique was fair and legitimate, and had highlighted issues and tensions of which they themselves were aware. At least one of the authors expressed the view that they had been let off lightly!

One of our motivations in writing this book was a desire to produce a text which would complement, rather than add to, the plethora of existing introductory methods texts. This would seem to be a growth market for many publishers, leaving both student and lecturer with a bewildering choice of potential texts upon which to draw. It is our belief that there are some excellent introductory texts now available (for example, May 1997 and Gilbert 1993 strike us as being particularly comprehensive and well-written books). Consequently, we had no wish to add yet another textbook to the long list of such books, neither did we feel that we could produce a book that would add anything substantively different to this existing body of writing. However, the idea for this book arose from what we saw as an inevitable weakness of many introductory texts, namely their tendency to focus on individual methods and broader methodological issues in isolation – a chapter on surveys here, a chapter on interviews there, a further chapter on ethics, and so on. While this would seem to be largely unavoidable within the constraints of an introductory text, it does have the unfortunate effect of playing down the strategic and mundane 'messiness' and blurred boundaries of most research. In contrast, by focusing in detail on recent examples of empirical research we have tried to convey some of the tensions and dilemmas which invariably arise within the research process. It is a rare research project indeed which does not involve some degree of compromise between its original design and its working out in practice.

In this final chapter we want to comment on three specific issues of which we have been conscious in writing this book. First, we have been struck by the methodological eclecticism of the authors of the eight studies. This has raised questions about the appropriateness of mixing methods, and the impact of doing so on research findings, both in terms of practical issues and in terms of the knowledge that results. Second, we are aware that some readers will view the task we have set ourselves in writing this book as creakingly 'modernist' in nature. Up until this point we have had little to say about the implications for the empirical research tradition of the 'postmodern turn' in the social sciences, and we will address ourselves to this issue in the second part of this chapter. Third, we have been reminded of the rich tradition of empirical research which exists within British sociology, and we hope that the book will be read as a celebration of that tradition. We end the book, however, with a plea for greater methodological transparency across the discipline.

Methodological eclecticism and the appropriateness of method

The classic textbook approach to research methods in the social sciences might lead some students to believe that a researcher is faced with a set of straightforward choices between one or other method in developing a research strategy. Thus, a researcher chooses either a survey or an in-depth interview strategy; he or she decides to use either documentary analysis or participant observation; and so on – one method is chosen, the other options are accordingly rejected. This is rarely the intention of the authors of introductory methods texts, but the abstracted nature of the introductory format, with the relative strengths and weaknesses of each approach delineated, may well lead some novice researchers to believe that a good research design should be based on a single method in isolation. Accordingly, the major challenge for a researcher is to decide what the best and most appropriate method should be. Of course, in many instances a researcher does indeed use only one method in exploring a sociological problem. This is perhaps more likely to be the case within the quantitative tradition, where a researcher may rely exclusively on various techniques of secondary analysis of large data sets, for example, and rarely if ever use any other method. By the same token, it is not unusual among qualitative researchers to stick to a tried and tested 'favourite' method.

However, these days it is not at all uncommon for sociologists to use a combination of methods, rather than one method in isolation. Indeed, in selecting studies for inclusion in this book, we soon realised that, even if we had wished to do so, we would have been hard pressed to find eight recently published sociological studies which relied exclusively on one specific research method. Figure 1.1 provided a summary of the methods used in each study. As this demonstrated, only two of our studies relied on one method in isolation: Wellings and colleagues' study of British sexual attitudes and lifestyles, and Saunders' study of home ownership. Both of these studies employed a social survey, Wellings using a national sample, Saunders a set of three local samples. Nonetheless, it is worth noting that Wellings and her research team used a number of different data-gathering techniques *within* the survey interview, while the pilot work was based in part on qualitative interviewing. All the other studies have combined an eclectic range of methods. The use by Roseneil, Hobbs and Mac an Ghaill of a combination of qualitative methods is very much a feature of the case study approach, and in these particular cases data were gathered from interviewing, documentary analysis, and diaries to complement the main investigative method, participant observation. Our other three studies, by Finch and Mason, Phizacklea and Wolkowitz, and Gregson and Lowe, are rather less conventional in that they combine methods drawn from two very distinct traditions. In all three cases, part of their research is based on data gathered via a quantitative survey, yet in combination with more qualitative methods such as in-depth interviews, case studies and documentary analysis.

In our discussion in Chapter 3, we noted that the use of a mixed method approach raises a number of technical issues, particularly relating to the integration of different types of data. While within this book we have focused chiefly on the challenges which this raised specifically for Finch and Mason, it is undoubtedly the case that Gregson and Lowe, as well as Phizacklea and Wolkowitz, will have faced similar decisions about how to deal with apparent inconsistencies between data sets, and whether or not one data source should take priority over another. Despite the difficulties and challenges of mixing methods, we argued in Chapter 3 that the combination of different methods within a single piece of research – if done well – can lead to a much more rounded and holistic view of the topic under investigation. Cohen and Manion (1985) are particularly strong supporters of a mixed method approach, arguing that it overcomes what they refer to as the problem of 'method-boundedness' in the social sciences. Quoting Smith (1975), they note that:

> Much research has employed particular methods or techniques out of methodological parochialism or ethnocentrism. Methodologists often push pet methods either because they are the only ones they have familiarity with, or because they believe their method is superior to all others. (Smith 1975, quoted in Cohen and Manion 1985)

There is, of course, a lot of truth in this statement, and we are both advocates of the need for methods training in the social sciences which provides students with a strong grounding in a broad repertoire of research techniques. Even if students never intend to use, for example, quantitative methods in their own research, it is nonetheless essential that they can understand the basics of quantitative data collection and analysis, at the very least allowing them to evaluate the work of others from a position of knowledge rather than ignorance or misunderstanding. Similarly, we advocate that quantitative researchers should be familiar with the basics of qualitative research techniques, in order to understand, for example, the different criteria used for evaluating qualitative, as opposed to quantitative, research. So much of the debate concerning the feasibility of mixing methods seems to be based on a lack of clarity and practical knowledge, on *both* sides of what is often perceived as the quantitative/qualitative divide.

However, much as we have sympathy with Smith's view, to reduce the debate about the feasibility of mixing methods to a simple argument about playing to one's strengths tends to ignore the philosophical argument that particular methods are linked to certain epistemological stances. Thus, far from being neutral tools which can be 'mixed and matched' with impunity, many social scientists regard certain methods as being inextricably linked to specific social science paradigms, and therefore believe that to combine methods is to be guilty of epistemological naivety. A distinction is usually drawn between positivist and anti-positivist or interpretive positions. The positivist paradigm aligns itself with a particular view of the mechanisms and assumptions of the natural sciences, underpinned by a belief that only that which is grounded in the observable can count as valid knowledge. In contrast, the interpretive paradigm – associated with intellectual traditions such as phenomenology, symbolic interactionism and ethnomethodology – stresses the dynamic, constructed and evolving nature of social reality. It rejects the positivist notion of knowledge being grounded in the objective and tangible, and instead seeks to understand social reality through the eyes of those being studied.

One could argue, therefore, that an adherence to positivism will necessarily lead a researcher to rely on quantitative methods such as surveys and experiments, which allow the researcher to draw conclusions about relationships and regularities between variables. At the same time, researchers who subscribe to a more constructionist interpretation of social reality will necessarily rely on more qualitative methods, which have a central commitment to viewing the social world from the perspective of social actors. Methodological purists would consequently argue that allegiance to a particular paradigm is the sole means of determining which methods a researcher should employ; conversely, the use of a particular method must surely imply allegiance to a particular epistemological stance. On this basis, we might conclude that Mac an Ghaill, Roseneil and Hobbs are interpretivist in outlook, and that Wellings and her colleagues and Saunders are positivist. But what of Finch and Mason, Gregson and Lowe, and Phizaklea and Wolkowitz, all of whom combine both quantitative and qualitative techniques within the same study? Does their choice of research strategy suggest that they are self-consciously sitting on the fence, or does it betray epistemological naivety? How can a researcher justify the combination of methods which have very different epistemological underpinnings? Indeed, this is a point which Mason herself addresses in her book *Qualitative Researching*, when she challenges researchers to ensure that the integration of methods is epistemologically legitimate, based on 'similar, complementary or comparable assumptions about what can legitimately constitute knowledge or evidence' (Mason 1996: 28).

A mixed method approach is certainly not unusual: indeed, it has been argued that 'if one looks carefully at the research actually conducted in the name of one or other epistemology, it seems that few working researchers are not blending the two perspectives' (Miles and Huberman 1984: 20). If we are not looking at mass epistemological naivety, then, does this rather suggest that it is possible to subscribe to the philosophy of one paradigm and yet still utilise the methods more commonly associated with an opposing paradigm? This is a point on which social scientists have argued long and hard, and many would still strongly argue against methodological eclecticism. Others, however, are less certain. Reichardt and Cook (1979), for example, address this issue by exploring the points on which the two paradigms are said to differ in order to see how far their respective attributes can in fact be *exclusively* applied to a particular paradigmatic approach. They conclude that few, if any, of the attributes are in fact inextricably and exclusively linked to one or other paradigm. Moreover, they argue that the distinctions which are commonly drawn between the two approaches are based on a false dichotomy; for example, the claim that quantitative research is necessarily objective is clearly a nonsense, as all research is based on decisions made as a result of human judgement. Others have added to this debate: the late Catherine Marsh, for example, argued that the survey research tradition is capable of encompassing far more than the conventional questionnaire study and can actually use a variety of methods, including observation, content analysis and the coding of recorded interviews (Marsh 1982). She rejected the view that surveys necessarily concentrate on causal explanations in favour of a broader view that they are capable of producing explanations that take account of social meaning. Delamont and Atkinson (1980) have also argued that ethnographers can 'serve several masters', and that while many researchers turn to ethnography as a reaction against empiricism, many in fact continue to bring a positivist perspective to their work.

These and many other writers (see Bryman 1988 for a thorough and detailed discussion) have demonstrated that the attributes usually associated with particular paradigms are not inherently and solely linked to one method or another, but are actually independent of the paradigms with which they are associated. However:

This is not to say that one's paradigmatic stance is unimportant in choosing a method; nor is it to deny that certain methods are usually associated with specific paradigms. The major point is that paradigms are not the sole determinants of the choice of methods. (Reichardt and Cook 1979: 16)

Others would go even further and argue that paradigms are not the determinants of method *at all*, and that to think they are is to muddle two separate issues: the practicalities of collecting data, and theories of knowledge. Thus, in practice, the choice of method is often largely determined by the demands of the research questions facing the researcher and the appropriateness of method to those questions. We have already seen how this was worked through in the case of Finch and Mason's *Negotiating Family Responsibilities*: normative beliefs were examined via a large survey, while an exploration of the dynamics of individual family negotiations was best achieved through in-depth interviewing. Similarly, the work of Gregson and Lowe and of Phizaklea and Wolkowitz was enhanced by relying on complementary methods and data sources, allowing them to get at different facets of the same phenomenon with each of their different approaches. A researcher's own epistemological viewpoint is not rendered irrelevant by this logic; indeed, it will probably determine the research questions which that researcher is prepared to consider in the first place and in turn will probably influence the extent to which methodological triangulation will lean more towards one tradition than another. It is similarly likely to influence the form of explanation the researcher will seek, and therefore the sort of argument evinced to justify the particular explanations given the evidence. Nonetheless:

> while a researcher may prefer to use one (methodological approach) to the relative exclusion of the other, if the research problem invites a combined approach there is little to prevent such a strategy, other than the usual reasons of time, money and possibly inclination. (Bryman 1988: 107)

What we conclude from all of this is that some of the best examples of sociological research have emerged from the creative and imaginative fusion of a variety of methods and data sources. While a minority of researchers may well be unaware of the broader issues raised by such an approach, we believe that this is not true of the researchers whose work is represented in this book. Methodological eclecticism is not without its difficulties, and the onus is placed on researchers to be aware of the epistemological issues which are thus raised and to draw them to the attention of their readers. Nonetheless, if it is done well, research which combines a number of different methods – whether mixing quantitative and qualitative techniques or, not uncommonly, mixing methods drawn from within just one of these traditions – can contribute to a much more sophisticated exploration of the sociological problems which lie at the heart of any given research strategy. In turn, our knowledge of the social world is all the more rich.

Social research in the shadow of the postmodern

Is it possible, though, to produce reliable knowledge of the social world, as implied by the previous sentence? This is, of course, a fundamental issue lying at the heart of the empirical tradition, yet some sociologists would argue that such a quest is a misguided enterprise. As with all other disciplines, sociology has felt the enormous impact of the 'postmodern turn' of recent times, and its implications for questions of epistemology and method are extremely far-reaching:

> At an epistemological level, converts to postmodernism regard it as nothing less than pulling the rug from under the feet of traitional scientific foundations. Although there remains definitional ambiguity over the term... postmodernism may be viewed as a critique of the values, goals, and bases of analyses that, from the Enlightenment onwards, have been assumed to be universally valid... Methodologically, the alternative to the complacent foundationalism of modernism becomes the maxim... that 'anything goes'. (Williams and May 1996: 158)

In particular, the postmodernist critique of research practice has confronted empirical researchers with a dual crisis: a crisis in representation, and a crisis in legitimation. The first crisis is based on questioning the expert status of the researcher, given that 'truth is contingent and nothing should be placed beyond the possibility of revision' (Williams and May 1996: 159). Thus, it is not possible directly to capture lived experience: the researcher is merely an interpreter, whose own account has no greater claim to 'truth' than anyone else's: 'There can never be a final, accurate representation of what was meant or said – only different textual representations of different experiences' (Denzin 1997: 5). Representation and reality can no longer be said to correspond to each other, therefore, and what becomes significant is an exploration of the textual devices used by researchers in attempting to create 'authentic' accounts. Stronach and MacLure (1997), for example, both worked with the same transcripts from a series of biographical interviews with 'Jack', a primary school headteacher, and produced two very different accounts of his life, which were then presented to Jack himself for a third interpretation. They conclude that authenticity is no more than a 'textual accomplishment'. Does this mean, though, that methodological questions are reducible to textual ones? They argue that methodology remains important to the researcher, if not to the reader: 'We do not seek to dismiss methodology, but rather to bring its textual properties to light; to ask what sorts of stories are implicated in a particular methodology, and what sorts of stories are suppressed or made un-tellable' (Stronach and MacLure 1997: 56).

The crisis of legitimation is closely related to the crisis in representation, and arises from a rethinking of concepts such as validity, reliability and generalisability. A claim to validity, based on rules concerning the production of knowledge and its relationship to 'reality', is the means by which an account is given legitimacy, and by which 'good' research is distinguishable from 'bad' research. Denzin argues, however, that attempts to claim validity for a piece of research 'cling to the conception of a "world out there" that is truthfully and accurately captured by the researcher's methods' (Denzin 1997: 6). Consequently, the postmodernist response to the legitimation crisis is based on a rejection of specific criteria for judging research: 'This position doubts all criteria and privileges none' (Denzin 1997: 8). Denzin distinguishes this response from that of an earlier critical perspective – poststructuralism – which contends that a new set of criteria is required, based on concepts such as subjectivity, emotionality and feeling. Emphasis may be given, for example, to the extent to which a text unmasks the operation of power and ideology, and hence serves an emancipatory purpose. In contrast, the postmodern position is more radically destructive of legitimating criteria.

The postmodern critique, therefore, sees the researcher as intrinsically implicated in the production of knowledge (Williams and May 1996). Moreover, centrality is given to texts, and to questions of power and authority which are inscribed within them (a text can be anything from a literary text, an official document, or an interview transcript, through to a photograph, a movie, or a building). On the one hand, this means that a pivotal concern of postmodern research is the deconstruction of texts and their embedded power relations: 'In this process, how the social world is represented becomes more important than the search for an independent "reality" described by such texts' (Williams and May 1996: 169). On the other hand, the accounts thus produced by the researcher in the process of deconstruction are as much the focus of the postmodern gaze as the initial texts upon which they based their analysis. The postmodern researcher is consequently caught in a hall of mirrors.

Two sets of issues relevant to the production of this book follow on from this discussion. The first set relates to the types of studies we have selected for inclusion, while the second set relates to our treatment of those studies. First, then, we shall consider the eight studies, all of which are based on a fairly traditional repertoire of methods. Moreover, in most cases the authors' deployment of these methods appears to be underpinned by an assumption of a large degree of fit between the accounts of respondents, the final research account and the aspects of social reality which they have sought to capture. There are, though, two exceptions to this. For the most part, Roseneil's methodology does seem to assume a correspondence between her respondents' accounts of Greenham and what Greenham was 'really' like. Thus, she provides a robust defence of retrospective interview data, citing Thompson (1988) as evidence for her claim that 'recall was probably little worse than it would have been had I been interviewing a day or two after the event in question' (Roseneil 1995: 193). However, she goes on to argue that: 'Recognising that *all* recalling is influenced by current beliefs, my interest has been more in the (current) social meanings of particular events and past experiences to the women, and less in reconstructing "factual" accounts of events' (Roseneil 1995: 194 – emphasis in original). We would venture to suggest, though, that more often than not she uses her interview data as a means of reconstructing past events, rather than deconstructing narrative, but she is clearly sensitive to questions concerning the limits of interview data.

Mac an Ghaill's research is the second exception. Once again, his research is largely based on traditional ethnographic techniques of observation and interviewing. However, he is the only one of our authors to draw explicitly on postmodern ideas in his writing. In particular, in theorising gender and masculinity, he argues that he has attempted to move away from essentialist notions of sex-role theories in favour of a position informed by 'the new politics of cultural difference', a position which 'resist(s) attempts to produce an account of the gender and sexual processes of schooling that (are) reducible to male and female voices' (Haywood and Mac an Ghaill 1998: 127). Thus his focus is very much on 'multiple subjectivities' and on the power relations underpinning the dominant discourses surrounding masculinity and femininity in the school. Mac an Ghaill uses his interview data not so much as a way of reconstructing events in the life of the school, but as a way of exploring the way in which 'dominant definitions of masculinity are affirmed within schools' (Mac an Ghaill 1994: 4). Of all the studies we have highlighted, then, Mac an Ghaill's comes closest to having considered the implications of the postmodern turn for the process of research.

We would have liked to have included within the book an example of research informed much more explicitly by postmodern, or at least poststructuralist, influences, such as a study based entirely on postmodern discourse analysis or the deconstruction of various types of text. Indeed, we discovered a number of interesting studies, particularly in the area of popular culture, which were based on these and similar approaches. However – and this applies equally to 'modernist' versions of discourse analysis and deconstruction – we were stymied by the tendency for research of this kind to be highly abstracted and thus relatively inaccessible in terms of our key criteria of methodological transparency. Many authors within this tradition do not write explicitly about their methods, even though it is clear that they have made decisions concerning the selection of appropriate texts for the deconstructionist project, and have developed systems for classifying and categorising those texts. These are important issues, yet they are invariably obscured from view, with the consequence that postmodern research strategies are currently subject to mystification in much the same way that qualitative methods all too often used to be. From a postmodern perspective, this in itself is interesting; what systems of domination are served by such a lack of transparency? A number of texts are now beginning to emerge which address themselves specifically to the implications of a postmodern research methodology (see for example Denzin 1997; Scheurich 1997; Stronach and MacLure 1997). However, it strikes us that their rather abstract styles and their invocation of 'methodologies of disappointment' and 'the practice of failure' are less than helpful for novice researchers who, like it or not, require rather more certainty than absolute uncertainty at the outset of their research careers.

The second set of issues is related to our treatment of the eight studies included in this book. Stronach and MacLure, drawing on Lather (1996), argue that most methods textbooks are concerned with offering problem-solving advice, 'on the assumption that better methodology will produce better accounts, clearer formulations of problems and more efficient solutions' (Stronach and MacLure 1997: 4). Thus, such texts are primarily concerned with offering a method-ology of certainty. From our perspective, this is largely attributable to what we noted earlier to be an inevitable weakness of many methods texts, namely their abstracted nature and their proffering of neat solutions to decontextualised research problems. In this book, we have tried to overcome some of these shortcomings, by demonstrating the messiness and tentativeness of social research. Nonetheless, we have done so from within a framework which firmly believes that it is still possible to distinguish 'good' research from 'bad' research, while recognising that the criteria for doing so will differ from method to method. Thus we have focused on issues such as the influence of a researcher's personal values on the research process, the appropriateness of different sampling strategies, defini-tional problems in survey research, self-censorship of research findings at the dissemination stage, and the logic of triangulation. We have not attempted to suggest that there is necessarily a definitive way to tackle any of these issues, but we have certainly argued that there may be better or worse ways.

We have, therefore, based this book on the premise that it is indeed possible to cultivate knowledge of the social world, and that the process of social research as worked out in the studies reviewed in this book has resulted in a series of important substantive contributions to our sociological understanding of society. That is not to say that we reject the validity of some of the arguments concerning the crises in represen-tation and legitimation. We welcome, for example, the debate concerning the limits of validity and the competing claims of alterna-tive accounts, and recognise the degree to which any knowledge of the social world which is thus 'produced' by empirical research is highly dependent on the methodological devices employed by the researcher (but then these insights are hardly unique to postmodernism; critical researchers, with feminist researchers at the forefront, have been engaged in these kinds of debate for many years). Nonetheless, we believe that the wholesale dismissal of conventional criteria for assessing social research can easily collapse into a rather hopeless relativism and, consequently, an inability to contribute to public debate. While acknowledging that many sociologists would not see this latter task as a proper, or necessary, goal of sociology, it is equally true to say that the influence of the eight studies highlighted in this book is derived in part from their undoubted contribution to contemporary policy debates. This, naturally, raises questions concerning the authority of the researcher in relation to those debates, but each of the researchers whose work is included in this book has been careful to state the limits of the work's generalisability and, in most cases, they have made it quite clear where they stand in relation to the topic being researched.

In praise of the empirical tradition

We hope that this book has demonstrated that the tradition of British empirical sociology is alive and well. It is as robust as Marshall's (1990) review of the 'classics' of postwar British sociology illustrated. It is our belief that the eight studies chosen for inclusion in this book represent some of the best examples of research currently being conducted within each of the sub-areas of the discipline from which they are drawn. Each has developed an imaginative research strategy in order to explore a particular sociological issue and, in addition to being methodologically exemplary, each is also well regarded for the substantive contributions it has made to their fields. Of course, we could easily have chosen to cover other sub-areas, and hence selected other equally strong studies. Moreover, it is undoubtedly the case that if we were to conduct an exercise akin to *Desert Island Discs*, and ask other academics to select eight highly rated pieces of research, we would be presented with as many different combinations as there were academics, reflecting the very specific research interests and methodological leanings of each individual. Inevitably, then, our selection is idiosyncratic, but we stand by our view that each of these studies, albeit in its own different way, exemplifies what is best about the British empirical tradition, and we very much hope that readers will be tempted to peruse at least one or two of the original studies.

A further strength of each of the studies we eventually selected lies in the methodological openness of the researchers concerned. Behind every piece of research highlighted in this book there is a researcher, or a group of researchers, with deeply held beliefs and personal research ethics which have not only influenced their initial choice of topic, but which have also shaped their responses to the twists and turns taken by their research project. Through their own reflexive writings, we are able to gain a sense of the intensely personal nature of the research process. More generally, however – and despite the growing emphasis on reflexivity over the last 15 years or so – we have been struck by the relative *scarcity* of methodological detail within many research monographs, although monographs based on certain types of research method are more likely than others to neglect such detail. Those based on survey research techniques or ethnographic methods almost inevitably include methodological detail somewhere within the text, yet as we have noted already there is often a lack of such transparency within research monographs based, for example, on methods such as documentary analysis and discourse analysis, particularly within the broad area of cultural studies. This results in an unnecessary mystification of the research process – particularly unhelpful for those wishing to conduct similar pieces of research. In contrast, all of the monographs chosen for this book include considerable detail of the research design and some of the issues of method which the researchers had to tackle. In addition, in most cases not only have the researchers included a wealth of such detail within their main text, but they have also published detailed reflexive accounts elsewhere, in journal articles and within edited collections.

We end this book, then, with a plea for greater methodological transparency within the empirical tradition, and the avoidance of opacity. There is a great deal of excellent research being conducted within British sociology, and we believe that the specific research strategies which have underpinned some of the best substantive contributions to the discipline can fire the methodological imaginations of students and of more experienced researchers alike. Often it is only by seeing how someone else has solved a particular dilemma that we are inspired to solve our own, yet we need always to be aware of the embeddedness of any given research project. By highlighting specific examples of good research, then, we have attempted to demonstrate the importance of context to the selection of appropriate research methods and to issues of methodology. Our job has been made easier by the reflexivity and attention to detail of the researchers whose work is presented in this book, and we hope that more researchers will follow their example.

As we have seen from our eight exemplars, the research process inevitably requires compromise and methodological flexibility. It involves serious setbacks and disappointments as well as triumphs and successes. It presents a succession of daunting challenges to our most cherished beliefs and values. However, the intense satisfaction to be gained from successfully meeting these challenges, and consequently contributing to a greater sociological understanding of the social world, more than compensates for the heartache and frustration that we might experience along the way.

Our closing injunction, then, is this: having seen how other researchers have met the challenge, now have a go for yourself!

Bibliography

Abbott, P. and Sapsford, R. (1986) *Women and Social Class,* London: Tavistock.

Abraham, P. (1995) *Divide and School: Gender and Class Dynamics in Comprehensive Education,* London: Falmer Press.

Aggleton, P. (1987) *Rebels Without a Cause? Middle Class Youth and the Transition from School to Work,* Lewes: Falmer Press.

Allatt, P. and Yeandle, S. (1992) *Youth and Unemployment: Voices of Disordered Times,* London: Routledge.

Allen, I. (1988) *Any Room at the Top?,* London: Policy Studies Institute.

Allen, S. and Wolkowitz, C. (1987) *Homeworking: Myths and Realities,* London: Macmillan.

Apple, M. (1994) 'Series editor's introduction', in A. Gitlin (ed.).

Ball, S. (1981) *Beachside Comprehensive: A Case Study of Secondary Schooling,* Cambridge: Cambridge University Press.

Barnes, B., Bloor, D. and J. Henry (1996) *Scientific Knowledge: A Sociological Analysis,* Chicago: University of Chicago Press.

Becker, H. S. (1963) *Outsiders: Studies in the Sociology of Deviance,* Glencoe: Free Press.

Becker, H. S. (1967) 'Whose side are we on?', *Social Problems,* **14**: 239–47.

Bell, C. and Newby, H. (eds) (1977) *Doing Sociological Research,* London: Allen & Unwin.

Bell, C. and Roberts, H. (eds) (1984) *Social Researching: Politics, Problems, Practice,* London: Routledge & Kegan Paul.

Bisset, L. and Huws, U. (1985) *Sweated Labour: Homeworking in Britain Today,* London: Low Pay Unit.

Blackwood, C. (1984) *On the Perimeter,* London: Flamingo.

Bonney, N. (1988a) 'Dual-earning couples: trends of change in Great Britain', *Work, Employment and Society,* **2**: 89–102.

Bonney, N. (1988b) 'Gender, household and social class', *British Journal of Sociology,* **39**: 28–46.

Box, S. (1981) *Deviance, Reality and Society* (2nd edn), London: Holt, Rinehart & Winston.

Box, S. (1983) *Power, Crime and Mystification,* London: Tavistock.

Bradley, H. (1997) 'Gender and change in employment: feminisation and its effects', in R. K. Brown (ed.).

Brake, M. (1980) *The Sociology of Youth Culture and Youth Subcultures,* London: Routledge & Kegan Paul.

213

Brannen, J. (1988) 'Childbirth and occupational mobility: evidence from a longitudinal study', *Work, Employment and Society*, **3**: 179–201.

Brannen, J. (1989) 'Childbirth and occupational mobility', *Work, Employment and Society*, **3**: 179–202.

Brannen, J. (1992) *Mixing Methods*, Aldershot: Avebury.

British Sociological Association (1993) *BSA Statement of Ethical Practice*, Durham: BSA.

Brown, R.K. (ed.) (1997) *The Changing Shape of Work*, London: Macmillan.

Bryman, A. (1988) *Quantity and Quality in Social Research*, London: Routledge.

Bulmer, M. (ed.) (1982) *Social Research Ethics: An Examination of the Merits of Covert Participant Observation*, London: Macmillan.

Burgess, B. (1991) *In the Field: An Introduction to Field Research*, London: Routledge.

Butler, T. and Savage, M. (eds) (1995) *Social Change and the Middle Classes*, London: UCL Press.

Byrne, D. (1991) *International Journal of Urban and Regional Research*, **15**(4): 1116–20.

Byrne, P. (1988) *The Campaign for Nuclear Disarmament*, London: Croom Helm.

Castells, M. (1977) *The Urban Question*, London: Edward Arnold.

Castells, M. (1983) *The City and the Grassroots*, London: Edward Arnold.

Chesser, E. (1965) *The Sexual, Marital and Family Relationships of the English Woman*, London: Hutchinson.

Christensen, K. (1985) *Impacts of Computer-mediated Home-based Work on Women and their Families*, New York: Center for Human Environments.

Christensen, K. (1988) *Women and Home-based Work, The Unspoken Contract*, New York: Holt.

Christensen, K. (1989) 'Home-based clerical work, no simple truth, no simple reality' in E. Boris and C. Daniels (eds) *Homework: Historical and Contemporary Perspectives on Paid Labour at Home*, Champaign, Illinois: University of Illinois Press.

Christie, R. (1976) 'Comment on conflict methodology: a protagonist position', *The Sociological Quarterly*, **17**: 513–19.

Cohen, L. and Manion, L. (1985) *Research Methods in Educational Research*, London: Routledge.

Cohen, P. (ed.) (1971) *Images of Deviance*, London: Penguin.

Cohen, P. and Taylor, L. (1972) *Psychological Survival*, London: Penguin.

Connell, R. (1987) *Gender and Power*, Cambridge: Polity Press.

Connell, R. (1995) *Masculinities*, Cambridge: Polity Press.

Cooke, P. (1989) *Localities: The Changing Face of Urban Britain*, London: Unwin Hyman.

Courtenay, G. (1986) *Survey of Family Obligations: Technical Report*, London: Social and Community Planning Research.

Crompton, R. (1993) *Class and Stratification*, Cambridge: Polity Press.

Crompton, R. (1995) 'Women's employment and the "middle class"', in T. Butler and M. Savage (eds).

Crompton, R. (1997) *Women and Work in Modern Britain*, Oxford: Oxford University Press.

Crompton, R. (1998) *Class and Stratification*, (2nd edn), Cambridge: Polity.

Crompton, R. and Harris, F. (1998) 'Explaining women's employment patterns: orientation to work revisited', *British Journal of Sociology*, **49**(1): 118–36.

Crompton, R. and Mann, M. (1986) *Gender and Stratification*, Cambridge: Polity Press.

Crompton, R. and Sanderson, K. (1990) *Gendered Jobs and Social Change*, London: Unwin Hyman.

Crow, G. and Allan, G. (1994) *Community Life: An Introduction to Local Social Relations*, Hemel Hempstead: Harvester Wheatsheaf.

Delamont, S. and Atkinson, P. (1980) 'The two traditions in educational ethnography: sociology and anthropology compared', *British Journal of Sociology of Education*, **1**(2): 139–52.

Denzin, N. (1997) *Interpretive Ethnography: Ethnographic Practices for the Twenty-first Century*, Thousand Oaks: Sage.

De Vaus, D.A. (1991) *Surveys in Social Research* (3rd edn), London: UCL Press.

Devine, F. (1992a) *Affluent Workers Revisited: Privatism and the Working Class*, Edinburgh: Edinburgh University Press.

Devine, F. (1992b) 'Gender segregation in the engineering and science professions: a case of continuity and change', *Work, Employment and Society*, **6**: 557–75.

Devine, F. (1994) 'Segregation and supply: preferences and plans among "self-made women"', *Gender, Work and Organisation*, **1**: 94–109.

Devine, F. (1996) 'The "new structuralism", class politics and class analysis' in N. Kirk (ed.) *Social Class and Marxism: Defences and Challenges*, Aldershot: Scolar Press.

Devine, F. (1997) *Social Class in America and Britain*, Edinburgh: Edinburgh University Press.

Dickens, P. (1990) *Urban Sociology: Society, Locality and Human Nature*, Hemel Hempstead: Harvester Wheatsheaf.

Ditton, J. (1977) *Part-time Crime: An Ethnography of Fiddling and Pilferage*, London: Macmillan.

Dorling, D. and Simpson, S. (1994) 'Gone and forgotten? The Census's missing one-and-a-half million', *Environment and Planning Series A*, **26**: 1172–3.

Downes, D. and Rock, P. (1993) *Understanding Deviance* (rev. 2nd edn), Oxford: Clarendon Press.

Downes, D. and Rock, P. (1995) *Understanding Deviance* (rev. 2nd edn), Oxford: Oxford University Press.

Dunleavy, P. (1980) *Urban Political Analysis*, London: Macmillan.

Dunleavy, P. and Husbands, C. T. (1985) *British Democracy at the Crossroads*, London: Allen & Unwin.

Economist (1994) 'Chain male: consensual gay sex', *The Economist*, 29 January.

Edgell, S. and Duke, V. (1991) *A Measure of Thatcherism*, London: Harper-Collins.

Epstein, D. and Johnson, R. (1997) *Schooling Sexualities*, Buckingham: Open University Press.

Farrell, C. (1978) *My Mother Said... The Way Young People Learn about Sex and Birth Control*, London: Routledge & Kegan Paul.

Felstead, A., Jewson, N. and Goodwin, J. (1996) *Homeworkers in Britain*, London: HMSO.

Finch, J. (1984) '"It's great to have someone to talk to": the ethics and politics of interviewing women', in C. Bell and H. Roberts (eds).

Finch, J. and Mason, J. (1990a) 'Decision taking in the fieldwork process: theoretical sampling and collaborative working', *Qualitative Methodology*, **2**: 25–50.

Finch, J. and Mason, J. (1990b) 'Divorce, remarriage and family obligations', *The Sociological Review*, **38**(2): 219–46.

Finch, J. and Mason, J. (1993) *Negotiating Family Responsibilities*, London: Routledge.

Finch, M. (1987) 'The vignette technique in survey research', *Sociology*, **21**: 105–114.

Foster, P. and Hammersley, M. (1996) 'Researching educational inequality: a critique', *Research Intelligence*, April, 18–20.

Foster, P., Gomm, R. and Hammersley, M. (1996) *Constructing Educational Inequality*, London: Falmer Press.

Franklin, M.N. and Page, E. (1984) 'A critique of the consumption cleavage approach and the growth of state employment: part 1', *Political Studies*, **32**: 521–36.

Fuller, M. (1980) 'Black girls in a London comprehensive school', in R. Deem (ed.) *Schooling for Women's Work*, London: Routledge & Kegan Paul.

Fuller, S. (1997) *Science*, Buckingham: Open University Press.

Gagnon, J. and Simon, W. (1973) *Sexual Conduct: The Social Sources of Human Sexuality*, Chicago: Aldine.

Gilbert, N. (1993) *Researching Social Life*, London: Sage.

Ginn, J., Arber, S. and Brannen, J. (1996) 'Feminist fallacies: a reply to Hakim on women's employment', *British Journal of Sociology*, **7**: 167–74.

Gitlin, A. (1994) *Power and Method: Political Activism and Educational Research*, New York: Routledge.

Gittens, D. (1993) *The Family in Question: Changing Households and Familial Ideologies*, Basingstoke: Macmillan.

Glaser, B. and Strauss, A. (1967) *The Discovery of Grounded Theory*, Chicago: Aldine.

Goffman, E. (1969) *The Presentation of Self in Everyday Life*, Harmondsworth: Penguin.

Goldthorpe, J. H. (1983) 'Women and class analysis: in defence of the conventional view', *Sociology*, **17**: 465–88.

Goldthorpe, J. H. (in association with C. Llewellyn and C. Payne) (1987) *Social Mobility and Class Structure in Modern Britain*, Oxford: Clarendon Press.

Gorz, A. (1985) *Paths to Paradise*, London: Pluto Press.

Gouldner, A. (1975) *For Sociology: Renewal and Critique in Sociology Today*, Harmondsworth: Pelican.

Greater Manchester Low Pay Unit (1986) *Homeworking: A Report on Homeworking Prepared for Manchester City Council,* Manchester: Manchester Low Pay Unit.

Green, P. (1990) *The Enemy Within: Policing and Class Consciousness in the Miners' Strike,* Buckingham: Open University Press.

Green, S. (1997) *Urban Amazons: Lesbian Feminism and Beyond in the Gender, Sexuality and Identity Battles of London,* Basingstoke: Macmillan.

Gregson, N. and Lowe, M. (1993) 'Renegotiating the domestic division of labour? A study of dual-career households in north-east and south-east England', *Sociological Review,* **41**: 475–505.

Gregson, N. and Lowe, M. (1994) *Servicing the Middle Classes: Class, Gender and Waged Domestic Labour in Contemporary Britain,* London: Routledge.

Griffin, C. (1986) *Typical Girls? Young Women from School to the Job Market,* London: Routledge & Kegan Paul.

Hakim, C. (1980) 'Homeworking: some new evidence', *Employment Gazette,* **80**: 1105–9.

Hakim, C. (1984) 'Homeworking and outwork: national estimates from two surveys', *Employment Gazette,* **92**: 7–12.

Hakim, C. (1987a) *Home-based Work in Britain: A Report on the 1981 Homeworking Survey,* London: Department of Employment.

Hakim, C. (1987b) 'Homeworking in Britain: key findings from the national survey of home-based workers', *Employment Gazette,* **95**: 92–104.

Hakim, C. (1991) 'Grateful slaves and self-made women: a review of recent trends and current issues', *European Sociological Review,* **7**: 101–21.

Hakim, C. (1992) 'Explaining trends in occupational segregation: the measurement, causes and consequences of the sexual division of labour', *European Sociological Review,* **8**: 127–52.

Hakim, C. (1995) 'Five feminist myths about women's employment', *British Journal of Sociology,* **46**: 429–55.

Hakim, C. (1996) *Key Issues in Women's Work,* London: Athlone.

Hakim, C. (1998) 'Developing a sociology for the twenty first century: preference theory', *British Journal of Sociology,* **49**(1): 137–43.

Halford, S., Savage, M. and Witz, A. (1997) *Gender, Careers and Organisations: Current Developments in Banking, Nursing and Local Government,* Basingstoke: Macmillan.

Hall, S., Critcher, C., Jefferson, T., Clarke, J. and Roberts, B. (1978) *Policing the Crisis,* London: Macmillan.

Hall, S. and Jefferson, T. (eds) (1976) *Resistance Through Rituals,* London: Hutchinson.

Hammersley, M. (1992) *What's Wrong with Ethnography?,* London: Routledge.

Hammersley, M. and Atkinson, P. (1983) *Ethnography; Principles in Practice,* London: Tavistock.

Hammersley, M. and Gomm, R. (1996) 'Exploiting sociology for equality?', *Network,* No. 65, May, 19–20.

Hamnett, C. (1991) 'Review of *A Nation of Home Owners*', *British Journal of Sociology*, **25**: 133–4.

Hamnett, C. (1995) 'Home ownership and the middle classes' in T. Butler and M. Savage (eds).

Harding, S. (1986) *The Science Question in Feminism*, Milton Keynes: Open University Press.

Harding, S. (1987) *Feminism and Methodology*, Milton Keynes: Open University Press.

Hargreaves, D. (1967) *Social Relations in a Secondary School*, London: Routledge & Kegan Paul.

Harrop, M. (1980) 'The urban basis of political alignment: a comment', *British Journal of Political Science*, **10**: 388–402.

Haywood, C. and Mac an Ghaill, M. (1996) 'What about the boys? Regendered local labour markets and the recomposition of working class masculinities', *British Journal of Education and Work*, **9**(1): 19–30.

Haywood, C. and Mac an Ghaill, M. (1998) 'The making of men: theorising methodology in "uncertain times"', in G. Walford (ed.) *Doing Research in Education*, London: Falmer Press.

Heath, A. and Britten, N. (1984) 'Women's jobs do make a difference', *Sociology*, **18**: 475–90.

Heath, S. (1997) *Preparation for Life? Vocationalism and the Equal Opportunities Challenge*, Aldershot: Ashgate.

Heath, S. (1999) 'Watching the backlash', *Discourse: Studies in the Cultural Politics of Education*, **20** (forthcoming).

Hebdige, D. (1979) *Subculture: The Meaning of Style*, London: Methuen.

Henry, S. (1978) *The Hidden Economy*, Oxford: Martin Robertson.

Hite, S. (1976) *The Hite Report on Female Sexuality*, London: Pandora Press.

Hite, S. (1981) *The Hite Report on Male Sexuality*, London: Optima.

Hite, S. (1987) *The Hite Report on Women and Love*, Harmondsworth: Penguin.

Hobbs, D. (1988) *Doing the Business: Entrepreneurship, the Working Class and Detectives in the East End of London*, Oxford: Oxford University Press.

Hobbs, D. (1993) 'Peers, careers and academic fears: writing as fieldwork' in D. Hobbs and T. May (eds).

Hobbs, D. (1995) *Bad Business*, Oxford: Oxford University Press.

Hobbs, D. and May, T. (eds) (1993) *Interpreting the Field: Accounts of Ethnography*, Oxford: Clarendon Press.

Hoinville, G. and Jowell, R. (1978) *Survey Research Practice*, Heinemann Educational Books.

Holdaway, S. (1983) *Inside the British Police*, Oxford: Blackwell.

Holdaway, S. (1991) *Recruiting a Multicultural Police Force*, London: The Stationery Office.

Holdaway, S. (1996) *The Racialisation of British Policing*, London: Macmillan.

Homan, R. (1991) *The Ethics of Social Research*, Basingstoke: Macmillan.

Huws, U. (1994) *Home Truth: Key Results from the National Survey of Homeworkers*, Leeds: National Group on Homeworking.

Irwin, S. (1995) *Rights of Passage: Social Change and the Transition from Youth to Adulthood*, London: UCL Press.

Jamieson, L. (1998) *Intimacy: Personal Relationships in Modern Societies*, Cambridge: Polity Press.

Jenkins, J. (1983) 'Resource mobilisation and the study of social movements', *Annual Review of Sociology*, **9**: 527–53.

Johnson, A., Wadsworth, J., Wellings, K., Field, J. and Bradshaw, S. (1994) *Sexual Attitudes and Lifestyles*, Oxford: Blackwell Scientific.

Jones, C. and Mahoney, P. (1989) *Learning Our Lines: Sexuality and Social Control in Education*, London: Women's Press.

Jones, G. (1995) *Leaving Home*, Buckingham: Open University Press.

Jones, T., Young, J. and Maclean, B. (1986) *The Islington Crime Survey*, Gower: Aldershot.

Kenny, M. (1996) *Daily Express*, 6 May.

King, R. (1984) 'The man in the Wendy House: Researching infants schools', in R. Burgess (ed.) *The Research Process in Educational Settings: Ten Case Studies*, Lewes: Falmer Press.

Lacey, C. (1970) *Hightown Grammar: The School as a Social System*, Manchester: Manchester University Press.

Lambert, A. (1976) 'The sisterhood', in M. Hammersley and P. Woods (eds) *The Process of Schooling*, London: Routledge & Kegan Paul.

Lash, S. and Urry, J. (1987) *The End of Organised Capitalism*, Cambridge: Polity.

Lather, P. (1986) 'Research as praxis', *Harvard Educational Review*, **56**(3): 257–77.

Lather, P. (1991) *Getting Smart: Feminist Research and Pedagogy with/in the Postmodern*, New York: Routledge.

Lather, P. (1996) 'Methodology as subversive repetition: practices toward a feminist double science'. Paper presented to the Annual Meeting of the American Educational Research Association, New York, April.

Laurance, J. (1994) 'Bedroom survey "can't be trusted"', *The Times*, 24th January.

Lea, J. and Young. J. (1984) *What is to be Done about Law and Order?*, Harmondsworth: Penguin.

Lee, R. (1993) *Doing Research on Sensitive Topics*, London: Sage.

Liddington, J. (1989) *The Long Road to Greenham: Feminism and Anti-Militarism in Britain since 1820*, London: Virago.

Lofland, J. and Lofland, L. (1985) *Analysing Social Settings: A Guide to Qualitative Observation and Analysis*, Belmont: Wadsworth.

Lovenduski, J. and Randall, V. (1993) *Contemporary Feminist Politics*, Oxford: Oxford University Press.

Mac an Ghaill, M. (1988) *Young, Gifted and Black: Student–Teacher Relations in the Schooling of Black Youth*, Milton Keynes: Open University Press.

Mac an Ghaill, M. (1991) 'Young, gifted and black: methodological reflections of a teacher/researcher', in G. Walford (ed.) *Doing Educational Research*, London: Routledge.

Mac an Ghaill, M. (1993) 'Beyond the white norm: the use of qualitative methods in the study of black youths' schooling in England', in P. Woods and M. Hammersley (eds) *Gender and Ethnicity in Schools: Ethnographic Accounts*, Buckingham: Open University Press.

Mac an Ghaill, M. (1994) *The Making of Men: Masculinities, Sexualities and Schooling*, Buckingham: Open University Press.

McCran, S., Joshi, H. and Dex, S. (1996) 'Employment after child rearing: a survival analysis', *Work, Employment and Society*, **10**(2): 273–96.

Macgregor, S. (1990) *Tackling the Inner Cities*, Oxford: Clarendon Press.

McGuigan, J. (1998) *Cultural Methodologies*, London: Sage.

MacKinnon, C. (1982) 'Feminism, Marxism, method and the state: an agenda for theory', in N. Keohane, R. Rosaldo and B. Gelpi (eds) *Feminist Theory: A Critique of Ideology*, Brighton: Harvester Press.

McRae, S. (1991) *Maternity Rights in Britain*, London: Policy Studies Institute.

McRae, S. (1993) 'Returning to work after childbirth: opportunities and inequalities', *European Sociological Review*, **9**: 125–37.

Maguire, M., Morgan, R. and Reiner, R. (1994) *Oxford Handbook of Criminology*, Oxford: Clarendon Press.

Mahoney, P. (1985) *Schools for Boys? Co-education Reconsidered*, London: Hutchinson.

Marsh, C. (1982) *The Survey Method*, London: George, Allen & Unwin.

Marsh, C. (1988) *Exploring Data*, Cambridge: Polity.

Marshall, G., Newby, H., Rose, D. and Volger, C. (1988) *Social Class in Modern Britain*, London: Unwin Hyman.

Marshall, G. (1990) *In Praise of Sociology*, London: Unwin Hyman.

Mason, J. (1994) 'Linking qualitative and quantitative data analysis', in A. Bryman and R. Burgess (eds) *Analyzing Qualitative Data*, London: Routledge.

Mason, J. (1996) *Qualitative Researching*, London: Sage.

Matthews, R. and Young, J. (1986) *Confronting Crime*, London: Sage.

Matza, D. (1964) *Delinquency and Drift*, New York: Wiley.

Matza, D. (1969) *Becoming Deviant*, Englewood Cliffs, New Jersey: Prentice Hall.

May, T. (1990) *Probation: Politics, Policy and Practice*, Buckingham: Open University Press.

May, T. (1997) Social Research: Issues, Methods and Process (2nd edn), Buckingham: Open University Press.

Maynard, M. (1994) 'Methods, practice and epistemology: the debate about feminism and research', in M. Maynard and J. Purvis (eds).

Maynard, M. and Purvis, J. (1994) *Researching Women's Lives from a Feminist Perspective*, London: Taylor & Francis.

Measor, L. (1985) 'Interviewing: A strategy in qualitative research', in R. Burgess (ed.) *Strategies of Educational Research*, Lewes: Falmer Press.

Miles, M. and Huberman, A. (1984) 'Drawing valid meaning from qualitative data: Towards a shared craft', *Educational Researcher*, **13**(9): 20–30.

Mirza, H. (1992) *Young, Female and Black*, London: Routledge.

Mitter, S. (1986) *Common Fate, Common Bond,* London: Pluto Press.

Morgan, D. (1996) *Family Connections: An Introduction to Family Studies,* Cambridge: Polity Press.

Morris, L. (1985) 'Renegotiation of the domestic division of labour in the context of male redundancy' in B. Roberts, R. Finnegan and D. Gallie (eds) *New Approaches to Economic Life,* Manchester: Manchester University Press.

Moser, C. and Kalton, G. (1971) *Survey Methods in Social Investigation* (2nd edn), London: Heinemann.

Oberschall, A. (1973) *Social Conflict and Social Movement,* Englewood Cliffs, New Jersey: Prentice Hall.

O'Connell Davidson, J. and Layder, D. (1994) *Methods, Sex and Madness,* London: Routledge.

Offe, C. (1985) 'New social movements: challenging the boundaries of institutional politics', *Social Research,* **52**: 817–68.

Pahl, R.E. (1975) *Whose City?* Harmondsworth: Penguin.

Pahl, R.E. (1984) *Divisions of Labour,* Oxford: Blackwell.

Pahl, R.E. (1988) 'Some remarks on informal work, social polarisation and social structure', *International Journal of Urban and Regional Research,* **12**: 247–67.

Pahl, R.E. (1995) *After Success: Fin-de-Siecle Anxiety and Identity,* Cambridge: Polity Press.

Panorama (1995) *Men Aren't Working,* BBC1, 16 October 1995.

Parkin, F. (1968) *Middle Class Radicalism: The Social Bases of CND,* Manchester: Manchester University Press.

Parsons, T. (1959) 'The school as a social system', *Harvard Educational Review,* **29**(4): 297–318.

Pearson, G. (1975) *The Deviant Imagination,* London: Macmillan.

Pearson, G. (1993) in D. Hobbs and T. May (eds).

Phizacklea, A. (1990) *Unpacking the Fashion Industry: Gender, Racism and Class in Production,* London: Routledge.

Phizacklea, A. and Wolkowitz, C. (1995) *Homeworking Women: Gender, Racism and Class at Work,* London: Sage.

Pilcher, J. (1995) *Age and Generation in Modern Britain,* Oxford: Oxford University Press.

Pollert, A. (1994) *Farewell to Flexibility,* Cambridge: Blackwell.

Pomeroy, W. (1972) *Dr Kinsey and the Institute for Sex Research,* London: Nelson.

Poster, M. (1989) *Critical Theory and Post-Structuralism: In Search of a Context,* Ithaca: Cornell University Press.

Power, A. (1999) *Estates on the Edge,* London: Macmillan.

Reichardt, C. and Cook, T. (1979) 'Beyond qualitative versus quantitative methods', in T. Cook and C. Rechardt (eds) *Qualitative and Quantitative Methods in Evaluation Research,* New York: Sage.

Reiner, R. (1996) *The Politics of the Police* (2nd edn), Hemel Hempstead: Harvester Wheatsheaf.

Reinharz, S. (1984) *On Becoming a Social Scientist,* San Francisco: Jossey-Bass.

Reinharz, S. (1992) *Feminist Methods in Social Research,* Oxford: Oxford University Press.

Rex, J. and Moore, R. (1967) *Race, Community and Conflict: A Study of Sparkbrook,* Harmondsworth: Penguin.

Rich, A. (1980) 'Compulsory heterosexuality and lesbian existence', *Signs,* **5**(4): 631–90.

Roberts, H. (1981) *Doing Feminist Research,* London: Routledge & Kegan Paul.

Roker, D. (1993) 'Gaining the edge: girls at a private school', in I. Bates and G. Riseborough (eds) *Youth and Inequality,* Milton Keynes: Open University Press.

Rose, D. and Sullivan, O. (1996) *Introducing Data Analysis for Social Scientists* (2nd edn), Buckingham: Open University Press.

Rose, G. (1982) *Deciphering Sociological Research,* London: Macmillan.

Roseneil, S. (1993) 'Greenham revisited: researching myself and my sisters', in D. Hobbs and T. May (eds).

Roseneil, S. (1995) *Disarming Patriarchy: Feminism and Political Action at Greenham,* Buckingham: Open University Press.

Roseneil, S. (1999) *Common Women, Uncommon Practices: The Queer Feminism of Greenham,* London: Cassell.

Routh, G. (1987) *Occupations of the People of Great Britain, 1801–1981,* London: Macmillan.

Rowbotham, S. (1989) *The Past is Before Us: Feminism in Action since the 1960s,* Harmondsworth: Penguin.

Rowbotham, S. and Mitter, S. (eds) (1994) *Dignity and Daily Bread,* London: Routledge.

Ruggiero, V. and South, N.(1994) *Eurodrugs,* London: UCL Press.

Saunders, P. (1979) *Urban Politics: A Sociological Interpretation,* Harmondsworth: Penguin.

Saunders, P. (1981) *Social Theory and the Urban Question,* London: Hutchinson.

Saunders, P. (1984) 'Beyond housing classes: the sociological significance of private property rights in the means of consumption', *International Journal of Urban and Regional Research,* **8**: 202–27.

Saunders, P. (1986) *Social Theory and the Urban Question* (2nd edn), London: Hutchinson.

Saunders, P. (1990) *A Nation of Home Owners,* London: Unwin Hyman.

Saunders, P (1995) *Capitalism,* Buckingham: Open University Press.

Saunders, P. and Harris, C. (1994) *Privatisation and Popular Capitalism,* Buckingham: Open University Press.

Savage, M. (1992) 'Women's expertise: man's authority: gendered organisation in the contemporary middle classes' in A. Witz and M. Savage (eds).

Savage, M., Barlow, J., Dickens, P. and Fielding, T. (1992) *Property, Bureaucracy and Culture,* London: Routledge.

Savage, M. and Warde, A. (1993) *Urban Sociology, Capitalism and Modernity,* London: Macmillan/British Sociology Association.

Scarman Report (1981) *The Brixton Disorders 10–12 April 1981,* London: HMSO.

Scase, R. (1991) 'Review of *A Nation of Home Owners*', *British Journal of Sociology*, **42**: 637.

Scase, R. (1992) *Class*, Buckingham: Open University Press.

Scheurich, J. (1997) *Research Method in the Postmodern*, Falmer Press: London.

Schofield, M. (1965) *The Sexual Behaviour of Young People*, Harmondsworth: Penguin.

Schofield, M. (1968) *The Sexual Behaviour of Young Adults*, London: Allen Lane.

Scott, J. (1990) *A Matter of Record*, Cambridge: Polity.

Seale, C. (1998) *Researching Society and Culture*, London: Sage.

Silverman, D. (1997) *Qualitative Research: Theory, Method and Practice*, London: Sage.

Skeggs, B. (1992) 'The constraints of neutrality', paper presented at ESRC seminar series, University of Warwick, November.

Skeggs, B. (1993) 'The cultural production of "Learning to Labour"', in M. Barker and A. Breezer (eds) *Readings in Culture*, London: Routledge.

Slater, E. and Woodside, M. (1951) *Patterns of Marriage: A Study of Marital Relationships in the Urban Working Class*, London: Cassell.

Small, S. (1983) *Police and People in London*, London: Policy Studies Institute.

Smart, C. (1977) *Women, Crime and Criminology*, London: Routledge & Kegan Paul.

Smith, D.J. and Gray, J. (1983) *Police and People in London*, London: Policy Studies Institute.

Smith, H. (1975) *Strategies of Social Research: The Methodological Imagination*, London: Prentice Hall.

Stanley, L. (ed.) (1990) *Feminist Praxis: Research, Theory and Epistemology in Feminist Sociology*, London: Routledge.

Stanley, L. (1996) *Sex Surveyed 1949–1994: From Mass Observation's 'Little Kinsey' to the National Survey and the Hite Reports*, London: Taylor & Francis.

Stanley, L. and Wise, S. (1983) *Breaking Out: Feminist Consciousness and Feminist Research*, London: Routledge.

Stanley, L. and Wise, S. (1990) 'Feminist practice and the academic mode of production: an editorial introduction', in L. Stanley (ed.).

Stanley, L. and Wise, S. (1992) *Breaking Out Again: Feminist Ontology and Epistemology*, London: Routledge.

Stanworth, M. (1984) 'Women and class analysis: a reply to Goldthorpe', *Sociology*, **18**: 159–70.

Stronach, I. and MacLure, M. (1997) *Educational Research Undone: the Postmodern Embrace*, Buckingham: Open University Press.

Taylor, I. (1981) *Law and Order: Arguments for Socialism,* London: Macmillan.

Taylor, I., Walton, P. and Young, J. (1973) *The New Criminology*, London: Routledge & Kegan Paul.

Taylor, I., Walton, P. and Young, J. (eds) (1975) *Critical Criminology*, London: Routledge & Kegan Paul.

Taylor-Gooby, P. (1986) 'Consumption cleavages and welfare politics', *Political Studies,* **34**: 592–606.

Thompson, P. (1998) *The Voice of the Past; Oral History*, Oxford: Oxford University Press.

Tooley, J. and Darby, D. (1998) *Educational Research: A Critique: A Survey of Published Educational Research*, London: OFSTED.

Touraine, A. (1981) *The Voice and the Eye: An Analysis of Social Movements*, Cambridge: Cambridge University Press.

Touraine, A. (1983) *Anti-Nuclear Protest*, Cambridge: Cambridge University Press.

Troyna, B. (1994) 'Blind faith? Empowerment and educational research', *International Studies in Sociology of Education*, **4**: 3–24.

Troyna, B. and Carrington, P. (1989) '"Whose side are we on?" Ethical dilemmas in research on "race" and education', in R. Burgess (ed.) *The Ethics of Educational Research*, Lewes: Falmer Press.

Troyna, B. and Hatcher, R. (1992) *Racism in Children's Lives: A Study of Mainly White Primary Schools*, London: Routledge.

Valentine, C. (1969) *Culture and Poverty*, Chicago: University of Chicago Press.

Wajcman, J. (1996) 'The domestic basis for the managerial career', *Sociological Review*, **44**: 609–29.

Walford, G. (1986) *Life in Public Schools*, London: Methuen.

Walker, J. (1988) *Louts and Legends: Male Youth Culture in an Inner City School*, Sydney: Allen & Unwin Australia.

Warde, A., Savage, M., Longhurst, B. and Martin, A. (1988) 'Class, consumption and voting: an ecological analysis of wards and towns in the 1980s' local election in England', *Political Geography Quarterly*, 7: 339–51.

Weeks, J. (1989) *Sex, Politics and Society: The Regulation of Sexuality since 1800* (2nd edn), London: Longman.

Weiner, G. (1994) *Feminisms in Education: An Introduction*, Buckingham: Open University Press.

Wellings, K., Field, J., Johnson, A. and Wadsworth, J. (1994) *Sexual Behaviour in Britain: The National Survey of Sexual Attitudes and Lifestyles*, Harmondsworth: Penguin.

Wellings, K., Field, J., Wadsworth, J., Johnson, A., Anderson, R. and Bradshaw, S. (1990) 'Sexual lifestyles under scrutiny', *Nature*, **348**: 276–8.

Wheelock, J. (1990) *Husbands at Home,* London: Routledge.

Wilkins, E. (1994) 'Survey explodes myth that schooling affects sexuality', *The Times*, 25 January.

Williams, M. and May, T. (1996) *Introduction to the Philosophy of Social Research*, London: UCL Press.

Willis, P. (1977) *Learning to Labour: How Working Class Kids get Working Class Jobs*, Aldershot: Saxon House.

Witz, A. (1995) 'Gender and service-class formations' in T. Butler and M. Savage (eds).

Witz, A. and Savage, M. (eds) (1992) *Gender and Bureaucracy*, Oxford: Blackwell/British Sociological Association.

Woodhead, C. (1996) 'Boys who learn to be losers', *The Times*, 6 March.

Yin, R. K. (1994) *Case Study Research* (2nd edn), London: Sage.

Young, A. (1990) *Feminism in Dissent*, London: Routledge.

Young, J. (1971) *The Drugtakers: The Social Meaning of Drug Use*, London: Paladin.

Young, J. and Matthews, R. (eds) (1986) *Rethinking Criminology: The Realist Debate*, London: Sage.

Young, M. and Willmott, P. (1957) *Family and Kinship in East London*, London: Routledge & Kegan Paul.

Index